Boope

'Real Policing in the Sixties.'

Graham L. Storr

Best Wishes
. Booper.

Published by Mr. Graham L. Storr

DEDICATED TO MY TWO LITTLE ANGELS:

Eleanor Jane and Isla Rose.

"To nourish children and raise them against odds is in any time, any place, more valuable than to fix bolts in cars or design nuclear weapons.'

Marilyn French

ACKNOWLEDGEMENTS

I acknowledge the help advice and assistance provided by many people in the preparation of this book.

In particular allow me to thank M.J. (Mick) Fowler for permission to reproduce his painting on the front cover.

I also acknowledge the help of Messrs. J.P. Bean, M. Currie, G. Tierney and R. Varey QPM.

To my Wife and family I say thank you.

CHAPTERS.

FOREWORD.

Greying detective superintendent Howard who had been involved in my prosecution and subsequent imprisonment leaned over the small table in the visiting room of H.M.P. Highpoint. Suffolk. It was autumn 1984. He carefully looked round the room before saying to me in a quiet voice .....

"I want you to give evidence against the other bent coppers involved or I will personally ensure that you lose your fucking pension and parole. That's a promise! "

Months before I would have started my reply with the words 'Sir' - but not now...

"You can fuck off, pal. I've just been sentenced to five years." I replied.

"If they find out in here that I'm a 'grass' - I'm dead. You were fucking useless as a sergeant on the crime squad and you're still a 'knob-head'. Don't expect me to do you any favours. I will do my 'bird' and pick up the pieces when I get out. You do what you fucking want". (Perhaps the daftest words I ever said in my life because detective superintendent Howard then 'arranged' for me to forfeit three-quarters of a police pension paid by me for some 25 years and I was turned down for my first parole.)

If you had to sum up your life in a quotation, which one would you choose?

For myself, I picked the above famous uttering by Scott. All that 'tangling', 'weaving' and 'deceiving' describes exactly the way I have lived for the past 25 years.

I was a provincial detective who was tried and convicted by his fellow 'peers' for a variety of crimes. I was then sent to prison.

This is a 'very' true story told by a disgraced northern copper who, as an operational detective in the busy industrial city of Sheffield, daily told lies on paper, and elsewhere, to both convict offenders and deceive courts, senior officers, colleagues and family alike.

This is not the story of a Scotland Yard 'mega-star'.

It is an attempt to paint a picture showing the whole spectrum of life as a provincial policeman in the 'sixties', who throughout his career was always at the 'sharp-end'.

So true, that I have been obliged to alter identities and disguise certain details to protect guilty police officers and others. Many who still patrol your streets, displaying massive egos of honesty and integrity.

Please remember this author has served two Masters - living on both sides of the fence.

A fact now, of which I am not proud. In reality my writings are a way of making my 'bird' pass more quickly and using the written text to erase many things from my conscience. It was a severe sentence handed down to me for my singular part in a catalogue of crimes committed in the main by others. Many serving and ex- police officers of varying rank were exposed criminally in the investigation but never prosecuted nor disciplined.

I have tried to be realistic, humorous and truthful as I recount my exploits. Writing from memory and in a prison cell I suspect is not the way other ex-coppers pen their memoirs, but in many ways I relish retracing my steps over a quarter of a century.

There will be criticism from the outside, dismissing my writings as the ramblings of a proven dishonest and unreliable person. A man who should have known better, whilst in a position of trust. However, remember I was considered a very successful albeit unorthodox practical detective, even by the same colleagues who convicted me.

My reputation and integrity are gone for now, so judge for yourselves, because you will never have a better opportunity to examine in detail the manner in which police officers in the 'swinging sixties' conducted both themselves and their investigations.

Please remember as I write this in 1984/5 it may never see the light of day again but I am sure it will help to pass the time in here.

H.M.P.
Highpoint.
Suffolk.
1984/5

Chapter 1 - 'Awaiting trial.'

"A moment's insight is sometimes worth a life's experience".

Oliver Wendell Holmes, Jr., 1841 - 1935

It wasn't cold by October standards as I waited outside the flat. There was plenty of time before my 'brief' was due to pick me up and I enjoyed the fresh air before the anticipated stuffy court that I knew we would endure. I should have brought an overcoat - it does look like rain. Hope I look the part in my dark grey clerical suit. Most detectives possess a dark suit to be worn at funerals, crown court and in the event of promotion.

I know I haven't got a chance of getting away with all the charges. The D.P.P. (Director of Public Prosecutions) wouldn't have authorized the prosecution if they were unsure of a conviction of some kind.

It was a pity I didn't get the chance to resign and leave quietly with my pension. After all I had worked almost 25 years for it. It happens all the time in the police - and not just in respect of bent coppers - more than you think - take your pension - official sick leave - disappear quietly from the public view. Mind you I don't think bent coppers are that newsworthy now. Oh I know judges and politicians still try to gain some mileage out of the situation- judges because of their position in society and politicians to attract votes.

I've picked a bad time in my life to get caught though. Well turned 40 and a classic example that life does not begin at that age. I used to play a lot of sport and kept myself reasonably fit, but the years of excessive drinking in C.I.D. have not helped. Irregular meals, lack of good sleep patterns, a bad leg injury sustained in a street brawl and a mysterious bout of hepatitis have left this body well and truly knackered.

I suppose some would think I had a pretty good life, before I blew it.

Married at an early age - separated and divorced.

Married again with two beautiful daughters. Like many other dedicated detectives though I found that the job and family life did not mix. Separated again and later divorced again.

Moved into a small flat with my female partner Marion and struggled to pay the £100 per month rent. Bathroom, central heating, one major bedroom. The flat was situated on Wortley Road Rotherham which led into the town. Rotherham was itself being swallowed up by nearby Sheffield city. I know the town was unhappy at the prospect of losing both its identity and autonomy as the constantly changing boundaries made their mark. It had always laboured under a second-class image being adjacent to the city of Sheffield but not having the commerce nor sociable facilities of its neighbour.

Heavy industry and steel-making had thrived in the area, but as with other crafts throughout the country, it was found cheaper to source goods in other parts of the world leaving the locals to look upon their futures with dismay and disillusionment.

The chamber of commerce used to make noises at national level about the hereditary skills and reputations being lost, but the world wanted cheaper goods and people did not even consider the past.

The town boasted Rotherham United a team in the third division of the football league who were destined to remain there forever. This, of course, did not prevent their supporters from being experts on the game with worldwide soccer knowledge.

Anyone reading Stan Barstow's novel - 'A kind of loving' set in a Yorkshire town in the 1960's can visualize my town in full detail. I don't have to remind you about Northern folk and their legendary 'friendliness' and this was so when my partner and I moved into the flat. Neighbours particularly and others seemed to think that I could get them off a speeding ticket or parking fine by simply lifting the telephone. Even after the local press had printed a small item about my suspension and covered my first court appearance they remained friendly. Headlines such as 'city detective charged' and 'detective sergeant accused in major fraud case' did not seem to persuade them to alienate me and it was good that I did not have to explain my charges to them because they were provided by the press. Naturally the press reports gave my full name, rank, address and age which many surprisingly did not know.

It sounds quite silly now but I was always known by my

nickname 'Booper' which I collected as a young detective and kept for over 20 years. I have been known more by that name in my police career, than by my real name and how I received it was simply that a C.I.D. typist once remarked how I resembled a young boy named 'Booper' who advertised 'Rowntrees' jelly tots in a television (black & white) commercial. The lad had black curly hair and was quite cheeky. In time the black curly hair turned grey, almost white, but the name stuck being used by friends, senior officers and villains alike.

If it had not been 'Booper' then it may have become 'Jack Regan' because I am told that I do resemble John Thaw (the actor playing detective inspector Jack Regan in the T.V series 'The Sweeney') and it was not unknown for me to walk in a pub and some loudmouth shout "Eh up, Jack Regan's here." I must admit to secretly enjoying this unique nickname of 'Booper'. I was a well-known character in the area where I kept law and order and my annual appraisal reports by senior officers were always satisfactory. Please note 'senior officers' and not 'superior officers' as often heard of in television programmes. You would never catch me referring to them as superior officers. Many of them gained promotion by nepotism and freemasonry connections rather than ability - but more of that later.

I looked up at the bedroom window of the flat. My partner Marion was still in bed.

She had not made a fuss when I left that morning but I was

confident of getting bail on the first day of the trial. I am going to miss my partner and the flat when I go to prison.

We have shared some good times there. Despite being near to the town a number of trees protected the houses from the wind that blew over the top of hill. Today the dark brown leaves were swirling alive in the strong breeze deserting the trees they had guarded since last spring. Each autumn the leaves gathered, ankle-deep in the corners creating dark soft carpets for me to walk on when I returned home usually in the early hours of the morning. I owe those leaves a favour as they prevented my footsteps from waking the neighbours who would have seen the drunken conditions I frequently came home in. Why should the neighbours suffer just because I worked the most unsociable hours known to mankind?

Why the hell does this morning have to be grey? Why can't the sun just show itself for a second or two? Has the sun deserted me with most of my colleagues? Everything I view at this time is grey - people - cars. The sky is like a grey fluffy bedding sheet from a low-class lodging house and I've seen plenty of those in my time.

Why is it only me on trial this morning? How many serving and ex-coppers should be in my position today? The reason I'm standing alone is because I kept my mouth shut. That's more than some of the others involved. A tip from the investigation team told me that one or two of the officers interviewed sang like birds. All of them had reason to worry just like me. I wonder how many shopped me to keep their positions. Surely everyone knew that I was not the only bad apple in the barrel? No, that can't be true. They had perhaps more evidence on me than the others but they knew they would need plenty to 'nick' one of their own and make it stick in court.

Let me tell you that the number of 'baddies' in the police service far outnumber the number of 'goodies'. Mainly in C.I.D. of course where it was necessary to bend the evidence to secure convictions. Almost 'every' operational detective I have worked with has committed some form of criminal act in his time. Many more serious than others. You think that's a bit strong? - Every time C.I.D. officers give evidence in court perjury is being committed unless contemporaneous notes (written at the time and signed by the accused etc) have been made. From 'guessing' the time the arrest was made, claiming to have cautioned the accused, recalling his exact reply at the time of arrest would always be perjury because most of these details would have been entered in the pocket book some days or even weeks after the event. The later appearance in court claiming, under oath, that the notes in the pocket book had been made as soon as practicable was perjury.

This is why you are witnessing the present haste by the government to bring in tape recording and video police interviews with suspects. Watch the crime detection rate drop then - you mark my words.

The judiciary have long intimated that they cannot ignore

any more abuses of the judge's rules by police officers.

Don't run away with the idea, by the way, that only Scotland Yard detectives are 'bent'. I'll agree, having known several, that they are the kings where corruption is concerned. They are expected to 'survive' in London where some of the richest people in the world live. Where villains are becoming millionaires and the Met. Police have to keep law and order. The difference being that in the Met. a 'freebie' would be £500-£1000, whereas in the North it would be a bottle of scotch. However there is life north of Watford and I relish the personal identification my birth provided me in both accent and values.

Just before my 'brief' arrives, let me tell you a story currently making the rounds about the recent violent clashes between the police and striking miners in the infamous pit strike. The scene is outside one of the Yorkshire coalfields where there had been serious clashes between the parties. In order to win the battle for the government, all available police personnel had been mobilised, even those just recruited and recently graduated from police training school. A brand new box of 'bobbies' had been opened and one very young and inexperienced officer found himself in the front row facing some very nasty pickets. The young constable did not know which way to turn. - 19 years of age - being verbally and physically abused with more mature officers going down like nine-pins all around him. The young copper could stand no more - he dropped to his knees and began to crawl backwards through the melee of other officers who were still trying to contain the mob. His path was suddenly blocked by a highly polished pair of shoes and a voice roared … "Young man - return to your position at the front - show some guts and courage, laddie". The young copper, who by then was thoroughly defeated and wishing he'd never joined the police clutched at the shoes pleading..... "Sergeant, I'm sorry. I can't take anymore." The voice above seemed surprised... "What do you mean 'sergeant'? - I'm your chief superintendent, laddie".

"Fucking hell" the young copper replied, "I didn't know I'd crawled that far back." The story, of course, is not true but it certainly took my thoughts away from the pending trial.

Hope my "brief" is on time, wouldn't like to upset the judge by being late on the first day. I wonder how many charges they will slap on me today? My counsel were going to have a word with the prosecution because not all the charges can be heard at this trial.

Perhaps now is the time to tell you what 'they' think I've been up to.

It all started with a relationship I formed with one of the city's top businessman.

We had been introduced by another serving detective who claimed that the businessman was actually and genuinely his uncle. It later transpired that this was a 'load of bollocks'' but many more police officers of greater rank than I were taken in by the claim and responded in a way to the businessman that now seems surreal. For my part I associated with the man for some considerable time, sharing a friendly and amicable involvement, despite the difference in our ages, affluence and position in society. He was the managing director of a Sheffield company which specialized in the manufacture of high quality steels and lived the life of a millionaire with money no object. He was a leading authority in the specialized field of his products and his family life was virtually impeccable.

His wife was the owner of one of the city's top private schools.

His eldest son was an executive with a county council in the midlands.

His daughter lectured in computer mathematics at one of the most famous girl's schools in the country.

His youngest son, despite being academically brilliant, was an alcoholic.

My business friend claimed to be an accomplished violinist and pianist although I never saw evidence to support his claims. He associated freely with all the leaders of commerce and industry in the city. Unfortunately his wealth had been obtained by defrauding his firm's parent company to the tune of almost £2m. Many thought that figure should have been nearer £10m., but it suited me to leave it at the lower estimate with the investigators thinking I'd been involved!

Then there were a couple of allegations suggesting that the businessman and I had conspired to set fire to a new private school in the city which had opened in competition to the school run by his wife. My upbringing had not schooled me in the vagaries of 'private' schooling but I do know that my friend's wife had prospered very well in this area as more and more parents sought to have their children educated to a level not available in the state system. When the second private school opened its doors nearby, the wife of my friend feared her livelihood was about to be threatened and it was thought necessary for action to be taken to remove the threat. The allegation was that I and my friend recruited a well-known villain from the city to set fire to the new school which would return things to normal for my friend and his wife.

Needless to say we denied these allegations, but it did not help our case when the new school did catch fire one night shortly after it opened. Damage was minimal due to a passer-by raising the alarm and the speedy response of the fire brigade.

The well-known city villain recruited - just happened to be my No.1 informant Brendan.

Then followed a claim that I had been involved in a burglary at a warehouse in Sheffield when platinum value £72,000 was stolen from the safe. The police apparently had evidence that I had kept watch whilst the raid took place. It was suggested that with my official police radio I could alert the burglars should that be necessary. What a load of 'bollocks'! I could prove I was on holiday, out of the country at the time and I experienced the feeling of many criminals when interviewed about crimes that the interviewers did not have a 'cat in hells' chance of proving. I told them to stick their evidence up their constabulary 'arses'.

Next came a fraud allegation which had netted my businessman friend and his accomplices some £250.000. Apparently false invoices had been passed between legitimate companies showing the sale and/or purchase of precious metals. How they expected a copper to be involved in that one I don't know.

A considerably more serious allegation was in relation to the shooting of man who lived in Derbyshire. It was pure coincidence, as far as I am concerned, that the man held an executive position in the parent company of my businessman friend. For some reason unknown to me, some person took it upon themselves to shoot him as he arrived home from work one evening. I vehemently denied the allegation and to my knowledge the crime has never been detected. Had the man been unfaithful to his wife or was there some other 'domestic' reason why the shooting took place? Perhaps we will never know.

There were the other 'normal' allegations of corruption and misconduct levelled at me, which gave the forces 'top' detectives some ammunition to have a go. I use the word 'top' loosely, indicating only their police rank not their ability.

The enquiry threw up many police disciplinary offences thus giving the investigators a weapon to threaten me with. I found myself admitting to some minor discipline offence simply to clear myself of some of the more serious criminal allegations. This was 'double-jeopardy' at the highest and a situation that the normal criminal does not face when being interviewed. However, it was comforting to know that the investigators could not 'verbal 'me and they knew it.

As with virtually all the detectives I worked with it was more than standard practice to 'verbal' an accused to make the case stick. In my case the many questions they asked me were laboriously recorded by a senior police officer. I added 'Sir' after every reply hoping that would convince a jury at a later date how honest and serious I was with the answers.

During the investigation and whilst I was suspended from duty my flat was 'turned-over' at 6am one morning by the head of the force C.I.D. and detective superintendent Howard. They were accompanied by six other junior officers who were totally embarrassed at being involved in the investigation of a detective who until then had been regarded as one of the best 'thief-takers' in the force. Armed with a magistrates warrant, apparently they were searching our small flat for 'evidence' despite the fact that I had been suspended from duty for months and had been kept informed on a weekly basis by 'friends' of any interesting points revealed during the enquiry. Needless to say they found nothing incriminating, although my partner did manage to conceal certain items in her underwear which just might have caused me some concern.

So, at the end of the day the D.P.P. came up with a list of charges to be put to me.

Ones they felt confident would obtain a conviction. There were a handful of corruption charges in respect of free meals, holidays and gifts from the businessman. They also added a conspiracy and incitement charge relative to the school arson offence. It was a massive enquiry and too many other individuals anxious to keep themselves free of criminal and disciplinary charges were eager to spill the beans. When you run with villains in the way that I did it is almost inevitable that as a police officer you will at sometime compromise yourself in your natural anxiety to detect crime. Additionally the name 'Booper' came up very often in their investigations which made their job much easier.

After several appearances before the local magistrates' court and committal proceedings the case was listed for trial at crown court. It was quite apparent that other fellow police officers found it more embarrassing to see me in the local court house than I did.

I had long decided that the press would not be treated to tearful remorse from me whilst in the dock. I am not without feelings but you control them - like royalty, politicians and news readers. Over the years I have become a hard bastard which shames me now, but I have to admit I still feel emotion when I hear 'Abide with me' played at the Wembley cup final and 'Land of Hope and Glory' at the last night of the proms. Many films have reduced me to tears in a darkened cinema. In the initial stages of my separation from

21

my wife and family the loss of my two daughters caused me untold misery even though it was self-imposed. I must, however, have a 'masochistic' streak somewhere inside, because after being locked up in my own police cells for 4 days I still emerged smiling, finding it hilarious that the custody constables insisted on calling me sergeant even though I was their prisoner. I managed to get bail from court, after a battle by my solicitor with a judge in chambers. One of the reasons given by the magistrates for refusing bail was my 'previous character and antecedents'. When you consider I had never been in trouble in my life, it is easy to see how untrained magistrates are easily manipulated - a point I should really know about because I have manipulated them on many occasions when trying to get some 'low-life' remanded in custody.

Certain 'Bail' restrictions were imposed to guarantee my final appearance at the crown court for the trial. Surrender of my passport was no problem because I was to venture no further than Cornwall during my final period of freedom. I was not allowed to communicate with any fellow police officers, which again was no problem because the majority were frightened to death to speak to me in case they were roped in.

Another hilarious situation was a condition of bail that enforced me to attend weekly at my local police station in Rotherham and sign a bail register. A picture of the bailee is available in case you try to get someone else to impersonate you and report on your behalf whilst you do a 'runner' to

Spain or elsewhere. This condition can prove restrictive to your normal villain but in my case it proved a boon. I have said that the majority of coppers did not want to know me, but there were, of course, several officers in whose interest it was to keep close to me out of mutual benefit. How many times when I reported for my bail did I just happen to bump into policemen (and women) who had warnings or information relative to the investigation? How many times was I able to pass onto other colleagues the theme of my last interview and facts that just might implicate them? I recall, whilst answering bail on one occasion a friendly officer tipped me off that my home telephone was being tapped. Rumours were circulating that a British Telecom engineer had spoken to a relative of being involved in a sensitive case at Sheffield police headquarters which involved a bent copper. Confirmation of this fact was academic though because I would have been really naïve to say anything incriminating on the phone. However, at the least it meant that the investigation team were playing for real!

So I served my period of suspension and bail whilst awaiting trial without any noticeable alteration in my behaviour pattern or life-style. I continued to play up to the image that 'Booper' had created for years as a joker and character. On one occasion whilst making an appearance at the magistrates' court I caused quite a furore in the public corridor by planting an affectionate kiss on a policewoman friend of mine. There cannot be many villains publicly showing that type of affection for the enemy!

I am still unconsciously watching the cars race past as I wait for my solicitor and a bad day will be set in motion. Still it is grey, grey and more grey…...

One of the main problems is that my trial will be held in the city of Leeds away from my force area. This is not unusual for bent coppers, sex offenders' council officials and other 'isolated' offenders. It is supposed to ensure fair play basically for the accused. Anyway my local crown court in Sheffield would not touch my case and sent it to Leeds crown court just up the M1 motorway. Perhaps it was for the best because the local press had reported other cases indirectly connected to mine and any jury member could not have failed to have been influenced by headlines such as…….

"Judge says he thought he was in Sicily when hearing one of the trials"

"The scandal that rocked Steel city"

"Secret underworld tapes that put three behind bars"

"£1.5m metals case denied"

"Steel fraud man jailed"

I was in receipt of legal aid allowing me to recruit legal representation and present my case in the fairness demanded by the British justice system. The world is only too aware of the enormous financial gains made by the legal profession so it was accepted that that I was unable to afford to finance any form of meaningful defence by myself. Ironically I have always been a strong opponent of legal aid, maintaining that guilty men go free too easily and lawyers become even more wealthy. However, I do admit I took full advantage of the legal aid assistance, even though in my heart I still hold the same views of the scheme! I first engaged a Sheffield solicitor who had not been on the circuit for too long but had already established himself as one who was very often found socially in the company of well-known villains and was rumoured to be more than willing to 'bend' the rules' to assist a client in trouble. My description of this legal representative proved only to be so accurate because after having represented me at only two of the initial police interviews the investigators refused to allow him to be present at any more after they found he was passing information onto another civilian suspect in the case who had fled to Spain.

I then engaged another firm of long-established Rotherham solicitors who subsequently engaged a Queens Counsel Barrister and a Junior. I knew the queens counsel very well from the time he had defended an accused I had taken to crown court. His knowledge of local criminals and their exploits were good and I felt we could use this to maximum effect during the trial. His attitude when defending was aggressive and I think he was quietly looking forward to cross-examining some of the top police officers in his area and making them feel as uncomfortable as could be. There was no doubt that my trial would not be a 'kindergarten-affair'. It had the makings of a 'Christians v Lions' contest with no holds barred. Even afterwards and in spite of my conviction, I could never have doubted the honest efforts made by my legal team on my behalf (perhaps they may emerge as the only ones in my writings to attract genial comment)

I am still outside my flat - what will the prosecution bring out today? They had already served me with hundreds of depositions (witness statements) which they were sure would lead to my conviction. When reading the statements I was amazed how previously friendly officers had become my enemies over-night - many of them with extremely serious 'skeletons in their cupboards' I may add. I spent hours going over those statements. Picking out salient points with an experienced and well-trained eye and typing copious notes for the benefit of my lawyers.

But the time has come for me to really stop dreaming and face stark reality. I'm in deep trouble this time and no mistake. I twisted and turned when interviewed searching for answers that would allow the D.P.P. to say 'no case'. But I was well and truly 'nicked'... broke the cardinal rule of coppers and villains alike... Never trust anyone!

There again the 'detectives' that nicked me would not have got very far without others squealing like pigs. The investigators were dealing with frightened rabbits who could not scream loud enough to try to save their own skins. Here I am not just talking about civilians involved in the crimes but serving coppers who had lots to lose and who sold their souls to protect themselves.

You would be amazed at the blatant inefficiency in the police service and the investigation and detection of crime is one department that falls sadly short. I know the media love to describe 'Brilliant detective work' 'Dedicated detectives' 'Painstaking enquires' which shows they are more concerned with selling newspapers than reporting the truth. If 75% of all suspects interviewed kept their mouths shut (as they are lawfully allowed to) it is difficult to imagine any of them ever facing a trial in court. It is human nature to respond to a verbal challenge at a police investigation. Replies given by an accused to detectives, whether they are made by frightened, inexperienced, untruthful or sick individuals can be simply or more deliberately misunderstood by the interviewers and thus justify a prosecution. When saying this I take into account cases where offenders have been caught in the act, 'verballed' or 'fitted up' by investigating officers.

Suspects in police custody are very often their own worst enemy and 'grasses' their next major problem. I am convinced that the detection rate figures for crime, upon which government base their successes (or failure) in legislating law and order would be consummately worse if it were not for the 'scum' who squeal on their colleagues.

Oh yes, I've exploited the system many times using the information gained from a 'snout' to crack some case, taking the view that it was a necessary evil of my working life. Perhaps it was poetic justice that one who so glibly exploited the misery caused by the system in the past should end up becoming a victim himself!

Just a minute though. Why am I getting all worked up about a system and occupation that I shall never follow again? Better compose my thoughts towards the problems facing me today. One part of me says that I should have 'grassed' all the other coppers involved, but another tells me that I did the correct thing in keeping quiet.

How the hell I got involved in the first place I don't know and how I fell so easily.

Certainly I had been disillusioned by the service for some years in common with many more officers. A combination, I would suggest of stagnation in the promotion stakes and the rough deal a copper seemed to get from everyone in society. Risks were taken by good detectives to put real 'villainous scum' behind bars, knowing that any 'slip-up' could lead to an enquiry and potential problems for that officer.

To most senior police officers of my era arresting villains was like a 'foreign language'

They knew it was somewhat different to the language they spoke
and perhaps they could utter a few phrases
but most never reached the point where they could speak it fluently!!

Consider disillusioned coopers with many years of service and experience behind them being supervised by officers who were *'only'* in a higher rank due to their links with freemasonry or other connections. You then have the ingredients of inefficiency that are all too apparent today and a recipe for disaster in the future.

Of course many coppers take the view that the money is excellent for the work involved.

Added bonuses such as rent allowance, free dental and optical treatment including privileged medical rates, remove many of the mundane domestic worries facing families today. All that remuneration, is, of course, supplemented by 'overtime payments', so imagine the rush to be included on murders and other major crime investigations.

The rush to be included, by the way, being for many coppers more financial than in the interests of detecting crime! It was always said that if a murder was not detected in the first 24 hours then the investigators had problems. Not that the 'un-detected' problems worried many officers because there were 'overtime payments' to be collected leading to a new car, caravan, overseas holiday. Many such pleasures have been financed directly by someone's gruesome deeds.

This was the blessing in being seconded to specialized units set up by most forces to combat major crime. I served two periods in the force serious crime squad and a length of time on the regional crime squad. This meant being automatically involved in any major incident the force dealt with. Attachments to these squads meant a decent financial return for the minimum of labour by the majority of officers.

Detective Superintendent Howard mentioned at the very start of this book fell well and truly into that category.

The actual hours spent on duty determined the size of your monthly pay-packet.

God forbid if they ever start to pay officers on actual results.

The time spent away from the marital home led to broken marriages, or at the very least domestic friction. The circumstances of the job encouraged adultery by most detectives either with female complainants, witnesses, prisoner's wives and fellow officers. I shudder to think how many affairs I have had - some quite lengthy - some so brief they are beyond recall. Details lost in the passage of time and fuelled by heavy drinking sessions. 'Part & Parcel' of the job was the ready excuse next morning to relieve a quickly sobering conscience. Internal 'police affairs' were rife at all ranks in the force. I have a mental list of now very senior police officers who would be hard-pressed to explain certain absences from home. But that was the attraction of being a detective - the unique demand for attention to some case or enquiry at the most unusual hours of the day or night was 'tailor-made' for the errant officer. There was a standard list of excuses to be used by officers when arranging for their colleagues to be away from home or for not having returned there. Short term excuses, or lies depending on your moral viewpoint, ranging from special observations or seeing an informant. Long term excuses that included a weekly course out of town, two or three days absence to collect a prisoner from another force area. One married detective took his girl-friend with him to Malta for two weeks whilst his wife thought he was on a bomb squad course in London.

As a young detective I recall going to the home of my detective sergeant one day to recall him to duty (he did not possess a home telephone). His wife had not met me before and quite cheerily replied that her husband had gone fishing for the day with a young copper he had nick-named 'Booper'. I always found it incredible when attending police social functions that there were so many wives who were quite prepared to openly criticize other police husbands for extra-marital activities when their own husbands were generally at the head of the field.

Why did I never get promoted further than sergeant? Routine appraisal reports were always good, containing excellent remarks about my detective abilities. Looks like I might need them at the end of the trial to show the judge I have not always been 'bent'.

'One of the best detectives in city'

'Has an unrivalled knowledge of city criminals and their habits which he uses to the best on everyday investigations'

'Is regarded as something of a character which he uses when educating junior officers'

'Has served satisfactorily in the acting rank of detective inspector on many occasions'

But the rank never came and perhaps that led to my rebelling against society and the force. My problem was that I played the 'detective game' my way. I know that sounds corny but it was true. In between 'nicking' villains, I used to drink to excess - openly chase the opposite sex and I did not give a 'shit' if the Bosses found out. I never let it interfere with my work though, but how many bigger and better men than I have said that before? On the quiet I got sound 'man to man' advice from friendly bosses.

It always followed the same pattern -"Booper get rid of the play-boy image and keep your cock in your trousers" but, of course, I was unwilling to accept such advice from a system and police service that seemed to welcome sustain and support failures. I really could not expect to knock the system so blatantly and expect kind overtures from the hierarchy. Most of the time I consoled myself with the thought

'Sod the lot of them. I'm all right as a detective sergeant '.

'Who the bloody hell wants a uniformed inspector's job anyway?'

I would have to wear 'fancy-dress' again and work regular shifts. The immense freedom I enjoyed as an operational detective sergeant would have gone. I know I am as good as any of them, so why worry?

Needless to say I used to open my mouth too much. There again, only if I thought it was justified. I've caused certain senior officers many embarrassing moments during their careers. I even embarrassed the Chairman of the Police Authority at an open meeting by asking a particularly meaningful question of him. It caused wild applause from the ranks, but like any good politician the chairman talked his way round it. The chairman and I knew each other very well with him being a Rotherham pub land-lord and we had a good laugh about the question afterwards.

Many was the time in an open office and with a 'freemason senior officer' present, I would publicly denounce the way the force had gone down in the eyes of the public due to the constant promotion of members from one 'lodge' or another. All these actions causing me notoriety and support from the ranks but creating enemies within the hierarchy. The more I persisted, the more enemies I created.

One of my pet complaints was that only junior officers appeared to be subject to the discipline regulations. Any breach by senior officers was invariably swept under the carpet or dealt with quietly and without public fuss. For example it would appear that only 'junior' ranks (i.e. constables and sergeants) indulged in 'extra-marital activities'.

Oh no - senior officers did not indulge in that sort of behaviour! If you were totally naïve you would think that when officers passed the rank of sergeant they automatically joined the 'celibate club'. Whatever their age, you would think that any normal sexual desire had been replaced by fetishes for computers, crime statistics and fantasies involving community work with ethnic minorities. Certainly there were a few senior officers having a 'pop' away from home on a regular basis, but they were invariably the guys who were not totally rank-conscious and got on well with the junior ranks.

How the hell did we get onto this subject? - I am on my way to court to face a trial and inevitably a prison sentence and I'm rabbiting-on about 'shagging'.

Although I said that most bosses would have you believe that only lower ranks were immoral, there are always exceptions to the rule. Whilst a detective constable, I attended a police promotion party held in a pub at Crookes an area in Sheffield. Also in attendance was a young policewoman who was engaged to a constable friend of mine. Rumour had it that the female was having an affair with a married and very ambitious male detective inspector. The inspector was not very popular with his colleagues, always promoting the image of clean-cut propriety that would grace his path to the top. As I left the pub that night, 'yes' in the company of another policewoman, we caught the female officer and the detective inspector leaving secretly together in his car.

That was it - the secret was 'out' - they had been seen together in public and what is more the inspector knew that I had seen him. A few days later I called in at Attercliffe divisional C.I.D. headquarters controlled by the detective inspector. He asked me to go for a drink and admitted the affair, swearing me to secrecy- which I did not have a problem with. Unfortunately for him a short time later he was on 'routine enquiries' with the policewoman when they came across trouble they could not avoid and in the struggle with a prisoner she broke her arm.

The inspector was quickly moved to another post and as usual due to his rank and prospects the 'affair' was all covered up. I never mentioned their 'affair' to anyone for years until the same detective inspector (then detective chief inspector and in charge of the task force team where I worked) had occasion to disagree with me in his office over some work-related matter. What upset me more than anything was that he decided to lecture me regarding MY 'affair' with a policewoman who worked in an adjacent office. In my case though the 'affair' was no secret. I took exception to his moral and 'work-efficiency' stand and told him so in no uncertain terms. Unfortunately the office walls were not that thick and several C.I.D. typists heard matters that had until then been only rumours about the 'affair' between the detective chief inspector and policewoman.

In the middle of the row I also reminded my boss about an 'affair' he had with another policewoman from a foreign force whilst he was at Bramshill Police College and which almost ruined his marriage. As a postscript to the story, the policewoman who had enjoyed her 'affair' with the male detective inspector continued her engagement to the male constable eventually marrying him, despite all our warnings. How strange is real life because the policewoman gained a divorce after a couple of years taking up with a female colleague? Strong lesbian rumours abounded as they moved in together, confirmed by vivid details of 'after-match' activities in pubs following force hockey matches.

I recall another male detective inspector (seconded to the regional crime squad) who was having an 'affair' with a very attractive uniformed policewoman. He was your pillar of respectability - married - children and a 'side-person' at his local church. The detective inspector was obviously destined for higher places, although it was his presentation and connections, rather than his ability or zest for police work that gave him an advantage in the promotion stakes. No-one in the crime squad begrudged him his bit of 'nookie' on the side, being an acceptable part of squad behaviour, but when you have achieved a level of supervisory rank you must exercise the greatest caution when adjudicating on the sins committed by lower ranks. In this case the inspector fell out with a detective sergeant named Lancashire and a detective constable who had been repeatedly 'misusing' a crime squad vehicle - taking their wives out shopping in the car and leaving it parked on several afternoons outside a local pitch and putt course. The inspector should have been more cautious when trying to bring the two officers to heel regarding their misdemeanours - but lacking in experience he tried to be clever with them causing them to retaliate. When the detective inspector next checked the 'official' notebooks of the two officers he was horrified to find they had been keeping observations on him in duty time visiting the flat of his mistress. Not only were times/descriptions of official vehicles etc. to be found in their recordings but particular note was made when the senior officer was on duty and even 'overtime' duty. The senior officer strangely confided in me what had taken place and I did feel sorry for him, but a noticeable change did come over him and he tried to stay clear of discipline matters until the time he left the squad. His association with the policewoman continued, as did his rise through the ranks until he finally left his wife and married her. Detective Sergeant Lancashire finished his career as a chief superintendent. Most will agree that his promotion through the ranks was undoubtedly one of the most blatant freemason 'scams' the force has ever seen.

I mention these seemingly minor matters ruminating in a massive organization to expose the calibre of many senior officers involved in running police forces nationwide.

One of the senior officers mentioned above will give evidence against me at my trial.

I wonder if it will cross his mind that he could have faced criminal and/or disciplinary charges himself following false claims for overtime and misuse of crime squad vehicles years before? I wonder if his conscience is ever troubled by his past deeds?

Perhaps the exalted rank he has achieved anaesthetizes the memories.

At this point I returned suddenly to the real world.

All my past thoughts forgotten as my solicitor drew alongside me in his car.

The past memories I had explored were gone and it was still a very grey day.

A bad day for my trial to start.

Chapter 2 - The first trial.

"Trial by jury itself, instead of being security to persons
who are accused,
will be a delusion, a mockery and a snare"
Lord Denham, 1876 - 1938.

We had expected the first trial to last about three weeks and I had agreed with my partner Marion that she would not attend court each day. I knew only too well that the first and second days would be taken up with legal arguments created by my defence counsel, on my behalf, to try and establish some form of advantage for me from the start of the proceedings. My other reason for not wanting Marion there, was that it was not definite that the trial judge would allow me bail to return home each evening. I must admit that I did expect the concession, but there was no guarantee it would be granted by 'His Honour'. Therefore the last thing I wanted was emotional scenes from Marion at the start of the trial and in front of the jury. Towards the end of the trial would be different. Then would be the time to try and gain sympathy by 'stage managed 'innocence and disbelief at the allegations which inevitably would have been made.

Secretly I had worried just how Marion would react when the trial finally started. After all, like me, she had lived with the whole thing from the beginning. Her composure on the first morning of the trial had been outstanding. We had embraced farewell in virtually the same way we had parted during our four years together. I found myself anticipating recriminations or regrets from her as the trial approached - but there were none. No signs of alarm anxiety or increased sexual activity. We were both fully aware that our co-habitation was in grave danger of being officially suspended for some considerable time.

Being of the Male species I found myself wondering if such a lengthy separation and enforced abstinence would cause problems on our reunion. Would it lead to a repeat of the teenage 'fumblings' both sexual and otherwise that were merely pleasant memories of a 'growing-up' period long ago?

The drive to the Leeds city crown court some miles away was uneventful. There were pregnant gaps in the conversation between my solicitor and me as we drove along the M1 motorway. Each harbouring differing thoughts I am sure.

I do not intend, for a variety of reasons, to outline or detail in any depth the exact offences to which I entered 'Not Guilty' pleas that Autumn Monday morning. My main aim in writing here is to create for the reader an overall picture of life among provincial detectives. I do intend to highlight a couple of incidents arising from the trial which supports my argument about the calibre of the nation's senior police officers and others. In reality, also, there is no point in my trying to discredit a complete prosecution case which leads

39

eventually to my conviction and imprisonment.

The crown court building was patently brand new, standing proud among decaying older Leeds city properties. It resembled a new recruit in a parade of older and visibly more experienced soldiers. The civilian crown court staffs were also obviously brand new also. Their imitation police security uniforms and their keenness in their duties were sound indications that the novelty of having some form of authority had not worn off.

I knew it was going to be one of those days as we parked in the basement of the court alongside an elderly gentleman and passed the time of day with him. He, in fact was the trial judge and I was not surprised to be told by my solicitor later on that first day that I was obliged to enter through the public entrance to the court like any other scoundrel. I accept that it would have made the old man's job more difficult to sentence someone to a period of imprisonment whom he had greeted daily.

The entrance foyer to the crown court was a mass of imitation sandstone brickwork, glass and newly smelling rubber carpets. My attention was drawn to a stainless steel plaque on the wall commemorating the opening of the building by some V.I.P. from the National Judiciary. I recalled a similar stainless steel wall plaque in the entrance to the Sheffield police headquarters where I had served. I began to examine the construction and interior format of the crown court building where the jury would deliberate in my case. I really do hate official new buildings. They lack character and appear as frigid domains of bureaucratic oppressiveness: imitation wood pine décor; hard-wearing, semi-industrial characterless carpets and a forest of exotic green foliage that died within the first few months. The blame for the death of the plants always falling on the poor cleaners.

If recent press reports are to be believed H.R.H. Prince of Wales and I share the same distastes in modern architecture, but the similarity ends there because I could not have married a bird like he did with skinny arms legs and shifty eyes. You will gather I am not a 'Royalist'.

The actual courtroom was large and airy which came as a surprise because I had expected it to be stuffy. There were no windows at all. The dock was separate and identified from the remainder of the room by a long low wooden fence resembling a pig-sty. Seating for some twenty prisoners was available, so I was able to occupy almost any part of the seating that I wished. Obviously for most of the trial I sat in the position which allowed me access to my counsel and the chance to hold whispered conversations with them when necessary.

The prosecution was led by a 'Q.C.' (Queens's Counsel) who was small, bespectacled and rarely smiled. Very early in the trial it became apparent how terrified the prosecution were that I would be able to eavesdrop on their private conversations. To cause them as much unrest as possible I occasionally slid along my seat to a position directly behind them. This would cause them to form a rugby-type scrum

41

each time they conferred. The sight of barristers complete with wigs and gowns trying to form a sound-proof arena resembled a cluster of penguins at feeding time. They were not pleased.

Completing the prosecution team was a rather plain looking lady who represented the D.P.P.'s office. She had a spotty complexion a pallid skin and clothes to match. I suspect as a child she had ignored her Mothers request to eat her vegetables resulting in an embalmed appearance. During the whole of the trial I never saw her smile once, not even when I got my two years imprisonment. So I remained alone in my vast wooden casket except for the two obligatory prison officers who were invariably asleep. The prosecution team lined the benches in front of me and to my left.

My legal team sat in front of me and to my right. Easily within calling distance should I feel that some challenge was required as the evidence unfolded? However most contact with my legal team during the trial was by scribbled notes written by me and handed eventually to the senior barrister via solicitor and junior barrister. Many notes were to change hands during the trial but not all were relevant to the proceedings. At one point my team had been joined by a female representative from my solicitor's office who was well-known to me. She was not directly involved in the case, but I was not surprised to see her there offering me moral support. During the time she was there some remark caused a ripple of laughter in the court which, in my untenable position I really could not enjoy and my face must have shown it. She quickly scribbled a note to me. It read 'Keep smiling Booper and don't lose your sense of humour.'

I digested the comments of the note for a minute and then returned my reply.

'Thanks love - but you're not sitting in the fucking dock.'

Why she passed it to my counsel I will never know but it certainly caused them some amusement.

No trial would be complete in this country without members of the jury. I refer to the twelve good men and true, although it does include females of course - who would subsequently decide my future. Whatever verdict they returned 'Guilty' or 'Not Guilty' was immaterial, because my life was about to enter one of two different phases.

I would either be found 'Guilty' and sent to prison or found 'Not Guilty' at this stage and have to fight the remaining charges at a later date. My life would certainly never be the same again.

Allow me to drift from the story a little......There have been several references in the press over the years regarding decisions by juries. Suggestions of 'jury-nobbling' which means that the accused (or his friends) have somehow managed to approach a member or members of the jury and persuade them either by remuneration or threats to influence their final decision in favour of the accused. I personally have never experienced this behaviour. It is more common for advantages to be gained by either the prosecution or defence teams by remarking about the case in the corridors of the court and in the hearing of the jury. It is not unusual in local crown courts to find your old school-teacher, neighbour or even a relative sitting as a jury member in the case you are involved with. In practice, of course, steps should be taken to remove that jury member and thus ensure a fair trial, but in practice it is not always as simple as that. Imagine being a police officer giving evidence in a court case where you are not called until the second or even the third day of the trial. Perhaps you have not been directly involved in the investigation which has led to the trial, but you have what is called a 'walking on part'. You answer by giving your full name rank and the police force you represent - standing upright in the witness box - clasping the Holy Bible in your right hand reciting the oath from memory - an oath promising to 'tell the whole truth and nothing but the truth' which means absolutely 'sweet F...all' to most police officers I served with. As you look at the jury trying to impress upon them how honest and decent you are - there is your Aunty Mabel sitting on the front row. She stops herself from waving to you (thank goodness). Now I know that our family and theirs have never seen eye-to-eye but blood is thicker than water if you know what I mean? Obviously Aunty Mabel should say something or the police officer himself declare the situation to the court. When the very same situation occurred to me neither Aunty Mabel nor myself said a word. The accused was convicted, would you believe, and the story caused laughter in the police canteen for months.

On a lighter note it was sometimes so embarrassing for officers, when taking the oath to be reminded of their full names as selected by their parents at Christening time.

I recall one detective who was blessed with the middle name of 'Flucker' and there was always laughter in the court when he announced his name in full. He used to tell the tale that it was the Vicar who had given him the name after he 'peed' all over the font at his Christening.

In my trial the jury were the usual cross-section of community just as the law envisaged or hoped for, unless some had been particularly chosen from the list by the clerk to the court after privately vetting the list prior to the start. One gentleman sitting on the front row was obviously ex-army and would undoubtedly be the foreman who would pronounce guilt or otherwise at the end. There were the usual couple of 'working-class' guys on the back row. Their absence from work on 'jury service' counting as a holiday so that each day they were attired in sports shirts and slacks. Each day it was comical to see them leaving the Sun newspaper open on the jury benches at page 3 much to the disgust of the lady members. One elderly lady on the front row snoozed through every afternoon session whilst another took copious notes in exercise books during the trial.

Each lunchtime, as my solicitor and I strolled in the Leeds streets outside the court it was impossible not to bump into one or more members of our jury. Most acknowledged our presence, but one lady was so anxious not to face us that she almost got knocked down rushing across the road.

Part of the evidence against me was contained in a tape-recording of an alleged damning conversation between me and my number one informant Brendan. In fact the case for the Conspiracy charge rested almost entirely on a small piece of the tape recording.

The remainder of the recording, in their eyes, positively identified my voice as one of the speakers and the reference to 'Booper' convinced them of my guilt. I know that readers will have heard many times that taped evidence cannot be used in British courts without stringent safeguards and no-one knows better than I as an ex-regional crime squad detective that it is almost impossible to allow this type of evidence. In my case we argued that it was 'NOT' my voice on the tape and we went to great lengths to prove this fact.

The prosecution sought to prove the tape in two simple ways. First they paraded several police officers in the witness box who had known me for many years and could identify my voice even on tape. They also included expert evidence from the 'Home Office Forensic Science Laboratory 'to show that the tape recording was genuine.

Do not be confused by the term 'Police Forensic Science Laboratory' which is, in fact, the same establishment. It is easy to see where the anomaly between the two can arise in a civilians mind and is perhaps promoted by the fact that in my experience they have overwhelming success in finding evidence to convict but rarely uncovering facts to prove someone's innocence. (Many mistakes have been made by the Laboratory in the past as the case of the recently discredited Doctor Clift proves - I just wish he had been involved in my case!) The scientists had re-recorded the tape thus removing all extraneous noises which left an almost perfect sound reproduction. This procedure may seem to the lay-person to be soundly biased against the defendant and I would agree with that argument but the foundations of British justice are so solidly deep that a minor observation like that would be ignored. After much legal argument the judge decided that the tape was admissible and so the trial could continue. There is little doubt that the trial could not have continued if the judge had dismissed the tape due to the lack of other substantial evidence against me. You may think then that the whole exercise was a waste of time.

Electrical sound equipment worth many thousands of pounds was installed in the courtroom so that the tape could be heard collectively by judge, jury, barrister, accused etc... Everyone connected to the case, and in many cases unconnected to the case, such as the press, appeared to have access to headphones. The most amusing highlight of the trial was watching barristers and jury members trying to get their individual head-phones satisfactorily attached to their heads. The judge removed his wig to listen. Two of the younger prosecution barristers, anxious to preserve the dignity of their profession fitted their head-phones on top of their wigs. This caused the equipment to slide over their eyes and eventually they removed their wigs. Many people think there is something indecent about a barrister or judge minus their wigs. The wig to a member of the legal elite is like a guardsman with his bearskin or a motor cyclist with a crash helmet. However, there was not one occasion when everyone in court heard the tape throughout. Many were slow to don the head-phones and the transcript had started. Others failed to operate the 'on' switch and could be seen knocking the equipment to get it to work. Some altered the noise control during the operation and almost lost their ear-drums. This was, without, doubt one of the most amusing asides to the trial.

Not wishing to veer from my original stance of not writing about the circumstances of the alleged offences in detail please allow me to recall a couple more incidents indicating the humorous side of the taped evidence and the questionable side that the press quickly identified. During one of the conversations on the tape, the career criminal Brendan is heard discussing with the detective (alleged to be me) his afternoon of pleasure spent in one of the cities massage parlours or brothel to more accurately describe the place. Brendan is heard describing in some detail the sexual offerings he had enjoyed free of charge being friendly with the management. He suggested to the detective, who also knew the management of the brothel very well, that if he wished to avail himself of the 'services' free of charge, there was a new lady there who was quite unique in the sexual 'menu' she offered. For once in my life (because I admit it was me on the tape) I replied with an answer to his offer that must have been blessed by the Almighty. In a loud voice I am heard to reply that I had no need of such services having only just met my new partner Marion. I added Marion was an excellent cook, kept me in clean shirts and was even better in bed - now when you consider the tape recording was being made without my knowledge and was some years later to be played openly to a packed crown court with Marion present, you will understand why I consider my reply blessed. Just imagine if I had succumbed to the invitation what repercussions there would have been at home.

The other more disturbing part of the tape recording revealed a situation that was of acute embarrassment to senior officers in the force and heralded banner headlines in the Sheffield Telegraph newspaper press...

"Questions that remain unanswered".

It became clear that senior officers of my force had been in possession of the tape recording some years before the investigation against me was started. Senior detectives from the Lancashire Constabulary had been making enquiries into allegations of police malpractice in my force and had interviewed Brendan. He had played his tape of the conversation with me to the investigating officers as proof that such malpractice was common in my force. Unknown to him they were also in possession of a tape recorder and so the text of his recording was in police possession very quickly and a long time before criminal investigations were commenced against me and several others.

The Lancashire Officers took their tape recording to Sheffield police headquarters, one would assume to try to identify the 'bent' detective speaking in the tape. It was played to three of the top officers in my force. At that time not one identified the voice on the tape as mine even though I had known all these officers personally for many years. This was also despite the fact that the career criminal on the tape Brendan was known by them to be my informant and there was direct reference to my nickname 'Booper'.

What reasons could those three original senior officers have for not identifying me all those years earlier? What caused them to deliberately neglect their duty?

Was it misguided loyalty to myself? Was it because they were aware that no other recent serving detective had been so successful in making headways into organized crime in the city and beyond? Without doubt if action had been taken at that time by any of those officers in the form of an official or unofficial approach to me there is no doubt that the later criminal trials would not have arisen. You will agree that it seems strange that they allowed an obvious corrupt detective to carry out his daily duties unchallenged, but this was so blatantly the case. Apparently they took no action at all to identify the corrupt detective leaving themselves wide open to all manner of accusations when the case broke. One charitable view was that they readily recognized my voice and convinced themselves that my actions were totally to secure the confidence and trust of a major criminal in the city. Perhaps they thought, because in all honesty none of the three senior officers had any real experience in dealing with villains of the calibre we are talking about, that it would be better if I was allowed to roam free in the criminal underworld, putting my neck on the line constantly but gaining results that they and society would eventually benefit from.

Another point to consider is that on the tape recording the 'bent' detective is heard discussing at length with the criminal the 'verballing' and 'fitting-up' of other villains by my police colleagues. In particular there was reference to a case where one local career villain had been 'fitted-up' by local detectives and subsequently received 12 years imprisonment. I was not involved in the case but fully aware of the circumstances and the unlawful tactics used by other officers to secure the conviction. Perhaps the three senior officers listening to that tape were not anxious to risk bringing the illegal actions of other detectives into the spotlight and thus quietly and jointly agreed to overlook things until my investigation some time later brought it all back crashing into their ' back-yard'. I am certain of one thing though and that is that we will never ever know the real reason for the silence of the senior hierarchy of the South Yorkshire Police and their lack of action all that time earlier. A silence and lack of action that could perhaps have saved me from myself in later years. How intriguing also that the local press after creating such a banner headline - "Questions that remain unanswered" did not fully pursue their scoop.

Perhaps it is correct, as I later learned later, that they were 'warned-off' by senior officers in South Yorkshire and reminded that their future livelihood depended on co-operation from the police to assist in producing their daily news!

Each evening, after the day's trial, I travelled home with my solicitor critically examining the gains and losses of the day and preparing for the next encounter. I always arranged for my solicitor to drop me off some distance from the flat so that I could enjoy the short walk across the small public park adjacent to my home. Later in prison I recalled vividly those walks. The trees losing their leaves. Children noisily playing games on the damp grass, their shrill cries carrying far in the afternoon air. I knew then that my incarceration was imminent and so I tried to recognize and remember the simple pleasure of freedom that we all take for granted. Perhaps a prison sentence would help me even further to appreciate the luxury and concept of freedom. Ashamedly at this point in my life I felt very little remorse. There were so many other overriding issues in my mind that a guilty conscience never got a look-in.

On a personal note there was the love and support shown to me by close friends, Marion, her parents and my Mother. I had absolute faith that some good would eventually come out of the catastrophe that I had created, even though I was totally unworthy of such a blessing. I convinced myself that my two daughters would never desert me for my misdeeds and the joint wealth of all these thoughts created a feeling that completely erased any conscience. As I entered the flat each evening following my walk across the park and embraced Marion, we were both aware in our hearts that the day was quickly approaching when I would not return carrying my briefcase and the damp grass from the park clinging to my shoes.

So the trial progressed at the accepted speed of most normal English crown court trials. To the casual observer and the jury members that was infuriatingly slow. The jury could be forgiven at times for assuming that their intelligence was being severely challenged when so much time was spent by both prosecution and defence outlining the obvious.

One senior detective giving evidence for the prosecution against me was forced to agree under cross-examination by my counsel that we hated each other. When pressed further he had to admit that on one occasion we had actually started brawling with each other in a Sheffield public house where a retirement party was being celebrated for the head of the force C.I.D. It must have been most enlightening for the jury to hear of police officers behaving in such an unseemly manner in public. However policemen are also human and that is why I write so openly here. A lethal combination of excessive drink and a strong clash of personalities led to our brawl - only brought to an end by the intervention of a detective constable who was friend of the other officer. You will imagine my chagrin therefore years later when both these officers were heavily involved in the investigation against me. On the outside the senior officer tried to appear that he was not directly involved in the investigation against me, but I am aware that he still remained in a proximate position to arrange ill-feeling and suspicion. I suppose he was only gaining revenge for the fact that I once nick-named him 'inch-high' due to his slight stature and I took the 'piss' out of him for his lack of humour. His Father had reached sergeant level in the adjoining force and certainly had pulled strings to ensure his son was appointed a constable in my force. I often wonder why he did not join the force his Father served in, maybe his old man did not think he would make the grade! The officer had made his reputation in Rotherham where stolen scrap metal was one of the major crime problems. His answer to this heinous crime was to sit outside a scrap metal dealer's yard and 'nick' anyone who came to sell the least amount of stolen metal. On paper his arrests looked considerable, but in reality they were normally the unemployed who were looking for some way to influence their state benefits. I think he would have died if he had ever seen a true villain. The fact of which I was aware, and told him on one occasion when we were in verbal dispute, that everyone was talking about his wife 'having it off' with another detective sergeant, did not really enamour him to me and so came his chance to give evidence against me and gain his revenge.

It was noticeable that almost all the officers involved in the prosecution were from the criminal investigation department, indicating that in reality almost all my police service had been in that department.

Senior officers of varying ranks paraded daily through the witness box giving the same rehearsed evidence and replies. Even though for many years I had personally taken part in such blasphemous conduct when trying to get some 'low-life' convicted it seemed so unreal for it to be happening to me. The majority of them were good enough to comment on my ability as a detective and everyone knew me as 'Booper' but all had trouble to look me straight in the eye. At this time though, these minor credits seemed lost to me among the overall trauma created by being a serving police officer accused in a criminal trial.

One very senior officer was questioned about accompanying me to meet an informant some years earlier. He was asked to agree that he was present at two meetings with me and the informant in a coffee shop. When he looked vague my defence council suggested that he should refer to his official pocket book because we were in a position to provide the actual dates and times of the two meetings. His reply to the judge was that he had 'lost' the note book concerned and believed it had been in papers 'misplaced' during a murder investigation. What a load of 'old bollocks'. The real truth was that he had never recorded the two meetings because he was idle and well-known for failing to keep records. In reality we should have pursued him more vigorously for his failings just to show how hypocritical senior police officers can be. They try to enforce the rules rigidly and yet break them in abundance.

Only a few months before I was suspended, a young policewoman in my division misplaced her pocket-book and could not give evidence in a shoplifting case.

I recall the poor young woman being put through hell by overbearing senior officers and threatened with disciplinary action for her loss. All the policewoman had to secure her books and documents was an old unlocked cabinet in a public corridor of West Bar police station whereas the senior officer had his own office, locked safe, secretary, desk and a number of civilian staff under his command. His excuse regarding the loss of the pocket book was accepted by the trial judge without any suggestion of reprimand or impropriety.

See what I meant earlier about senior officers being a 'breed apart'?

How many coppers over the years have fallen into disgrace over failings in respect of their pocket-books? How many good detectives have been returned to uniformed duties for sins including misdemeanours with their official books? Officially entries in a police officer's pocket-book should be recorded at the time or as soon as possible. 'Contemporaneously' is the correct description of the practice. In reality this rule was 'never' observed. It was virtually impossible to achieve and defending counsel are waking up to that fact and pursuing police officers and their recorded notes more and more in the courts. The time must come when taped evidence will be the norm in police interviews and as I said earlier watch the effect on the crime detection figures.

As a very young detective I made the National newspapers in relation to my pocket book when I told the Quarter Sessions judge (Pre- crown court) that I did not carry it at 'all' times in C.I.D. - ' because it was too big to fit in my suit pocket'

That comment went down like a bomb with senior officers, because for years and years the police had always maintained that pocket book entries were made as soon as possible because note books were always available. For me to hint at the truth really put the cat among the pigeons. It did not affect the result of the case and four very clever London 'pick-pockets' were convicted. It was also the first and perhaps only time I have seen a defence lawyer silenced by a civilian witness in a trial. My colleague and I had been keeping observations on bus queues in the Sheffield city centre because there had been so many complaints of 'pick-pocketing'. An unusual crime in the sixties perhaps, because the working-man took great care of his wages having worked all week for them and he was not akin to losing them by theft. It was Friday afternoon in the city when the buses were full of working men going home for the week-end. We watched as the four accused surrounded a man in working clothes as he tried to board a bus in Waingate. It was a very well worked plan where two stood on the bus step asking the

57

bus conductor if it went to a certain location and thus preventing anyone else boarding. The other two accused behind then pushed at the back of their target, as if angry they could not board the bus, but at the same time one would slip the wallet or purse out of the victims pocket. My colleague and I had not seen any of the four suspects actually stealing a purse or wallet but their actions were sufficient for us to arrest them on suspicion. They were taken to the C.I.D. office where their previous records indicated that we had captured a well-known London gang of 'dippers'. It was at the Quarters Sessions court later that I dropped a 'bollock' trying to be cute. I told one defence lawyer that my colleague and I had been so close to the accused when they we trying to steal from the man at the bus stop - "As close as a cricket pitch length" I said. When the defence asked me how long a cricket pitch was I could not remember! When asked why I had not entered details in my pocket book at the time I said my pocket book was not in my possession. When asked why it was not in my possession, I uttered the reply that was to haunt me for many years:

"It won't fit in my suit pocket, sir. That's why I didn't have it"

National newspapers murdered me with comments like…………

'Detective too smart for words'

'Detective claims pocket book spoils the cut of his suit.'

The four accused were convicted anyway so my 'faux pas'

was overlooked.

I mentioned that I had never seen a defence lawyer humbled in such a way as in that case.

The four accused had engaged a London barrister of many years standing who looked old and haggard. He wore a barrister's wig that was stained and dirty. He had a large hump-back and when questioning witnesses snarled and tried his best to aggravate them.

He tried it with the man in working clothes who had been accosted by the four accused at the bus stop, suggesting that because the man wore spectacles he may have a problem with his sight. The man went silent and looked round the court room. In a rough Yorkshire accent he said to the barrister "Ah tha trying to say I'm blind? Beco's I'll tell thee this - I can see as well as I can see that hump on tha back!"

The barrister looked shell-shocked and sat down.

Back to MY trial the witnesses for the prosecution were coming thick and fast.

Another senior officer from my force gave evidence against me. He had earlier achieved national fame in the press and on television after leading a murder hunt in which three members of the same family had been found slaughtered in their own home. The man responsible had been sentenced amid a welter of media coverage. The detective in the case was considered by his rank and experience to be at the top of the professional tree. An authority in the eyes of the public representing the organization he worked for. Unfortunately or fortunately all men are equal and are fallible in life despite the incongruous titles in front of, or the decorations after their names! This 'paragon of law enforcement' told lies on oath during my trial

By many standards it was not a serious case of perjury, although my limited criminal knowledge of the law of this land understands that perjury is perjury - like it or not. We knew the evidence was coming because we had been served notice in the form of deposition statements prior to the trial. In essence the officer claimed that he had 'never' socialized with me away from duty. He accepted that we had worked together and attended police functions, but recognizing that to admit closer social links with a rogue officer could possibly affect his future, he therefore chose to tell lies to the court.

One incident more than others gave us chance to test his integrity and we were all set to reveal how on one occasion the senior officer and I had escorted two married ladies out for the evening. All arranged, I might add, by the senior officer.

We had worked together for some considerable time in the force serious crime squad based in the Sheffield police headquarters. At the time, as detective inspector he was head of the squad. He was always regarded as one of the boys and liked to take a drink at any time of the day or night whether on duty or not. I knew him well from his detective sergeant days when he was heavily involved with a married store detective in the city, albeit being married himself at the time.

His marriage was on the rocks, only kept alive in public for family and future promotion prospects. We used to indulge in heavy all-day drinking on the serious crime squad and it was following such an event that we returned to the squad office early one evening and the Boss made a phone call. That night I found myself making up a four-some with two married ladies from Barnsley and a good time was had by all. The brief 'affair' I started with my 'date' was to finish after a few weeks but I know the Boss continued the association with his for some considerable time. You can imagine, therefore, how annoying it was for me to read in the depositions served on my defence team prior to the trial that the Boss and I had never socialized. It would be difficult to describe a more social liaison with a male colleague than that I think?

There had been other excursions to support my claim against this senior officer.

Local detectives, including the Boss and myself, used to frequent a dance hall in the Manor district of Sheffield, lovingly referred to on Thursday evenings as 'Grab a Granny Night'. The event basically catered for males over 30 years, where uninhibited ladies could enjoy sexual encounters without strings attached. I know of many senior officers in the Sheffield force who must hang their heads in shame when passing the place in broad daylight. The dance hall on Thursday evenings created an environment all of its own, being invariably full and emitting a distinct odour created by a mixture of heavy bodies, intoxicating liquor and cheap perfume. Many officers have been forced to get rid or fumigate their clothes before returning to the marital home.

As my ex-Boss gave evidence against me, I wondered if his conscience troubled him at all. In view of the fact that his evidence was designed to convict me of 'corruption crimes' did it cross his mind that he too could have been prosecuted, with my assistance, for a similar crime?

It was a London enquiry involving H.M. Customs & Excise and our serious crime squad. We had become involved in the massive customs & excise investigation where the payment of V.A.T. had been evaded on silver metal melted down and sold in Sheffield. The fraud had netted a local silver-smith many thousands of pounds before he was arrested. Whilst it was necessary for us as the local police to be on hand at the arrest and at other times, it was basically the job of the customs & excise to prepare the case for court During the period of the investigation the customs and excise branch based in London held their annual dinner and the Boss myself and another detective were invited as guests. It was a superb and lively occasion held at the Connaught Rooms in Great Wardour Street. London. It had meant 'inventing' an enquiry in London relative to the V.A.T. enquiry to get us there on full expenses, but the Boss arranged all that. Accommodation was gained through a London-based friend of mine who was the night-manager at the Park Plaza Hotel in Bayswater. We had a fabulous time, all at the tax-payers expense and my friend the manager arranged for the accommodation to be entirely free. He also secured us inflated receipts so that on our return we picked up a nice few quid when we submitted our expenses. There was little danger of being detected because the Boss signed our expenses and they went through as normal. The conspiracy between my Boss and the hotel night-manager in obtaining false and inflated receipts were clear criminal offences. Did those thoughts cross the mind of this senior officer as he struggled to give evidence against me, but pointedly avoided looking across at me in the dock.

A rather humorous event actually took place at the Park Plaza Hotel in the early hours whilst we were helping my friend the night-manager to dispose of a large bottle of scotch. We were all drinking in the splendour of the rather spacious lounge when it was reported that there was an 'intruder' in the hotel. What a heaven-sent blessing for my friend the night-manager and the hotel staff to be in the company of three of the finest detectives the North had ever produced! The arrest of the 'intruder' was virtually certain with such a galaxy of 'thief-takers' on hand. We all left our drinks and rushed to make a thorough search of the hotel corridors and floors. After some time and with no evidence of any 'intruder' we returned to the lounge to find that in our absence someone had 'stolen' our bottle of scotch!

Many thoughts, grievances and memories were to ghost through my mind day after day as I sat in the dock in sullen observation as the bevy of witnesses passed by for the inspection of the jury. It was ironical that the only witnesses called by the prosecution who appeared nervous were police officers. Their faces, ghostly pale. Their hands visibly shaking as they took the oath in voices that I would never have recognized if they had not been before me. These trained experienced individuals showing inherent fear that I might be tempted to maliciously expose some skeleton in their cupboard or embarrass them with some murky deed from the past. Let them beware of this animal trapped and caged who could so easily cause them maximum discomfort in court or even serious repercussions at work or home. How many visibly breathed a sigh of relief as they left the witness box unscathed and still with their many secrets because we did not pursue that type of defence.

One of the detective sergeants involved in the investigation against me had known me most of my service and we were quite friendly. Due to his position in the Fraud squad he was given the task of exploring my Bank and Building society accounts when the enquiry started. He apparently found several transactions that he considered 'suspicious' and worthy of investigation. One 'suspicious' transaction was a cheque for a reasonable amount made payable by me to a well-known character in the city. The man had no previous convictions but was on the fringe of villainy in Sheffield and his associates and life-style led to several entries about him in the crime intelligence system. I was told later that the investigation team really thought they were onto something in respect of this transaction where they had proof of a detective sergeant paying money to a city rogue!

The humorous irony of this event was that the cheque was

in payment to the rogue for several gents' two-piece suits I bought from him 'at the right price'. Where they came from I don't know, I didn't ask, but the price was right and they sold like 'hot cakes' to members of the criminal investigation department. The laughable part though, was that when the fraud squad detective went to interview the rogue about the transaction the man corroborated my claim that gents suits had changed hands but he could not help noticing that the sergeant was actually wearing one of them!

As I sat in the dock of the court my mind often drifted away from the proceedings to list a catalogue of police officers and incidents that could have put them in court with me.

You will recall that I earlier referred to my association with the wealthy businessman in the city and my downfall was directly attributed to that friendship.

His criminal activities, when exposed, caused the investigators to dig deeply into his past and as they examined his lifestyle and tried to account for the thousands of pounds stolen from his company, other 'police' liaisons were detected.

I know that other officers (and one particular ex detective sergeant) were heavily involved in criminal behaviour together with and on behalf of the corrupt businessman.

The fact that no-one except me ever appeared in court and no disciplinary action was taken against any other officer strongly suggests that deals were done and facts suppressed for various reasons.

Let me outline briefly some of the behaviour that I am aware of between the businessman and other officers and you tell me why no-one else ever faced trial.

It was my duty being close to the corrupt businessman to distribute free gifts to fellow police officers. During the festive season 1980-81 I placed several cases of very expensive wines and spirits in the boot of a car owned by a detective superintendent who was in charge of the West Bar division C.I.D. where I was then posted. Later, when the same officer had been transferred to the Woodseats division, where the businessman lived, the superintendent was able to return the favour by arranging for police cover to be restored to his home. It had been withdrawn earlier due to numerous false burglar alarm calls and in accordance with police policy, where the police will refuse to attend alarms that continually operate incorrectly. In fact the alarm installed at the home of the businessman was extremely expensive and sophisticated but was no match for the antics of the young alcoholic son of the businessman who returned home daily pissed out of his brains. Other meetings between this superintendent and the businessman also took place but I was never privy to the details.

Over the same Christmas period 1980-81 I rendezvoused with a fellow detective sergeant on the M1 Motorway and handed over several cases of expensive wines and spirits again on behalf of the businessman. These were gifts from the corrupt businessman to the sergeant and a chief inspector who had been transferred to an outer division.

Both the sergeant and chief inspector had been friendly with the businessman when we had all worked together on the No.3 regional crime squad. Despite the fact that we had all moved on, the businessman never forgot his 'police friends' ensuring of course that favours could be demanded later in life. I am aware that the chief inspector received other gifts from the businessman including an expensive and complete kitchen re-fit at his family home. All free of charge of course. I know that the investigation team were fully aware of these events but never got the chance to pursue them in depth because the chief inspector was tragically killed when his petrol-mower suspiciously exploded in his garage shortly after the investigation commenced. Apparently the officer was smoking as he filled the machine with fuel............. Suicide or what?

So many other police officers of all ranks, had been entertained free of charge by the businessman over many years before I came on the scene that the list was impossible to formulate.

One officer regularly chauffeured the businessman around the country, when his duties permitted, as well as acting as security for the many premises owned by the man.

He was, of course, well rewarded for his involvement. The same officer and another policeman were instructed by the businessman to follow one of his many 'girl-friends' after she had offended him. The lady was subject to quite serious harassment and threats, but no action was ever taken against any officer in respect of this.

Another police officer, who was also a qualified pilot, flew the businessman to several venues in the UK. The same officer also flew other well-known businessmen across the country. Some of these men were later to be charged with criminal offences revealed by the investigation against myself. The investigating officers actually took possession of a photograph of the same pilot police officer posing alongside the aircraft with a major career criminal from Sheffield and our businessman friend before he flew them to some venue. Towards the end of the investigation the pilot police officer had his home searched by detectives armed with a warrant issued under the Firearms Act. The same pilot police officer was also interviewed about his association with a man who had just been arrested bringing gold Krugerrands value almost £100.000 into the country from Jersey and avoiding the V.A.T payments.

I here remind you again that I am and probably always will be the only police officer to face prosecution from the investigation.

The investigation team became aware that the businessman and others involved in his company fraud had been used by metal squad detectives to pose as informants and claim the rewards after court cases. The metal squad detectives on several occasions had recovered quantities of stolen metal by other means and without the help of an informant. The offender(s) were arrested and taken to court and any rewards being offered by the losers were claimed by the police officers stating the use of an informant. It was unnecessary for the businessman or others to appear in court or sign any statement as long as they indicated they were the informant should any enquiry ever develop.

One metal squad detective became so close to another city businessman that he frequently borrowed the man's holiday home in Spain taking family holidays there.

Another metal squad detective actually sold a quantity of expensive scrap metal recovered from a thief to my businessman friend and was handsomely paid for it. I know because I arranged that deal. This was one event I admitted to the investigation team when I was interviewed, but it never formed the basis of a charge against me, my businessman friend or the metal squad detective. One wonders why no action was taken by the investigating team in respect of this?

I know I have gone to some length describing corrupt events by police officers and others simply to highlight the point - why only me?

A small, but quite significant, fact was being discussed by my defence team in court.

I was certain that detective superintendent Howard leading the investigation against myself, the businessman and others had been very close to the businessman when he had served as a detective sergeant in the No. 3 regional crime squad. I too was serving in the squad at the time, hence my comments at the start of this book about the capabilities of the officer whom I described as 'a fucking useless sergeant on the crime squad'.

Even to a lay-man it will be clear that this senior officer should never have been in charge of an investigation against someone with whom he had socialized. Conflict of interest - or what? During my suspension I had been able to make certain enquiries and I was convinced that at least on one occasion, in our crime squad days, detective sergeant Howard (later to be detective superintendent) had been dined by the corrupt businessman. My defence team put this fact to the prosecution team long before the trial started indicating a massive 'conflict of interest' but they strongly denied our claims.

It was incredulous then that as the trial against me had started, the very day before the detective superintendent was to give evidence; we received a statement from the prosecution admitting that he had, in fact, dined, free of charge, with the businessman some years previously during the crime squad period. He claimed to have accepted the gift of a free meal because he thought that he could persuade the businessman to become a police informant in the scrap metal world. He already knew that the businessman was heavily involved with a detective constable (later promoted to sergeant) serving on the regional crime squad and any benefits in respect of information would come through that officer. His declaration was a complete tissue of lies. Detective superintendent Howard had enjoyed a 'freebie' and maybe more, many years before which, in his wildest dreams, he never thought he would be asked to account for.

To support his claim the detective superintendent produced his old pocket book from more than 12 years previously which duly recorded the meeting. I knew exactly what he had done. He had never made such an entry in his pocket- book all those years before.

Recognizing the importance of the point and the allied 'salvo' being prepared by the defence in that there was a blatant 'conflict of interest' by his senior role in the investigation, the detective superintendent had obtained a new pocket book rewriting the events of the day in question when he met the businessman all those years before and ensuring that his pocket-book notes corroborated his claim.

To the uninformed the obtaining of a new pocket book and ensuring that it fitted events correctly (even many years later) was not as difficult as it sounds. It was a ruse I had used on many occasions. Yes there was the tedious bind of re-writing the script in the pocket-book to fit the evidence accordingly but it was always better than being open to accusations of perjury. A sequel to this part of the case was that many months later I met the convicted businessman where he was serving his sentence in H.M.P. Featherstone. He admitted having been approached whilst on remand by Howard and asked to corroborate the facts that were outlined earlier, including Howard asking the businessman to become an informant. The businessman thinking that his co-operation and agreement would ensure some support from the superintendent when his case went to court - agreed.

The businessman was sentenced to 7 years imprisonment!

Despite many rules and regulations regarding the issue of police note-books, to prevent the sort of behaviour I now describe, there have always been ways to get round the problem by wily detectives. Let me tell you how police pocket books can be blatantly misused.

I recall in my early C.I.D. days attending juvenile court as a detective constable to give evidence against some children accused of 'shop-lifting'. It was a typical Saturday afternoon case where some kids had gone into a Sheffield toy shop stealing pencils, rubbers, crayons and the like. The kids were detained and I attended at the store with my detective sergeant and brought them back to the C.I.D. office. After a short interview the children were taken home and left with their parents who were more concerned that their afternoon had been spoilt rather than the criminal activities of their kids. Nine times out of ten children pleaded 'guilty' at the juvenile court, were given some minor punishment and that was the end of the matter. The shop from where they had stolen the goods were contacted and told of the result of the court case. The stolen property, instead of being returned to the shop as force policy demanded, was usually 'nicked' by the investigating officers to be used in the C.I.D. office or even featuring as Christmas stocking fillers for officers with young families.

On this occasion, however, the parents decided that their kids had done nothing wrong, had been wrongly accused by the shop and police alike and they should not reach maturity with a criminal stain against them. They pleaded 'Not Guilty' to the thefts. It was most unusual for detectives to be called to give evidence in a 'Not Guilty' plea at juvenile court so my experienced detective sergeant did not have a scrap of evidence in his pocket-book! Plus the fact that the sergeant had left early that day and was never there when the interviews took place anyway. It was necessary for two officers to be present when the kids were interviewed so the file was submitted showing my sergeant present at all times. We were now about to be called to juvenile court and to give evidence on oath-was it going to present problems? At the juvenile court I gave evidence first and produced my pocket book - told the magistrates that I had recorded the actions and replies of the accused kids, accurately and as soon as possible in the company of my sergeant. The magistrates allowed me to use my notes (as always) and I left the witness box. What no-one saw, was that as I left, I secreted my pocket book under a shelf in the witness box for it be collected and used by my sergeant when he was called as the second witness. The sergeant took the oath, asked the magistrates for permission to read from 'his' pocket-book and that was that. I do not recall the verdict of the court in respect of the kids but as a young detective I recognised this behaviour as being 'taught the ropes'. Oh by the way the detective sergeant went on to become a detective superintendent!

As the end of my trial drew near, my partner Marion began to look desperate sitting in the public area of the court. We both knew that I had never stood a chance and in reality the end was something of an anti-climax. The jury foreman (the ex-military man I described earlier) returned a 'Guilty' verdict on two of the three charges. The jury had retired for a sufficient period of time to satisfy their consciences and thus consider themselves justified in returning to normal life leaving the strange world of British justice behind them.

I was pleased that the judge had little to say to me personally when passing sentence.

You can rest assured that any form of judicial observation at the time a prisoner is sentenced means absolutely nothing. My observations are that any judges indulging in lengthy post-trial sermons to the accused on sentencing do so only to justify their authoritative positions in society and to create and promote a feeling of public confidence in the system.

"You will go to prison for two years etc." said the judge.

I turned, nodded distinctly to Marion who was surrounded by friends at the time and I then descended the stone staircase at the rear of the dock.

So that was it. A serving detective sergeant from the South Yorkshire police had been convicted of crime by his fellow peers and in accordance with the laws of the land

What lay ahead? I have been asked by many people to describe my feelings at that particular time. I have seen some prisoners collapse in the dock. Some hurl abuse at the judge and jury or seek comfort from their family and friends across the court-room.

My emotions remained intact and constant. I had known

for some two years that this day would eventually come and I was more than prepared for it. Unashamedly I was still not remorseful or even concerned about the events. I knew that I had to serve time with the sort of people I had sent to prison for the last 25 years and I had to prepare myself for that experience Perhaps my decision to act this way paid off because within minutes of receiving the sentence I was full of humour offering to finger-print myself and save the prison officers a job. I also offered to remove my belt, knowing prison rules, but the prison officers told me to keep it, adding that they would be very disappointed if I tried to 'top myself'. I was then placed alone in a clean cool cell beneath court. The walls bore none of the graffiti that would certainly follow in times to come. What did the future hold for me? An ex-police officer in prison is as welcome as a pork-chop at a Jewish feast, so my past occupation put me in a category apart from other prison inmates.

Chapter 3 - To court again.

"It's strange that men should take up crime when
there are so many legal ways to be dishonest."
Author Unknown, quoted in 'Sunshine Magazine.'

As all my waking and sleeping hours registered the novelty of prison life, my thoughts were troubled in the knowledge that I had further charges to face.

Following a meeting with my counsel it was jointly decided to enter pleas of 'Guilty' to certain of the remaining charges. The reasoning here was twofold.

One, I fully anticipated some credit for this action by saving the court time and expense.

Secondly it was certain that the basis of evidence which had convicted me at my first trial would undoubtedly have the same effect at the second.

So, a few days into the New Year of 1985, I was taken from the Suffolk prison where I had already served several months of my initial sentence and driven to the crown court in my home city of Sheffield. It was a bad winters day, but I enjoyed the freedom from prison as the taxi made its way North. We passed fields with a slight covering of snow which gave them a neglected and deserted appearance, but it was bitterly cold and as we approached Sheffield I found myself uneasy. The sun had occasionally exposed itself thinly from behind clouds bringing a cold brightness to the day. When it did begin to snow heavily I reached the decision that the Gods had decided not to look kindly on me this day.

The Sheffield crown court building was quite distinctive in that it was old and dilapidated. The complete opposite in appearance to Leeds crown court where I had been sentenced a few months previously. I was quickly taken, in handcuffs, from the taxi by two prison officers, who were obviously anxious to enjoy their bacon sandwiches and placed in an old cell at the rear of the building and below ground-level.

It was still bitterly cold. What a bad day to attend court I thought as I sat shivering on the wooden bench in the cell watching snowflakes dash themselves to death against the small frosted barred window. The cells in this crown court were not the most comfortable I had ever experienced and perhaps you would not find more old and neglected cells in the country. I was aware that a civic building programme had been announced by the city council some years previously which included a new crown court. Obviously, therefore it was pointless spending revenue on repairs to the existing building.

I examined the filthy tiled walls……..

"John Smith expecting 18 months. Got 3 years. Hope the fucking judge dies of Cancer"

"Billy Brown expecting 5 years. Got 18 months. Silly fuckers. Can do it on my prick"

I looked for an entry on the wall from the notorious Charlie Peace or Mary Queen of Scots written at the time of their detention but found none.

77

These cells have been a brief home to thousands of scoundrels over the years. How many dramas have been played out in the courts above and these cells over the years? How many lives and relationships have been forcibly changed forever following a court appearance like mine? How many prisoners have rejoiced at the leniency of British justice and how many more have been bitterly disappointed?

'That detective constable Thompson is bent. The dirty slag" (Even villains have been known to get it right on occasions)

The next graffiti meant something to me.......

"Sergeant Ellis - drug squad - the bastard fitted me up but superintendent Fraser squared it and got the filthy pig some bird- serve the bastard right - ask for Fraser he plays it straight for a copper."

Oh yes, he played it straight all right because superintendent Fraser was investigating detective sergeant Ellis who was not a member of his own force. The case almost ruined relations between the two police forces for good. Detective sergeant Ellis (drug squad) attacked crime and criminals in the same way that I had done. His 'forte', like mine, was to mix with the villains - scratch their backs and look for a return from them with information and the like. I was quite friendly with D.S. Ellis playing football with him in the divisional soccer team and enjoying the occasional drink. Ellis had allowed a major drug dealer in the city a free rein in return for information and a few bodies now and again. All this being condoned by senior officers.

You may argue that to behave in that manner is wrong but without such behaviour crime detection results would suffer and the drug squad would have no chance in combating this type of crime that I feel will haunt society forever. I never served in the force drug squad so my knowledge of this particular criminal enterprise is limited. I do know, however, that it is becoming a major threat and the time cannot be far away when this country will be aghast at drug-related crimes and events. Every town and city in the country now braces itself for the advent of major criminal drug activity - the bigger the drug squad - the bigger the problem.

In the case of detective sergeant Ellis it was simply that a drug user had been captured and sent to prison. Unhappy with that and being aware that it was the dealer used by Sergeant Ellis as an informant who had 'grassed' him up, he complained to superintendent Fraser who served in the Humberside police. The superintendent made no contact with our force, completely ignoring protocol and secretly entered our force area arresting the drug dealer friend of Sergeant Ellis. Fortunately for the superintendent he got lucky in catching the drug dealer with a large quantity of drugs. The dealer was arrested and revealed all about the arrangement he enjoyed with the drug squad and in particular detective sergeant Ellis. The superintendent submitted a file to the D.P.P. alleging conspiracy and corruption by Ellis and the officer stood trial. He was convicted and sent to prison for three years. The dealer received seven years imprisonment, despite having given evidence for the crown against his one-time protector sergeant Ellis (let that be a warning to others). A collection by fellow-officers was taken on behalf of Mrs. Ellis and a large party held when the ex-officer left prison after serving half of his sentence. There followed a 'shake-up' in the force drug squad with several officers being moved to other departments.

No other officers were ever taken to court or even disciplined over the case.

Another one swept under the carpet……..

There won't be any 'bleeding' collections and parties for me that's sure!

I was alleged to have profited from my crimes which apparently is repellent.

What a funny lot coppers are. Break the law in the manner of Ellis, go to prison but still qualify for friendly financial support and parties. Break the same criminal laws as in my case and be branded a 'fucking leper'. Some writing on the wall caught my eye -

'That Judge Clark is a nice guy. Expecting 3 years. Gave me 12 months. Fucking mug."

I hope Judge Clark is still a nice guy because I am due to appear before him this day.

Any further thoughts were interrupted by the cell door being opened and I climbed the familiar stone steps into number one court. The same route travelled in the past by murderers, rapists and corrupt policemen. I was escorted by three 'screws' that appeared to be ready for trouble. 'Bloody Hell' you won't have those sort of problems with me.

If he gives me 20 years I won't go over - composed-correct and collected all the time.

Play-acting. Playing a character. Don't show them what you are really thinking.

As a detective over the years how many plays have I acted in?

I've raged at Prisoners - laughed with them - prayed with them- assaulted them- lied to them - 'verballed' them - threatened them, even shedding tears on one occasion with a female to secure an admission. All these activities designed to elicit the information that would help to detect crime. I have witnessed more violence towards prisoners than I ever want to recall. Violence to prisoners in my service became as common as wishing them 'good-morning.' but perhaps we can talk about this later.

Judge Clark had not arrived in court so I waited alongside the dock. By standing on a low wooden bench I was able to see into the courtroom. I acknowledged Marion sitting in the public gallery. It was good to see her and in the company of so many friends.

Even a friendly fellow detective sat unobtrusively in one corner of the court. So they didn't all desert me in the end. Marion has done well since the trial. She took some 'stick' after I went to prison with the local press publishing pictures of her and me together. It is not much of a recommendation to be branded as the 'mistress' of a bent copper.

Having been interviewed by officers during the investigation against me she had survived with flying colours. She refused to answer any of the questions that were put to her by a pompous 'prick' of a detective superintendent, apparently causing him to throw his pen down in frustration. (Mind you she had been coached by an expert.) The superintendent had no answer to her 'No Reply' comment each time he asked a question and the interview apparently turned into a farce. This was another senior police officer who had made it to the top via freemasonry and the chief constables office.

I noticed some of my friends waving from the back of the court. Smiling broadly and supportively as one would a Bride and Groom walking down the aisle. The kind of 'teeth-baring' nod of the head which signifies their loyalty accompanied by a silent declaration that they can do 'F-all' for you. I don't know where I would rather have been at this time - in the dock or getting married. In both cases you are going to end up with something you never bargained for. One of my friends put his thumb up, as if he had just had a good win on the horses. A lady-friend winked and mouthed the words 'All right love?'

The silly sod - I've been in the nick for the past 3 months and I'm back again today to cop for some more bird– how can I be all right? Still, at least they took the trouble to come to court. I'll never forget them for that.

But 'friendship' can be a double-edged sword and that is where, perhaps, I went wrong trying to extend the hand of friendship albeit for the right reasons, towards the wrong people in the jungle that is the 'criminal world'.

Back in court I was still blatantly aware that many more 'friends' had not shown their faces or their support. Where were all the police colleagues that had begged me to keep them out of the investigation? Where were the few that promised that if things went wrong for me they would ensure Marion was taken care of?

I'll tell you where the spineless 'bastards' will be ….......

The C.I.D. will be chasing some mug for screwing his gas meter.

Or capturing some poor old lady who absent-mindedly put a tin of John West salmon in her shopping bag without making payment for it!

That is, of course, if they are actually doing any work at all. Many will be 'boozing', 'shagging', doing personal shopping.

Some will have nipped off home, after 'signing-on' to dig the garden or decorate the house. With the luxury of personal radios and a car outside they can be back at the station in a short time should the need arise.

What about the 'Uniform' - where will they be? Probably asleep in a 'Panda' car depending on the shift they're working. Or 'officially' visiting licensed premises having worked up a thirst and knowing a friendly land-lord. Maybe the 'Uniform' will be 'stuck-up' some bored housewife. It always amazed me how the uniform held an attraction for certain women. They would ring the station complaining about a lost dog or an obscene phone call they had received.

Anything that would mean a visit by a uniformed officer.

On several occasions I've had the door opened to me by women in different states of undress.

"Oh, come in officer, didn't get time to get fully dressed. I'm sure I'm safe with a Policeman."

How many female complainants have met a copper at the door deliberately wearing a dressing gown and obviously nothing else?

On one occasion I was invited into a council flat by a lady with long blonde hair. She was wearing panties and nothing else. Her nakedness did not bother her at all and perhaps it was good that I was very young then and in the company with another officer.

Going back to the complaint of the lost dog or obscene phone call, all this would be forgotten as lust took over.......

"Oh, you're so different. I hope you don't think I go round jumping into bed with all the ladies that ring the station."

"My Wife really doesn't understand me. Mind you being a copper doesn't help. It's the fault of the bloody job it makes you feel so insecure. I mean each day might be my last!"

"That scar on my shoulder? Oh, it was nothing. Tried to arrest twenty blokes single-handed. They all had knives. We caught some of them. Happens all the time. I did get a commendation from the chief constable? Oh, I also got a bit of criminal compensation which made me feel a little better."

"Yes, I agree the courts should lock the bastards up. Dangerous? No, not really, all in a day's work."

"Well I've been a copper for 12 months. Hoping to get in

84

the C.I.D. soon. On your first day in C.I.D. they teach you how to take witness statements, submit a crime report and then for the rest of the time you go 'boozing' and 'shagging'"

"I wish I'd met you ten years ago. I think I told you the Wife and I don't get on. We're only staying together for the kid's sake. Yes, I'd love to take you out. No, I'm not worried about being seen out and about with you. I can always think of an excuse. As long as you don't mind being seen out with a copper. Of course I look different in civvies. I'll wear my jeans and a UB40 T shirt. I can tell the Wife I am on observations to catch the Yorkshire Ripper. Well she doesn't mind when the pay packet comes in and there's plenty of overtime in it."

"No, love, I'm sorry to have keep the radio on. Never know when I might get called to a Murder or a Rape. Very messy that type of case I can tell you. No, the radio won't scratch the bed-side cabinet. Hush a minute love - they're calling me …..(Panda 4 from Control - what is your QTH?) Oh bloody hell, Sarge. Not 'now', please…………."

"It's all right love they can't hear me unless I press the button on top of the radio. What does QTH mean? - It's the sergeant asking me to state my exact position. Bloody hell he would have a heart attack if only he knew......"

Whilst my thoughts had been basically somewhere else, the judge had entered the court, bowing to all and sundry but pointedly not in my direction. I stepped into the dock being fully aware of the procedure and remained standing whilst the charges were read to me.

The crown court clerk was a woman named Brenda. I knew her quite well. In fact we were on first name terms. Very attractive really in her own way. Many is the time we had shared a coffee in the crowded corridor of the court house. She was reading my name out loudly enquiring if it was me? Silly cow, of course it's me. The prison authorities will look sick if it's somebody else. Like me I bet you always find it strange when you are referred to by your full Christian name. All those Victorian sounding middle names that your parents blessed you with as a baby to keep all members of the family happy.

Brenda was addressing me again. I suppose it was a little embarrassing to her, knowing me so well. She showed no signs of that though. Very professional. I wonder why she took the case? Curiosity perhaps? I'm sure she could have found another crown court clerk to do the job who did not really know me. I wonder if she still lives in the small cottage on the outskirts of the city? Rumour had it, in fact confirmed one night when he was very drunk, that she enjoyed a very strong passionate relationship with a married detective sergeant friend of mine. He described her as 'very grateful' for his attention which I suppose means she was a good 'shag'. Good job he's not in the dock with me! He quite easily could have been when I think of some of the strokes we've pulled in the past.

Anyway there was nothing Brenda could do to help me. At least she was always pleasant and sociable towards the police which is more than could be said for some of the judiciary staff. Some of them were right obnoxious 'pricks' acting as though you were beneath them. High court judges, barristers, solicitors and clerks and even the court caretaker considered himself in a league of his own.

To a certain degree it was the same in the police force. I think while I am having a go at the legal profession I'll include the feelings held by most operational police officers in respect of the 'headquarters shiny-arse brigade.' They used to prosecute in the magistrates' court the minor offences that clogged the legal system in every town in the land. Traffic and drunkenness offences. Breaches of the licensing regulations and other trivial crimes. Overnight these ordinary coppers became Perry Mason or Sir David Napley. Overnight they all started wearing those silly half-moon spectacles favoured by the legal profession, but making them look real 'pillocks' in uniform. A cross between Benny Hill and a car park attendant. Then what about the accent? In the county of Yorkshire any deviation from the famous accent branded the speaker a foreigner. Suddenly Oxford accents were heard in the police canteen. The word 'remand' became 'remarrnd' - a 'cat' became a 'carrt' and a 'rat' became a 'rarrt'. Silly bastards, how would they present the word 'fat'!

I turned my attention back to His Honour Judge Clark. After studying him for a second or two I resumed my thoughts seeing no visible reaction from him to me in the dock.

It was the Judge Clark whom I had read about on the walls in the cells that morning. He certainly looked fierce and I was already harbouring misgivings about coming up in front of him despite the assurances from my counsel. Do I fake an illness and adjourn the trial to get another judge? I'm 'skint' so I can't offer him a bribe and I don't have anything on him to blackmail him so I'm stuck.

A couple of guys I know in the city did get a good result though. They went up on a serious Conspiracy charge that should have netted them at least 4 years imprisonment each. The sum of £12.000 changed hands between the guys and a representative of the judge and they walked away with a suspended sentence. Nice work eh?

On the question of blackmail I do know of one or two judges and barristers that their 'perversions' leave them wide open to getting screwed. Being close to the management of one of the city's saunas, as I mentioned earlier, alerted me to the type of sexual gratification that some of the local legal gentry enjoyed. I recall the sauna being raided the day after a very well-known barrister had spent the afternoon there as a customer Even though the sauna had been under police and camera surveillance for days prior to the raid the barrister was never interviewed although his identity was well-known.

Mind you there was one judge whom I had known personally for years before he moved onto higher things. Having drunk quite a lot at the annual chambers Christmas party he was caught having it off with a young female member of staff on one of the office desks. That was bad enough but the dirty old sod had her trussed up like a chicken with the telephone wire.

Of course the police have to approach judges on occasions for various reasons or even, occasionally judges ask for the personal views of operational police officers in respect of certain crimes.

In my force we had a very successful 'stolen metal squad' - necessary due to the abundance of steel firms and industry to be found in the city and adjacent areas. Officers seconded to the squad were responsible for the investigation of crime where highly expensive metals had been stolen. As with the drug squad though, you are not fully aware of the extent of the problem until you have investigated it. Then like drugs the bigger the metal squad - the bigger the stolen metal problem. One of the issues in creating this type of 'expert' team though is that the officers become 'narrow-minded' and tend to neglect other crime than the ones they specialize in. In my mind this is a problem that needs to be addressed by the police hierarchy.

I know of one very experienced and successful detective constable, seconded to the stolen metal squad who was approached on several occasions by one particular judge asking for his views on cases before him. I am convinced that heavy sentences, coupled with severe warnings to potential metal thieves by this judge, were directly attributed to advice expressed by the detective. A good idea, I hear you say!

Only on one occasion have I personally approached a judge and this was in support of a prisoner in the dock. The prisoner was my number one informant named Brendan. (I refer later to him and one of the most successful operations I undertook which came about through his information and assistance. Stolen jewellery was recovered which had Royal antecedents-See Chapter 11). Brendan had found himself before a crown court judge charged with causing actual bodily harm to a city taxi driver. The attack following a dispute between him and the taxi driver who suffered a broken jaw.

The arrest and prosecution of my informant had been handled by uniformed officers from another division who were convinced that in view of his previous convictions and violent nature my informant was to go away for a very long time. The two uniformed officers were totally unaware of my relationship with the accused. They were certain the law would imprison Brendan who had assaulted the taxi driver only days after being released from prison after serving a six years sentence (reduced to four years on appeal) for glassing a man in a restaurant. I appealed to South Yorkshire senior officers that the informant was more use to us, the police, on the outside rather than being locked up, but they were unwilling to support me. I appealed, without my own force being aware, to senior officers in West Yorkshire force area where we had cleared up their big jewellery crime and they made the decision to approach the trial judge. A full report was submitted to the judge outlining the circumstances of the jewellery case and stressing the part played by Brendan. A meeting was held in the judge's chambers with myself, senior police officers and both prosecuting and defence counsels present. Back in court the two uniformed officers were astounded to see the accused released with a suspended sentence and to this day do not know what strings were pulled to achieve that result. It was ironical that Brendan the 'grass' never reached his potential in helping the police, other than his recovery of stolen diamonds mentioned later in the book. Brendan now serves a term of imprisonment directly and indirectly connected to my crimes.

I was back with Brenda the crown court clerk. She was reading the charges out to me and I was trying to remember which five I was pleading guilty to. Two of the charges I entered 'Not Guilty' pleas after an agreement with the prosecution and this was accepted. All the time my eyes were turning to my junior barrister who, with a deft nod of the head indicated which way we had decided to plead to each individual charge. The judge had already asked my counsel if I had abandoned my appeal against the first term of imprisonment imposed on me at the previous crown court. We confirmed this and thus and expected some form of temperance in respect of the sentence the judge would pass. How wrong a conclusion that turned out to be.

The 'twat' of a prosecuting barrister opened the crown's case against me. I said earlier he was also a Q.C. like my senior barrister, but I wondered as he opened the case how he had ever reached such dizzy heights in the judiciary. Perhaps due to family or other connections. Again - no smile ever crossed his face.

There was no need for him to be over-vindictive to me

because my counsel had warned him before the Christmas vacation that we would plead guilty to certain charges and the prosecution were happy with that. He must have enjoyed his Christmas break not having to prepare a long case against me that would have been challenged, but I saw no credit from him towards us for that concession. I didn't like the little 'twat' and I didn't trust him. I think if he had been defending me we would have parted company ages before the trial started. He lacked character and humour, but I have to agree his case presentation was solid. Rumour had it that he was soon to become a 'circuit judge' which is one way of getting rid of an inefficient barrister. At least my Q.C. had some flair and bounce as he defended my case but one would expect that with it not being him going back to prison at the end of the day. I was hoping, of course, for some credit from Judge Clark for pleading Guilty and saving time and expense for the court. Surely even a 'bent' copper can expect that?

I looked up at the massive round face of the old wooden clock secured to the front of the upstairs gallery. I had looked at that clock on so many occasions in better times when appearing in the court as a witness. Now it had a strange disturbing effect on me sitting as an accused and experiencing the loneliness that only someone in my position knows. I wonder how many prisoners have looked up at that clock and wished their lives away?

I thought again about the snowflakes I had left on the underground cell windows. There was a fan-light window in the court but the heavy frosted glass prevented my friends the suicidal snow-flakes from saying their individual goodbyes to me. How many snowflakes will die before today is out?

This court many years before had been the city magistrates' court and only became a crown court when a new building was built nearby. I recall vividly times I have appeared in that witness box giving evidence against some 'low-life' from the city.

"The loneliest place in the world" coppers called the witness box.

It's a sight more fucking lonely in the dock I can tell you.

I realized that little had changed in that room since I had been sworn in as a brand new constable over twenty years ago. Visiting regularly after that to give evidence against drunks, thieves motorists and the like. The clock was the centrepiece.

The colourful coat of arms behind the judge seemed out of place against the dark wood panelling. 'Dieu et mon droit' which I thought was French turned out to be Latin - 'God and my right'. I suppose that comment is about right.

The court seating had not changed over the years for the public and those that mattered. Varnished wooden benches that played hell with your arse after twenty minutes for the 'commoners'. Cushions were provided for the defence and prosecuting counsel and their teams. In the dock where I was seated were cinema-type chairs, securely fastened to the floor to prevent them being thrown at the judge or others if some accused took exception to his sentence. When anyone moved the whole room creaked in protest.

Quiet mutterings as if the past took exception to being disturbed. Dark sombre wooden echoes from a past life-time spent witnessing a city's depraved and degenerate being paraded before it. What could those sturdy walls tell us?

What counselling or influence could they impress upon us?

Does crime really pay?

Is the 'big one' really worth it?

Was it worth it in my case?

Decidedly 'No' even before sentence is passed.

Pension almost gone. Liberty gone. Reputation and integrity well and truly 'knackered'.

But I am fortunate to have retained a nucleus of firm friends.

The close relationship I enjoyed with a magistrate and his wife from childhood days stood the test of time and they showered me and Marion with Christian love from the early days of my problems. Friends and relatives have remained loyal. Several serving and ex-coppers took the time to make contact assuring me and Marion of their support at all times. Or was their close attention to detract from their own misdeeds? Perhaps the stigma of being a 'bent copper' is not as meaningful as it was. The public read of corruption in public life every day of their lives, why should the police be any different? Wholesale corruption in the corridors of Whitehall, Downing Street, Town Halls, Buckingham Palace, The Church, Society and Industry. Don't try and put all the blame on my shoulders. I'm a small insignificant copper who got caught acting stupidly and without real thought, in a society that always demanded more. At least my misdeeds did not jeopardize the safety or welfare of the nation like others.

Oh yes, senior police officers are often heard to remark that they need to weed out every corrupt strand in a dishonest web - every bad apple in the barrel. They talk of pursuing corrupt coppers ruthlessly but like everything else in this Life it depends on who you are and what connections you have. For people in certain positions strings can be pulled when danger looms and we all know the proverb 'how long is a piece of string?'

In respect of certain criminal activities, avenues can be opened which provide an easy escape route not generally open to lesser mortals. The full weight of the law and its punishments can be avoided for those with the right connections.

If the public only knew half of what goes on at the top?

Recently, as disgruntled coppers civil servants and other public sector employees have started to leak information to the press, the scale of the dishonesty of those in power is becoming apparent. A general rule of thumb in their case though being - No prosecution unless absolutely necessary and a conviction is ensured. Is that the way the general public want law and order to be administered? Is the man in the street happy that action is not taken against certain members of society because their parents are senior police officers, judges, local counsellors, members of parliament royalty or freemasons?

Would society be happy that prosecutions are not pursued against certain police officers because it would hold a police force open to ridicule or expose failings within its own systems? In my case, look at the serving 'suspect' officers left behind?

Guarding the public daily and gleefully taking home their salaries provided by tax-payers they are duty bound to protect. Many remaining free because Booper kept his mouth shut. He followed the unwritten code saying nothing to incriminate himself or others.

A dishonest statement you say? Well, maybe it is, but that's the way I feel at the moment!

Most police officers are, by nature very self-critical.

Not, you understand in an effort to improve their efficiency in policing society but more to improve their positions in the promotion stakes. In the old days you were promoted after proving yourself. If you were good at 'nicking' villains you gained entry to C.I.D. possibly remaining there for the whole of your career. Gaining promotion in a specialized department that benefited greatly from your zeal and experience.

Officers specializing in road traffic, dog section, mounted section and scenes of crime followed a similar pattern. If you did not want to specialize then you remained a 'plod' for thirty years during which time your service flew past, encompassing a bit of sick leave now and again - annual leave - a training course or two and presto there was your protected pension. Gained by not really putting yourself out at all. In the old days it was quite simple. You started on the shop-floor - worked hard - learned 'how the milk got into the coconut'. Your seniors then considered you for advancement.

Unfortunately things are changing as we speak with the bloody freemasons and other nepotism.

Looking round the court my eye quickly settled on the members of the press.

I knew most of them personally. One or two I did not know and I assumed they were 'free-lances' ready to supply the national papers with a juicy 'filler' story.

Whilst on bail they had taken photographs of Marion and me when I appeared at the lower court, plus I had been tipped off by a friendly local reporter that the press in general were anxious to get snaps to supplement their reports. I did not receive much help from my friends in the press, although in fairness I don't blame them. They had their careers to pursue and needed to be close to senior officers at headquarters so it would have been unwise to show a liaison with a 'bent' copper. I remember the day I was suspended.

Newspaper placards in the city streets that day showed 'detective sergeant suspended' and I wondered how they got the news so quickly? As I bought a copy of the local newspaper that afternoon and read the headlines I heard two locals go by exclaiming 'Only one copper suspended. What about the others?' A comment perhaps that sums up the public attitude to the police. The press, must to some degree, carry the burden for the degeneration of the police in the eyes of 'Joe Public'. The police themselves are obviously not without blame also. For many years the police were autonomous in revealing information to the press. The press in general resented this, claiming to be muzzled in their efforts to keep the public abreast of matters of importance. It was inevitable therefore that journalists throughout the country would seek information in other ways thus creating new areas of their profession such as 'cheque book' and 'investigative journalism'.

Senior officers from my force many years ago were under intense pressure to openly admit facts relative to a case infamously known as the 'Rhino Whip Affair'. To me personally it remains imprinted in my memory forever.

When people ask the question 'When did law and order begin to break down in this country?' I often point to 1963-4 when the 'Rhino Whip Affair' occurred. This case, together with other events, really caused the public to question the role of the police in society.

Oh yes, other infamous cases also hit the headlines causing serious mistrust in the forces of law and order but having knowledge of the 'Rhino Whip Affair' I can safely argue that it greatly contributed to a state in society which will only get worse before it ever gets better.

In the early sixties, as throughout the country, crime was on the increase and in my force area 'housebreaking' was becoming common. ('House-breaking' being a term used under the Larceny Act 1916, which was in force at that time) The head of C.I.D. formed a local squad of 'hand-picked' detectives to combat the 'house-breaking' problem and other associated crimes. They were told to be as ruthless as necessary.

It was rumoured that national regional crime squads were to be formed and there is no doubt our local C.I.D. chief tried to precipitate this by forming his own squad and securing personal glory and recognition by the move. The team set about their task with some relish. Within days they had received information suggesting two brothers and another man were involved in the majority of serious 'house-breaking' crimes and they were arrested. I understand that the police had no evidence whatsoever to directly implicate the suspects in any specific offences and simply set about 'beating' admissions from them. When interviewed, over some considerable time, the prisoners were assaulted by the detectives using feet, fists a wooden towel rail and a rhino whip in an effort to gain confessions. The presence of the 'rhino-whip' in the police station was later explained away by it having been recovered by one the detectives from some local 'yob' and kept in his desk as a 'memento'.

As I write this I am reminded that my appearance now, some twenty years later is in the very same dock occupied by the three suspected 'house-breakers'. In fact I had been present in the magistrates' court that morning, when the three men appeared and the police asked for them to be remanded in custody. My presence in court was in respect of an old drunken Irishman I had arrested during the night and I was there to give evidence should he plead 'Not Guilty'. My case with the drunken Irishman took second place when the three 'house-breaking' suspects appeared in the dock represented by a well-known local solicitor. Encouraging them to remove their shirts in the dock there were gasps from the public gallery as their bodies showed wicked blue and red weals across their torsos. I could see that many officials were shocked, including the chair of the magistrates who was known to very 'pro-police'. A riot almost broke out as members of the prisoners families screamed abuse at the detectives in court.

The solicitor representing the three men made allegations that they had been seriously beaten whilst in custody and complaints would be made against the investigating officers.

The incident later led to questions in the House of Commons a public enquiry and the resignation of the chief constable and some senior detectives nearing retirement.

Other detectives were posted to uniformed duties never to occupy a position in C.I.D. again. Two lowly detective constables from the hastily assembled 'squad' pleaded Guilty to assaulting the prisoners and if my memory serves me right were each fined £75.00 and dismissed from the force. No senior officer ever faced any charges which supports several of the points I have made earlier about 'cover-ups' and having the right connections.

The only good thing to come out of the 'Rhino-whip affair' was that I was transferred into C.I.D. as a trainee detective to replace one of the constables who was sacked.

The press crucified the force at local and national level and even today the famous case arises when allegations of malpractice against the police are voiced.

As I sat facing His Honour Judge Clark I knew that I would not escape today with a fine of £75.00. ....

The prosecution had finished their case and the little Q.C. had sat down. No favours had been shown to me by that little swine. He had lost himself several times in his presentation, which surprised me, but caused me to hope that the judge would pass sentence only on the bare facts of the charges.

I had becoming increasingly aware that Judge Clark had started to look more often in my direction. Was he working himself up for the attack? I was beginning to think my counsel and I may have misjudged appearing before him and I feared the worse when he adjourned for lunch instead of putting me out of my misery and passing sentence.

So it was back to the freezing unfriendly cells for an hour with only the snow-flakes as playmates.

On my return I was speedily dismissed with three years imprisonment AND it was to run consecutively with the term of two years I was already serving.... 'Bastard.'

The judge made a speech trying to blame me for every recorded crime committed in the North of England. The silly bastard even suggested that my actions gave encouragement to the striking coal- miners to attack and violently challenge the police. At the time I could not see the logic in that argument and he was proved to be a real stupid 'twat' when later all charges against the miners brought to court were dismissed.

My physical reaction was a shake of the head and I was taken back to my cell.

Oh boy here was my chance to add to the graffiti on the wall about that 'fucking Judge Clark'. What's the point? What will I get from that, the building will be gone soon. Forget it.

A tearful five minutes with Marion through the small cell window was all that was allowed. Then it was in the taxi, handcuffed to a 'screw' and a drive through the tea-time traffic. It was a winter fare-well to the area that had been my home and life for over forty years. My sanctuary for some time was to be a prison cell many miles away from home and the taxi driver seemed anxious to get me there as quickly as possible as he accelerated into the darkness of the snow-bound countryside.

Chapter 4 - Puberty to Policing

"And in the end, it's not the years in your life that count.
It is the life in your years."
Abraham Lincoln, 1809 - 1865.

I was ten years of age riding my pedal cycle down Darnall Road in the East end of Sheffield and back to my home during the lunchtime school break. I had been to the bakers for my Mother. An errand I was obliged to make almost daily. I was following a large motor lorry down the steep incline of the road when suddenly the passenger door flew open and a small girl tumbled from the cab, her head and top part of her small body going directly under the rear wheels of the lorry. My bicycle collided with what was left of her body. I fell from the machine and sat in the road unhurt, but inches from what was left of a precious daughter. A never-to-be-forgotten experience in many ways but the first time I had encountered police officers in real and close action. I can remember being shocked at the time and my Mother wanting me to take the rest of the afternoon off school. I am now ashamed to say that I had to go to school that afternoon so that I could recount the incident in so much detail to all my friends and each time the tale was told it became more gruesome and I assumed a bigger and more important role in the event.

I was the centre of attraction having been a witness to the

tragedy and for days I was called upon to recount the accident more and more.

My life had been destined to follow the path created by others who had grown-up in the Attercliffe and Darnall areas of the large steel manufacturing city that is Sheffield. Working class folks in working class housing surrounded by large working environments.

The city had a world-wide reputation for manufacturing high quality steel and cutlery but even in my younger days successive governments had allowed foreign competition to erode its monopoly on such specialized merchandise.

Yorkshire had one of the finest cricket teams in the land so as a child I watched fascinated by the likes of Bradman, Hutton and Trueman as they performed in front of an acknowledged humorous, yet learned crowd of spectators at Bramall Lane cricket ground. The satirical and intensely serious advice offered publicly, yet never in those days obscenely, by followers of the game was something always to be remembered. I was fascinated as a youthful Trueman roared into bowl from the pavilion-end showing a total disregard for the opposing batsmen and as an impressionable juvenile this to me made a good game of cricket into a great game. I dreamt of the day when I would emulate the cricket masters and memorized the strokes actions and antics to be repeated later in the more mundane surroundings of the local park. In the those days there were no drug scandals, no cheating, no excessive drinking nor controversies that distracted a nation from its favourite summer sport.

Perhaps you can recall those idyllic days when all the seasons of the year were guaranteed to fall into the pattern described by songwriters. One summer I sat all day in the blazing sun, completely absorbed in the cricket at the Bramall Lane ground until I was felled by 'sun-stroke'. A miserable journey home on the tram-car, short-cut by spending some time in the cool front room of my grandmother's house allowed me to recover. I can well recall the room although it was rarely used except for Christmas gatherings and where my grandfather lay before his funeral.

In the winter months there was football where it was absolutely necessary as a child to support one of the two professional football clubs in the city - Sheffield Wednesday F.C. or Sheffield United F.C. I used to attend matches in the company of two sisters who were friends of our family. They were only three of four years older than me but we never encountered any trouble whatsoever. I find it difficult in my short life to understand how public enjoyment of sport has been so drastically curtailed and in many cases ruined by certain elements of our society. I was able to stand as a child behind the same goal every match watching my favourite keeper display his talent.

I could wander at will in the parks and woodlands close to my home without any fears of being molested. Why have 'dirty' old men become such a problem to children over these last few years? There were paedophiles in my day, although I have always questioned why such behaviour is regarded as 'criminal' as opposed to 'medical'? As society uncovers and indeed accepts more of its own secrets will this type of sexual perversion multiply? The grounds-man employed at my school often invited lads into the changing rooms to look at nude pictures whilst masturbating himself, encouraging the kids to join in. I was terrified when he showed them to me and left very quickly. (In prison this behaviour is known as 'shaking hands with the unemployed' which speaks for itself!)

Puberty advanced upon me as these first sexual encounters occurred. I was soon to learn that sex was not always about boys exciting other boys or men, but there were girls as well. To this day I don't know if I was lucky, or not, to be seduced at the age of 16 by a friend of my parents. She must have been 20 years older than me. My girl-friend and I were at her house one evening, when it was suggested that we have fish and chips and that the wife and myself fetch them whilst my girl-friend and the husband prepared the table.

We went in her car; because I was not old enough to drive and en-route she stopped in a local wood and my '*cherry*' got picked. The relationship went on for some time but perhaps I have said enough about this particular memory.

As I studied the Criminal Law as a young constable, I was amazed to learn that a boy under the age of 14 years cannot be convicted of rape or offences involving 'the sexual act'. He is presumed incapable of intercourse at that young age. How 'out of touch' the laws of the land have become in reality. I recall well before my 14th birthday taking a girl of a similar age to me into some bushes close to the local railway line. We put our 'things' together and I worried myself silly for some weeks after when some older boys tormented me with the fact that she could have a baby.

Coming from a solid working-class background it was considered something of an achievement for me to pass the '11' plus examination and be enrolled at Firth Park Grammar School in Sheffield. I learned to smoke, but hated it, particularly when I set fire to my school blazer on the top deck of a bus as the inspector came to check our bus-passes. I got a good-hiding from my Mother and did not smoke again for many years.

My parents were very strong Baptists and therefore as long as I can remember in my childhood I attended church three times every Sunday. I used to walk with my brother and my parents to chapel until my Father managed to buy a Ford Popular motor car later followed by a Ford Anglia. The church, in those days, was a thriving institution and whilst it has suffered set-backs over the years I think that a revival is more than imminent. Although three times at church every Sunday never really alienated me from my parents, I have to admit that becoming a police officer and working unsocial hours allowed me an escape route so that my visits became less. I realize now that this did upset my parents. I do consider myself a Christian although my life can never be cited as an example of goodness. When my debts to society have been paid and my sins purged I can perhaps return to an existence where I can make amends for an adult life-time of wickedness. Please allow me to return to a normal life and put behind me a blatant disregard of the Christian criminal and social law. If anything, I owe it to the memory of my dear Father who passed away suddenly a few years before my imprisonment. A man who was the most sincere Christian that I have ever met and who would have certainly turned 'the other cheek' if the occasion arose. His death had a most profound effect on me and I wept unashamedly when I kissed him goodbye in death. A man who never refused to help a fellow human being, even at the expense of his own comfort.

My Mother and I remained close even after my crimes had been brought to the attention of the general public. Another true believer in Christianity and one whom I will never seek to offend again by my misdeeds. She too must have watched devastated by my moral decline over the years but her love and affection for me never faltered. Oh what sleepless nights I must have caused my parents. Is there any wonder that friends of my parents could not understand how such a 'degenerate' as me came from such fine family traditions. During my police service, unfortunately, I have encountered several occasions where honest god-fearing families have been torn apart by the actions of their children.

So church Whitsuntide parades were followed by Boy Scout summer camps and Saturday afternoon cricket matches where, eventually, I played in the same team as my Father.

To drop a catch from his bowling was akin to having committed murder.

Remember those days when it snowed like hell in the winter but the summers were always guaranteed wall-to-wall sunshine. With several other children from church I used to visit the Attercliffe Corporation swimming baths every Saturday morning. It was better to go early than risk being bullied by the estate lads later in the day. We would call at a small shop after the baths and buy a one penny slice of bread and dripping. Many arguments ensued as to who would get the crust or the slice of bread with the jelly from the bottom of the dripping bowl. On winter mornings it was not unknown for a runny nose to add to the flavour of the bread and dripping.

My Father, at the time was an insurance agent employed by the Liverpool Victoria Insurance Company and had successfully built up his 'round' close to home so that the cost of travel did not interfere too much with his salary and costs. Frequently on Friday evenings I was deputed to accompany my Mother as she collected insurance payments on behalf of my Father. Being a working-class area it was imperative to call at Friday tea-times so that the wages drawn that day by the 'man of the house' were still available before he went to the local 'ale-house'. It was not a fortune that my Mother collected but in the dark, poorly-lit streets she always felt more secure with me around. Our house did in fact border a really low-class housing area. With so many regular

Friday tea-time visits many of the houses became known to my Mother and me by their own peculiarities. I think the most memorable being 'the pie in the pot house' or when my Mother was not listening 'the pie in the piss-pot house'. One Friday evening we called as usual to collect their insurance payments just as the family were sitting down to the evening meal. In the centre of the table was a steaming meat and potato pie contained in a very old and battered child's enamel potty. The lady of the house, on seeing our expressions, explained how her normal glass dish had been smashed in a family dispute and knowing that her husband always expected a meat and potato pie on his return from work at Friday tea-time she had made use of the next best thing. She did assure us that the potty had been well and truly scrubbed before use as a cooking item.

Next in my young life came the pedal-cycle craze. I was very lucky when my parents, with some financial sacrifices, managed to buy me a Claude Butler racing cycle complete with three gears. In my dreams my new cycle would lead to success in the Tour de France and other major cycle races. I bought some second-hand cycle shoes from a friend, despite the fact that they were far too small they really looked good. I made a shoulder bag from cloth supplied by my Mother and used it for the shopping. Wearing it across my chest as seen in cycle magazines. For my birthday I was bought a pair of plastic water bottles complete with plastic straws which fitted to the handlebars of the bike. There was no way you could drink from them whilst in motion and the water always tasted

110

of plastic. In this day and age I cannot think of a more unhealthy device. These were the days of eternal youth where I was able to cycle in the morning, play soccer or cricket in the afternoon and attend the Sheffield city hall dance at night without feeling any ill-effects.

Sex was of some interest then, but it came a poor second to sport and local girls and those from church had to really put themselves out if they wanted any physical reaction from me. Not that I was slow when volunteers were required to lock the chapel up after the service. I got the job frequently and it was not unusual for me to have help from one the girls. My parents would never believe what happened in the vestry after morning or evening services. Then I fell in love with the girl next-door and later married her, although our separate upbringings were poles apart. I suppose the guarantee of a nightly 'shag' on the door step made real sense in those teenage days. Three years later we were divorced after she did the 'dirty' on me with a guy who she worked with.

Having left Firth Park grammar school, excelling in sport, but little else, meant it was time to seek employment. I was attracted to the police cadet scheme although I never really knew why. I think now that the first real seeds of a police career were planted when I used to stay at the home of my uncle in Rotherham. He was the caretaker of the waterworks headquarters which was situated in the centre of the town and opposite the main Frederick Street police station. At weekends when I slept there my small bedroom window overlooked the police station yard and I found it fascinating each Friday and Saturday night watching drunks and other miscreants being wheeled inside. Many of the prisoners showed a willingness to fight and there was never a shortage of police officers to accommodate them. Unfortunately as my interest in the police 'goings-on' increased, so did my attention to my female cousin who was three years older than me. When I was found in bed with her one Saturday morning by my Aunty that was the end of my week-end visits even though we had never done anything more than kissed.

As a police cadet I did enjoy the sense of identification that the uniform brought. Even though my uniform flat-hat never did fit me and was only kept in place by layers of newspaper, it was enough to cause a young teenage boy to feel elated. Our uniform which was identical to the normal police issue had light blue flashes on the epaulets and hat to indicate to the public that we were only really 'apprentices' and not really 'bobbies' From birth I was blessed with rather large ears which were really accentuated when I wore my police cadet hat thus prompting comments such as 'F.A. cup' or 'looks like a taxi with the doors open'. I think my pride in the uniform and perceived position in society did little to allow the comments to register.

I found it exhilarating at 16 years of age to be publicly identified as a representative of the police organization. In those days it was not considered prudent for police cadets to be seen to much extent in public, although school crossing patrols were often manned by us and in later years cadets did accompany beat constables and even as secondary observers in police patrol cars. To the experienced officer landed with a young cadet for a shift was often considered a punishment as it tended to limit their freedom in more ways than one.

As I write, government 'cut-backs' have decimated cadet schemes in most police forces.

I cannot argue against the cuts which are obviously political and financial but I note that in some twenty years the scheme has gone 'full-circle' and police cadets have become a thing of the past. 'Good job' - I hear you say when you consider how I turned out in later years. The police service seems unique in introducing schemes promoted as 'life-changing' - applauded and recognized as fine innovations until they are exposed to practical reasoning and public examination. The circle turns completely and the schemes disappear forever - 'police cadet scheme' - 'unit beat policing' are examples which support my point. However, I cannot knock the experience I gained as a police cadet.

Although an onlooker would perhaps describe my duties as an 'office-clerk', it was still useful for someone at my age and with my limited knowledge of life to gain an idea of what happened on the 'shop-floor'. Police cadets were posted to several divisional police stations during their service and were allowed to control the public reception desk where 'lost' and 'found' property and dogs would be handled,

113

together with motorists producing driving documents and the like. This in itself gave the young cadet the ability to recognize all the driving documents required by the law and undoubtedly gave the young man an in-depth knowledge of motoring legislation. The ability to make a good cup of tea was paramount as was the love of 'lost' and 'found' dogs. Frequently, and usually for a laugh at my expense, I would be sent from the West Bar police office to the nearby R.S.P.C.A. kennels down Nursery Street dragging behind me a dog almost my size. Normally the larger 'found' dogs would be taken to the kennels by police van, but if I had been unusually cheeky to the station sergeant this was his way of reminding me who was in charge. I soon found out though, that if the dog gave me any trouble it was easy to let it run away - rip up the report and return to the station assuring the station sergeant that my task had been fulfilled.

A significant mention must be made here about the role of female police cadets.

They were not to come until much later in my police career and I, for one, am rather pleased that such a definite distraction to someone like me was avoided. I have no wish here to speak disparagingly about the role of females in the police service. Later I hope to refer to some of the occasions I have experienced their unique ability and value on the job

Older officers, together with myself, I am sure will pay respect to their specialized supportive roles in dealing with offences and investigations involving children and females.

However, the advent of the Sex Discrimination Act removed totally and wholesale what had become an efficient self-contained unit. You will gather from my writings by now that I preferred the 'old days' where female officers did not command such a place in the force that it was necessary for the required number to be promoted and avoid any suggestion that they were being discriminated against because of their sex. I must question their role as a senior or promoted officer because it simply did not work. Most male officers I know, did not take kindly to taking instructions from a female and in particular one who did not have the service, outlook or indeed the experience to command respect. Having watched the T.V. series of 'Juliet Bravo' on occasions, I have squirmed in my seat witnessing the bowing and scraping portrayed by the two station sergeants towards the female inspector. A sad indictment of the future of the police service.

If I was truly honest though, when I was sixteen years age and a police cadet I fell in love with almost every female police officer I came into contact with. Perhaps it was the uniform skirts and black stockings that revved me up. I was always fascinated, but a little wary and somewhat afraid of the most senior female officer in the force. She was a spinster, as ugly as hell, but immaculate in uniform. I was told that she was a 'lesbian' which at my sixteen years of age was something of a novelty and rarity. She shared a house with another single female so the 'lesbian' part was confirmed by older friends of mine. If I am honest I really did not know what 'lesbians' did any different to other people. When I compared her living arrangements with certain of my family and other people I knew, it was obvious that I should stay away from the subject of 'lesbianism' as long as possible.

Whilst, as I said earlier, police cadets were not encouraged to make many appearances in public there were other ways that they could be useful and create a feeling of being an asset to the police service. Being given a pair of overalls and pushed under the floorboards of a house to recover a large quantity of stolen silverware was one event. My youthful figure and agility being distinctly more suited to the task than those of the obese detectives in the case. Imagine my excitement one morning being ordered to run, in cadet uniform, from Hillsborough divisional police headquarters to the nearby police box at Malin Bridge carrying a fire extinguisher. Some children had lit a fire at the rear of the box and I was full of pride at being able to put out the fire without any real damage to it.

The pleasure of working in the scenes of crime department at headquarters where I could see all the photographs taken at some gruesome murder or accident. Several photographs of females subject to sexual offences were often around and I wonder if the victims ever were aware that a young man was beginning to enjoy puberty at their expense. My time in the scenes of crime department came to a very abrupt end though when I failed to take care one morning as I was trimming photographs of some crime scene and chopped the end of my finger off with the guillotine. The office policewoman promptly fainted and I was rushed to hospital. I recall my next attachment as a police cadet was working at the police stables and spending most of my time mucking out the horses. Maybe it was a punishment but no-one ever admitted so.

I gained some recognition one Sunday evening on my way home from church by telephoning for assistance from a police box on seeing two uniformed constables being attacked in the Darnall shopping centre. The two officers were battling with some twenty youths and with the arrival of assistance several were arrested, given a good hiding and locked up for the night. The divisional superintendent thought I had been 'very quick-witted' but in reality what else could I do?

As I approached the end of my period as a police cadet and began to dream of life as a fully-fledged constable, one event taught me that officers did not always work 'by the book' and I would most certainly have to change if I was to survive in the force.

I mentioned earlier that officers and operational detectives in particular, need to be actors on many occasions to achieve the desired result.

I was attached at the time to Attercliffe police station in the east-end of the city. The area had attracted many Arab and Pakistani immigrants who sought employment in the highly successful steel industry. They worked hard but brought with them a culture and life-style that was entirely different to ours and the local population found it difficult to adapt in such a manner that true integration would ever be possible. The police force did, I think, make an effort to accept the presence of a different 'breed' in their midst who demanded 'policing' just as existing society did. Most older police officers, however, were not happy with this influx of people from strange lands, unable to speak our language and who created a criminal environment all of their own. Quarrels between the 'immigrants' were normally resolved by knife fights and the statistics for this type of crime rose steeply in the division to the consternation of the local police chief. Older officers took a more philosophical view saying……'Fuck them. Let them kill each other and we'll get rid of the bastards.'

I arrived at work one afternoon to find that a particularly nasty fight had taken place the previous evening between two Pakistani men. One was in 'intensive care' at the local hospital and not expected to live. The other Pakistani had been arrested and was being 'interviewed' by three of the local detectives. The prisoner would not admit the offence and the C.I.D. men were losing patience. During the early evening I was sent to find one of the detectives in the case. I toured the station but unable to locate him I decided to try the parade room. What a shock was to come…….

The room was very dimly lit. In attendance I found one detective constable wearing a dark suit, clergy-mans 'dog-collar' and carrying a Bible. He was quietly muttering religious passages that meant no sense at all. The Pakistani prisoner was blind-folded and his hands tied behind his back. A noose was around his neck, the remainder of the rope leading up to rafters in the room. The prisoner was standing on a trap-door in the floor (which I was later told had been opened in his view to demonstrate to him just what was about to happen.) The 'Vicar' was reading the 'last-rites' as the detective sergeant in the case was telling the prisoner (who apparently spoke good English) that....."You can't come to our fucking country and behave like an animal or we'll fucking treat you as one" I noticed a stretcher laid at the side of the trap-door and for a minute I really thought the cops were going to hang him. I was then spotted by the detective sergeant who yelled at me to get out - later collaring me and warning me in no uncertain terms never to speak of the incident again. I went home that evening terrified that the news would report how a man had died in police custody and how I would become a witness. I returned the next day to find that the prisoner had made a 'full and frank' admission to the wounding offence and was in the cells.

If I were asked to point to any distinct advantage in having been a police cadet before joining the real force it would be that I was 'known' by most senior officers and considered to be reliable which could only serve as a bonus in time to come.

There is no doubt my ideals and credibility were at their

highest when I was a police cadet. If my life could have stayed in that mode perhaps I would not be in prison now.

However, all things must come to an end and at the age of eighteen and three-quarter years I was packed off to the police training school at Pannal Ash, Harrogate, Yorkshire.

The course of three months was designed to teach me how to be a policeman and enabled the authorities to unleash me onto the streets and an unsuspecting public exactly on my 19th birthday. As I filled my suitcase ready to attend the course, I examined, with pride the uniform that replaced the police cadet dress.

Helmet (far too big requiring paper to be stuffed inside).

Truncheon (perhaps 100 years old and riddled with wood-worm - I broke three).

Handcuffs (very heavy that were never carried by any officer because of their weight).

Whistle (never ever used in my career, except when I once refereed a cadet football match).

Boots (always needed 'wearing-in').

Pocket Book (the biggest liar manual in the World).

Personal 'Collar' Number(in my case - 301).

It seems now as I sit in my cell that my whole life has been governed by numbers...

My school locker number.

Number on my free bus pass.

Telephone number on the instrument installed at home whilst I was still quite young

The registration number on the first motor car that my Father owned.

The registration number on the scooter and then first motor car that I owned.

We could go on, you and I about numbers, but now I have an unwelcome advantage in that I have a prison number and you don't. Society knows you by your Christian and surnames whereas I am a just a number.

A situation that I never, ever, expected to be in when I first set out from home as a teenager on my journey to becoming a real 'Bobby'.

Chapter 5 - Early Policing - Learning the ropes.

*"Without deep reflection, one knows from daily life
that one exists for other people."*
Albert Einstein, 1879 - 1955.

The police training school or 'College' as the instructors liked to call it was a beautiful imposing grey stone mansion set amongst sports fields and rolling North Yorkshire countryside. It was approached from the main Leeds - Harrogate road, a few miles from Harwood House which in itself is another country mansion that has been objectively raped in the interests of tourism. By vehicle you would travel through beautiful and interesting countryside at any time of the year and as one turned down a small lane a quick glance across the fields and woodland would expose the college as it stood guard over the surrounding area. It was easy to imagine how the building had absorbed the changing domestic and social habits of the local people over the years.

This was an area that following the war, the affluent from Leeds and Harrogate sought to establish themselves and their ideals. In some cases it afforded the residents a country squire title and lifestyle whilst still allowing them to pursue their business interests and ideas in the local towns and cities. I mention the area in some detail because some 15 years later as a detective on the regional crime squad I was to travel through the area each day whilst seconded to the investigation to track the infamous 'Black Panther'. (You may recall that he had shot Mr. Donald Skepper, a postmaster at Harrogate, and was later arrested many miles away in the West Midlands.)

Oh what memories Pannal Ash police training college holds for me - although the criteria for becoming a good police officer seemed to rest on the ability to memorize and recite word-perfect definitions of offences and duties. Even now, some 25 years later it is still easy to recite those dreary definitions, although in reality the Acts promulgating them have long been repealed....

'A person steals, who without the consent of the owner, fraudulently and without a claim of right made in good faith, takes and carries away anything capable of being stolen'
Larceny Act. 1916.

'A constable is a citizen, locally appointed, but having authority under the crown for the protection of life and property etc...'

There were many others, of more obscure definition embracing the crimes of Infanticide. Coinage, Rape, Embezzlement and Sacrilege. I wonder how many officers from my course ever came upon these offences on a regular basis when they returned to their respective police forces?

Thirty trainee officers to a class and four classes starting at the same time every three months. Considering these numbers and recognizing there were several other police training colleges throughout the country gives you an idea of the number of new officers being thrown to the public annually The classes contained youths (and more mature students) from all walks of life. The college itself was staffed by serving police officers as instructors, seconded from the various police forces. If you were lucky enough to come across an instructor from your own force then you were guaranteed preferential treatment and certain acceptance at 'passing-out ' time. In my case there was no instructor from my force, so for success on the course I relied on the expertise I had gathered as a police cadet. I found myself sharing the training school facilities with ex-miners, ex-guardsmen, ex-farmers and in my class one ex-convict. He had apparently slipped through the vetting procedure and his embarrassed force quickly moved to discharge him when it became known. Three students found the absence from home too much to bear in the first 24 hours and resigned. The remainder of us were glad to see the back of them.

The first day of the course followed the same pattern as every course follows.

The 'do's and don'ts' lecture by the school commandant disguised as a 'welcoming talk'.

It seemed all we had to do was to work hard and totally avoid the 'domestic girls' who worked in the school canteen. One of the young constables from my force who had preceded me on the course obviously did not pay much attention to the 'welcoming talk' because some weeks after he 'graduated' one of the 'domestic girls' followed him - with child...

I was more interested in sport at this time, so instead of 'tackling' the domestic or village girls, I was more often to be found in the gymnasium, cross- country running or playing soccer. I did study hard though so that my graduation would lead me to full-time employment as a 'guardian of the peace'. We were forced to endure 'square-bashing' under the watchful eye of an ex-army sergeant major. Designed to instil discipline in us we were led to believe. Like many others on the course I had just missed conscription so I assume the authorities thought of it as a good way to knock us into shape. We became quite good at drill by the end of the course and in time for the 'passing-out parade'.(Later as an 'under-cover' detective on the regional crime squad I had difficulty in working out just what we did achieve by all that marching.) We were, in many ways 'brain-washed' by the drill to the extent that we would practice our marching at the most unusual times. The class drill leader was in fact an ex-guardsman who loved to get us practicing even at night time dressed in pyjamas and boots. As a soldier he perhaps was quite good but academically he was useless.

One of the physical training instructors was a sergeant from Leeds city police force and had a weird obsession with blood. Apparently he had been a very good amateur boxer before joining the police and his facial appearance supported this.

One of his duties was to train us in First Aid so blood got a mention regularly. Unfortunately he was also a 'bully' and enjoyed antagonizing one of the biggest constables in our class who was from the Lincolnshire force. Things came to a head in the gymnasium one day when the constable lost his temper and punched the sergeant on the nose causing him to fall to the ground covered in blood. Normally he would have been over the moon with all that 'claret' around but when he realized it was his own he was not that happy.

In those days I rarely drank any kind of intoxicating liquor, so it was inevitable that following a class celebration at the local pub one evening, I drank too much and became 'leg-less.' I could not stand up without help and was sick in the foyer of the public house, much to the disgust of the landlord. Two of the biggest coppers in the class came to my rescue, carrying me back to college where we all were 'put on report' for being late, entering the building through a back-window and for me again being sick in the school office.

So the college did it's job producing a young, inexperienced and very nervous constable which they thought fit to patrol the streets of the West Bar division of the Sheffield City Police. It was September.1960.

Following two weeks in the company of another more senior constable I was then on my own.

My first tour of duty alone was on Nights. (11pm-7am).

It was a strange part of the city to me and I commenced my

126

career by being late on my first shift because I could not find the police box. It was necessary at the start of each shift to make contact with divisional headquarters by using the telephone from the police box and also at certain designated periods during the patrol. Remember there were no police radios in those days so if a constable did not 'ring-in' at the correct time then a search-party would be sent out to ensure that he was safe.

On my second night alone I found the London Road police box in good time but walked into a massive brawl outside the Locarno dance hall opposite. I don't recall feeling nervous and waded into the centre of the fight waving my truncheon about, but not particularly hitting anybody with it. It was not long before the 'Police Cavalry' arrived to assist me, some kind passer-by having telephoned that a lone P.C. was in trouble.

Then followed a speedy baptism into the practical side of policing that did not change for some 25 years. Two of the youths arrested for fighting were dragged into the police box and given a good hiding. Please don't ask me why.

When the police van (or Black Maria as it was then called) arrived, the two youths were thrown inside and given another 'pasting' just for good measure.

The Black Maria was in fact an old ambulance with the fittings removed and a chrome bell attached to the front designed to clear traffic in an emergency. In real terms no-one could hear the bell ringing beyond a distance of some twenty yards. An illuminated letter 'P' was fitted above the front windscreen again to warn of an emergency. The van was also used to collect dead bodies from sudden and suspicious deaths.

The youths got another good hiding in the back of the van en-route to the police charge office in the centre of the city. Again please don't ask me why.

On arrival at the police charge office, which was to become so familiar to me in years to come, the two youths were bundled out of the back of the van - slapped around the head a few times and then dragged up the stairs. I am positive they would have walked unaided but apparently it was the accepted thing to slap, kick punch and throttle them until they reached the charge office desk. I was assured that in this type of 'incident' the police always won and any damage caused during such a fracas either to the police box, the police van or to windows of the charge office were classed as 'wilful damage' (later called criminal damage). The accused would then be charged with the damage offences in addition to the usual 'drunk and disorderly' allegations. One important consideration was that if the accused suffered any obvious bodily markings or wounds from the conduct of the arresting officers then a charge of 'assault on police' against them would be included as a matter of course.

The principle in taking a prisoner to the charge office was primarily for his conduct and actions (unlawful or otherwise) to be assessed by a senior officer. This officer would then sanction the charge(s) and the person would invariably be placed in custody.

Technically if the senior officer was unhappy with the allegations against the accused he should release that person, without charge and as soon as possible.

"In almost 25 years service I have never known a charge to be refused by a senior officer for the type of anti-social offences being described here. It was not unusual for the inspector or sergeant not to even bother leaving his office to see the accused or query the circumstances of their arrest."

Before we leave this subject let me apologize for seemingly always referring to the arrested as male persons. Let me assure you it was a very similar course of conduct when females were detained.

Officers who worked in the charge office were generally those with years of experience. Most had never been interested in promotion and most had not even taken the promotion examinations. Many carried 'king-sized chips' on their shoulders.

One particular sergeant, who came across as a very nice man, had his own way of dealing with violent or awkward prisoners. He would pick up the extremely heavy large ledger from the desk and smash it on their heads. I never saw many prisoners retaliate after that.

I once arrested a very large and drunken Irishman who was always in trouble. Like many casual labourers in the city he used to dig trenches during the day for a living and start drinking after work at tea-time. His clothes were muddy and filthy, his trousers were fastened with string around the ankles (a practice observed by all the Irish labourers I met who explained it was to stop soil going into their boots). With some help from another officer I managed to get him to the charge office, although he was more awkward than violent. The man could not stand without assistance and leaned across the charge office counter 'fucking and blinding' at the desk sergeant who had heard it all before.

A terrible smell told me that he had 'shit' himself and the sergeant was telling me to search him, adding that as a young copper that would teach me not to bother bringing drunks like him into custody. I started going through the man's pockets whilst the sergeant was shouting at him to untie the string round his trousers.

The smell was beyond belief...

The sergeant was shouting at the drunk "You're a fucking disgrace and you've shit yourself."

The Irishman just kept repeating, "I haven't, sir. I haven't" as he staggered about the charge room.

There was no way the man, in his condition, could even bend over and the sergeant took great pleasure in telling me to untie the string round his ankles - adding that the man could perhaps hang himself in the cells if left with the string. I pushed the drunk against the counter, held my breath and quickly untied the string from round the bottom of his trousers. Immediately there was 'shit' all over the charge office floor released from his trouser bottoms. The smell was overpowering. The sergeant was shouting "I told you.

You've fucking shit yourself"

The drunk was shouting "No, sir. No, sir."

The sergeant concluded the episode there and then by pointing to the mess on the floor and shouting……………. "I suppose that's fucking gold-dust"…………..

Despite the violence I witnessed in my early police days there was not the aura of 'evilness' that exists today between accused persons and the police.

A sober prisoner would fight a policeman to escape. If successful he would leave the scene as quickly as possible. The youth of today would not be happy with simply escaping; they would have to seek instant retribution by injuring the officer also.

After some two years on the beat, one night I tried to arrest three, drunken Irish brothers in the Wicker, Sheffield, who had been celebrating St. Patrick's night. They were not particularly well-built, but young fit and very drunk. I was alone.

I tried to take one of them to Nursery police box some 50 yards away from where they had been fighting but all three turned on me. I drew my truncheon and lashed out at all of them. The earlier fears of using the baton had then been well and truly conquered.

I hit one of the youths on top of the head and the truncheon broke. I said previously most of the batons issued at my time were perhaps over 100 years old and full of wood-worm.

I was left with about six inches of the staff in my hand and the youths were dragging and pulling me to a wall which ran alongside the River Don. There was a drop of some 30 feet over the wall into the water and it was quite obvious they were going to throw me over. I was screaming and fighting back as best I could, but rapidly losing the contest.

Suddenly what remained of the baton was pulled from my hand and I thought my end had come. But I was lucky............

The landlord of a public house overlooking the river had come to assist me. He was only a small guy and it was he who had pulled the broken truncheon from my grasp. I am told that the landlord went berserk, attacking the three youths with the broken truncheon staff and picking up my helmet which had been knocked off in the struggle he used the metal badge side to smash it into the face of my attackers. Within minutes assistance arrived in the shape of the 'police cavalry' and all three youths were detained.

I was not in a condition to witness much afterwards but I am told the youths were kicked all round the street by the officers. Taken into the nearby police box and given another good hiding. They got further beatings in the police van and charge office and each received three months imprisonment some time later for 'assault on police' and drunkenness offences. I went to hospital for the night and later acquired a new set of top teeth damaged in the fracas. The pub landlord received a letter from the force thanking him for his assistance. Well deserved I might add because he undoubtedly saved me from serious injury that night. My shift inspector, on his way home, called at my home to tell my Wife that I was being detained overnight and that she was not to worry. I am led to believe she showed little interest in my welfare.

Violence had become a way of life to me by then but I think you will find that I stand alone in exposing it in the manner I do now.

I cite violent happenings that were inflicted on fellow human beings simply because they were unable to defend themselves, some officer needed revenge or as in the case of the already mentioned 'Rhino Whip Affair' admissions were required.

So life on the beat continued in a busy city where three shifts were manned.

There was an unwritten rule that only 'tall' officers could work in the city centre and with the number of ex-guardsmen in the force that was not difficult to achieve in the years prior to my service where concentrated recruitment had been aimed at the armed forces.

This rule though, was becoming difficult to maintain and less-tall probationary constables, like myself, working the outlying beats were moved closer and closer to the Sheffield city centre. Outlying beats are not, as the name suggests adjacent to the countryside, but simply away from the main part of the division.

All city police forces have operational divisions. Each division has a headquarters to control its operations. The city centre division West Bar, was the smallest division in the force covering basically the centre of commerce and local government and the more up-market shopping areas. Feeder roads into the city centre had spawned residential areas that were home to lower paid workers who found it easy and less expensive to reach work in the city. Most of these areas have deteriorated and decayed during the past twenty years causing them to become 'ghettos' where social unrest breeds. Many have now totally become immigrant colonies with their own cultures and ideals leaving the local authorities, including the police, to rethink strategies. Burngreave and Pitsmoor areas in Sheffield in the early sixties had reached the point where perhaps as many as 60% of the residents were West African and Jamaican. Young white girls had been attracted to the area, for a variety of reasons, causing social unrest.

I found it significant that whilst the West African and Jamaican immigrants chose to spawn in the areas butting onto the city centre and shied away from employment, the Arab and Pakistan element frequenting Attercliffe area in the East end of the city sought full-time employment in the steel works and other heavy industries.

It was in this type of environment that any young copper had to learn quickly to survive.

Most of the time whilst on the beat you were alone. No personal radios and only one small patrol car and two motor scooters to get to you quickly if you were in trouble.

As with the pub landlord who assisted me when I was

fighting the Irishmen there were generally members of the public who would at least telephone headquarters for assistance should the need arise.

Another 'baptism' in my early uniform career occurred one afternoon in Burngreave. It was just after 3pm and all public houses were obliged to close at that time in conjunction with the Licensing Laws - normal service to be resumed early in the evening until 10.30pm.when they were obliged to close again. (How things have changed and one may think not for the better).I was making my way to carry out school crossing duties when several passers by called me to a fracas at a nearby pub. As I reached the scene, I found the largest, very black West African lady I had ever seen in my life. She was almost as wide as she was tall. Her blouse was open displaying the biggest white 'bra' I had ever seen in my short life which supported the biggest pair of 'bazookas' in the World.

Oh yes, as well, she was as 'drunk as a skunk' - knocking the landlord from the pub all over the road. Traffic was swerving to avoid the melee and the kids were coming out of school. I joined in..........First she knocked my helmet clean off my head with one swipe. Then the pub landlord, the lady and me fell into the road all three of us rolling about as if we were all drunk. A large crowd had gathered including the children leaving school. A cheer went up, mainly led by the blokes from the pub every time the lady tried to kick us as her skirt by then was round her neck showing the biggest pair of white silk knickers ever seen. Again, fortunately, someone had telephoned the police and assistance arrived in the shape of the Black Maria and two constables. After killing themselves with laughter at the sight of the landlord and myself lying on top of a semi-naked drunken black woman we threw her into the back of the van and took her to the charge office.

On arrival at the charge office there was another scene for the public as it was almost tea-time and workers were passing on their way home. It took three of us to lift and carry the woman into the office. By this time her skirt was completely missing and her blouse was torn and hanging onto only one of her arms. Charging her with drunkenness was a brief formality and then she was placed in the cells. She did plead guilty later in court, making no reference to the way she had been arrested or the state of her clothing - thank goodness.

I have lost count of the times I was assaulted in the early days. I was only 5' 9" and weighed eleven and a half stones. The minimum height for male police officers being 5' 8". Not everyone who assaulted Policemen were caught. I always seemed to end up in the middle of three or four fighting men - one would wallop me at the side of the head and run off. I soon learned that if I could hang onto one of them he could pay for the sins of the others when we got him back to the police box or charge office.

In the first three years of my service I broke three truncheons, which I suppose speaks for itself and confirms that my earlier fears of actually hitting someone with it had long disappeared. Older and more sensible coppers than me adapted a sound strategy in dealing with fights in that they would wait round the corner until all the fight had gone out of the battlers before moving in to arrest them. Even so it was not always possible to avoid a fracas and with the city centre division full of the tallest coppers in the force anyone looking for trouble soundly got it! But with 'midget' coppers like me starting to patrol West Bar division, it proved a signal for abuse from the public and colleagues alike.

Every Friday or Saturday night some drunk in a taxi or bus queue could not resist the urge when I walked past…….

"Does your Mother know you're out at this time of night, Sonny?"

"You don't look old enough to be out in the dark, Son?"

This was the men, the women made comments that would make your head spin…….

"Do you want me to sit on your face for ten bob, officer?"

"You can use your truncheon on me anytime, officer."

I did have my uses though because the older and bigger coppers would send me out alone usually into Fitzalan Square after 'turning-out' time. When the drunks started on me, seeing my size and thinking I was alone, my colleagues would come flying round the corner walloping anything in sight and arresting who they could lay their hands on.

Night-life in the North was just finding its very successful feet during the early sixties.

Unemployment was not at the level that it is now in 1984/5 The initial effects of unemployment felt after the ending of the War had diminished and many people had secured employment allowing a reasonable way of life. Apprentice schemes in the early sixties were the norm and successful providing a well-qualified male and female workforce. Friday and Saturday nights were universally acknowledged as the time to unwind after a week spent down the pit, in the steel-works or behind a desk or shop counter.

In the case of the lads it comprised of as much ale as you could get down your neck before the pubs closed at 10.30pm. A newspaper full of fish and chips with loads of salt and vinegar. The vinegar after a while running through the paper and onto your best suit and shoes.

In the case of the girls it was the time to wear the most daring and outrageous dresses (that your parents would allow). Care had to be taken how much you drank and you always carried condoms in your handbag 'just to be sure'.

Before the last bus home the necessary 'pee' in a shop door-way (this applying to both lads and lasses) or even a stand-up 'leg-over' if you had been lucky enough to pull a bird.

The last bus home, the 'pee' and fish and chips, always being more important than the sex. How many youths have escaped an inquest from parents when arriving home smelling of vinegar instead of 'the other'? Should you be slow in finishing your fish and chips, having a 'pee' or completing 'the other'- then you had to walk home and in the sixties that was not always a good idea.

Walking home late at night was often guaranteed to get you

a 'pull' by some keen copper. Do not allow me to paint such a bad picture of the Sixties copper, because after verifying your name and address and checking your trouser 'flies', the officer would be convinced that you were not about illegally and allow you to go. However, any person unable to prove he was on honest business and verify his name and address was well and truly 'nicked' (I agree, quite illegally by the officer). The miscreant would be taken to the nearest police box and detained (I agree, quite illegally by the officer) whilst further enquiries were made. All police stations held electors lists so it was quite easy to determine the name and address of someone by checking the list and then getting them to describe the details of their neighbours so you knew they were telling the truth.

But other events also took place whilst I was a young copper. Someone once said:

"The first look at something immoral can be dismissed as inevitable, but the second look is a sin."

This thought never came into my mind late one evening in Sheffield City centre when an older copper whom I was patrolling with, asked me if I was into 'Piking'.

Rather sheepishly and a little embarrassed I told him I did not know what it meant.

He decided to show me. We crept up the alleyway alongside the Museum public house in Leopold Street and into the rear enclosed yard. It was very dark in the yard surrounded by large office buildings rising up into the night sky. There was muffled music and general pub chatter coming from the building. My colleague told me to be very quiet and not to use my torch as he crept towards a ground-floor window, which although being of frosted glass, was obviously the ladies toilet. The officer removed his helmet and bending down peered through an air-vent some three feet from the ground. I could easily make out the figure of a female sitting on the 'loo' facing the air vent. I could see her pulling her pants up and her skirt down before flushing the toilet and leaving.

Now you might not believe this but I was shocked. I agree it would not trouble me now all these years later but I was only 19 years of age and I certainly had never seen anything like that before. What was I to do? I wanted to be 'one of the boys' and I did not want it to get back to the rest of the shift that I had 'no bottle' and was not a 'piker'. So we waited until the next lady came into the toilet and it was my turn, but I had quickly made a plan - I would look but close my eyes and my colleague would never know......... With so many things going through my mind I bent down quickly to peer through the air vent but I had forgotten to remove my hat and as I bent forward the metal helmet badge crashed against the toilet window. Honest - I still had my eyes closed but as my helmet almost fell-off, the woman screamed and my mate loudly hissed that I was a 'Stupid twat'. As he yanked me up I opened my eyes and looked through the air-vent to see a young lady with obviously natural black hair and a pair of red knickers round her ankles. By then, though, I was being pulled across the yard by the other officer in an attempt for us to reach the street before the landlord came to investigate. I could still hear the lady screaming, but my colleague seemed only concerned with calling me a 'Stupid twat' and running as fast as he could down the alleyway and onto the street. We were lucky because it was some minutes before the pub landlord and some customers came running out of the pub. On seeing us the landlord was over the moon to see two policemen on hand and we all rushed back to the yard searching for the offender(s).When the scoundrel(s) had not been traced we left the area agreeing with the pub landlord that whoever got up to that sort of behaviour were, in the words of the landlord "fucking perverts" In the police canteen some days later mention was made that the air-vent had been bricked-up at the particular public house and I swear there was a real mood of disappointment among those present.

Many years later as a detective sergeant I returned to that scene of my first 'pike' at the Museum pub when the new landlord shot an intruder who was breaking into his living quarters. The officers accompanying me at the time could not understand the smile on my face.

Any police stories told by officers who have regularly worked the 'beat' always include incidents in toilets. In my early days I found it somewhat embarrassing to search the ladies public toilets when on night duty. However the checks did pay-off because I once found a man asleep in the Pond

141

Street bus station ladies toilets and took him to nearby police box to check his identity. He was wanted throughout the country for all types of crimes and was surprised to have been caught, believing he was safe in a ladies 'loo.'

You would be surprised at the number of females to be found sleeping rough. Most of them trying to keep warm huddled on the floor of some filthy public toilet. I never could understand why some of my colleagues found it such a joke to throw buckets of water on them in the middle of the night. Oh, by the way the graffiti to be found on the walls of the ladies toilet is something to behold. Written obviously by females but aimed at men so it can only have been intended for visiting policemen who search the toilets in the dead of night. Public toilets required attendants during the day and invariably were some of the best contacts a copper could make. There was always a cup of tea. A glance at the girlie magazines the attendant had recovered from the cubicles where some bloke had 'relieved'' himself. In one of the public ladies toilets in the city all the wash basins had to be reinforced to prevent them from coming away from the wall Apparently ladies constantly used to 'pee' in them instead of using the cubicles. Who described ladies as the 'fairer sex'?

Back to the 'piking' again reminds me that too many coppers I worked with the three shifts each contained an identity of their own. On the morning shift it was generally traffic patrol in the city centre. The end of the afternoon shift and beginning of the night shift were for 'piking' and dealing with anti-social drunken and violent behaviour.

Certain coppers I know used to come to work early on nights just to visit all the alleyways and doorways where they knew courting couples would be 'shagging'. I know of one copper who used to wear soft-soled boots simply to creep up and catch couples in some form of sexual act.

In the city centre was Sheffield Cathedral with numerous deep and dark doorways.

You will probably not know this, but under the Ecclesiastical Courts Jurisdiction Act. 1860 it is an offence to commit any indecent act in the grounds of a church or sacred building. I do not recall many coppers ever reporting anyone for such an offence but, of course, there is always the exception and there had been complaints from the clergy about used condoms and the like being found all over the sacred grounds. Special attention was paid to the complaint by officers on that particular beat and one winters evening a constable caught a couple having sex against a tombstone. Both had been drinking heavily. The constable separated them - took details of their names and addresses and reported them for the offence as described above. In graphic details the officers report described the couple engaged in sexual intercourse The report went on to describe that when he caused them to separate the man's penis was 'erect, wet and steaming'.......... The mind boggles.

I shudder now when I think how dishonest I have become over the years.

It was not always the case. About 2am one morning I was

143

waiting to ring the office from Burngreave police box. I was standing under a nearby bus shelter to protect me from the rain. As I idly shone my torch at the debris on the floor I noticed a five pound note and naturally picked it up. I submitted a 'found property' report and left the money with the report in the police box to be collected. Never ever did it cross my mind to keep the money. I took some 'real stick' from the rest of the shift when they heard about it and I suppose in its own way a little of my honesty disappeared afterwards.

Being on probation for two years encouraged me to work hard and try to get involved in every type of incident that would benefit my later career.

Humour was often to be found on 'beat' patrol.

Take for instance one constable who must have been on the force for some 15 years when I first met him. He was the quietest man I had ever known and whose nose always seemed to be running be it summer or winter. He never, in the three years I knew him arrested or 'booked' anyone. He would patrol his beat on the morning shift taking in traffic duty and maybe school crossing patrol. He would deal with any road accident that he came across and accept found property and the like and that was it. On afternoons again it was traffic duty at tea-time and patrol until it was time to go home avoiding any 'trouble spots' near pub closing time. On nights he examined the 'lock-up' property on his beat to perfection but again was never to be found in any situation where police intervention may be needed. (A point here that you may not be aware of, was that in the Sixties, householders would report to the police station when their house was unoccupied due to their annual holiday etc. A card would be made out and left in the police box on the relevant beat and officers were expected to check the house once every shift, so the properties sometimes were visited three times a day. If anything untoward was found there was a 'reference' such as a neighbour or family member who could be contacted and deal with the problem. I cannot think of any better way to let the local criminal fraternity know that a person's house was unoccupied than this system which has now been discontinued.) Anyway back to the 'quiet' constable. He always came to work by bicycle, in all weathers, leaving the cycle behind any shops or offices that he knew it would be safe. He was never selected at weekends by the inspector to work 'double' with another officer at trouble spots because it was known that he could not be relied upon to support a colleague in trouble. Some of the lads became a bit 'pissed off 'by him considering he drew the same wages as them but never took his fair share of the work and danger. Their unrest was made clear to him one morning at 7am just as dawn was breaking and he was finishing a night shift. He went to collect his bicycle from the rear of a department store in the city centre only to find it was missing. Within a few minutes he had located the machine at the top of the massive flag pole on the cenotaph memorial in Barkers Pool where some of his colleagues had raised it during the night. Early-morning workers had a surprise seeing a uniformed officer trying to lower a bicycle down the flag pole at that time of the day but he was unmoved and never tried to find the culprit or remonstrate with anyone. Why keep him on the Police force I hear you ask?

Simply, because it would have been more difficult and costly for the force to get rid of him.

Apart from the humour though, other events on beat patrol were bitterly sad.

Having just passed the police driving examination I was looking forward to being able to drive the small Hillman Husky vehicle allocated to our division. The only way the vehicle could be identified as a 'police' vehicle was by a small illuminated box 12" x 6" showing the word 'police'. I should have known better because constables with more service than I were generally given the driving job and real friction in the ranks was caused if the shift inspector designated the task to any youngster. My first 'drive' was one lunchtime after I had I walked through the station and the desk sergeant instructed me to attend the scene of a road accident at Brookhill near to the Sheffield University buildings. A corporation bus had run over a small child killing him instantly. My mind went back to the little girl killed many years before as I rode my pedal cycle back from the shops and she fell from the passenger door of the lorry I was following.

I dealt with the accident involving the little boy, assisted by one of the sergeants. I then went home and cried myself to sleep that night but went to work next morning as if nothing had happened.

Over the years I became so hard that I am ashamed to say peoples dramas and traumas affected me very little. Despite all the training in the world no-one can teach you how to break news of a bereavement to a relative. I had the task on some three of four occasions but it never became any easier

Some of the most pleasing memories of working the beat were the characters that brought variety onto the streets of the city. The British Rail and Sheffield Star newspaper van drivers who would lean out of their vehicles and throw sweets to you whilst you were on traffic duty in the centre of the road. The newspaper driver would also push the latest edition of his paper in your pocket if he had any spares left.

Hospitals were a favourite haunt of beat policemen assuring you a cup of tea and even a 'cat-nap' in the boiler house on night duty. A good rapport developed between casualty department staff and officers who were frequently called to deal with the injured from road accidents or assaults. Many drunks have been thrown out of the hospital at the request of the night sister and then given a good hiding round the corner.

> *"There are only two certainties in life. Death and a*
> *Nurse."*

.........whoever coined that saying must have been a copper!

Many is the time though that dawn has been breaking when leaving a party at the nurses quarters and romances between officers and Nurses often flourished. Later as a young detective officer I visited living quarters known as 'Sisthome' at the Northern General Hospital in Sheffield, which, as the name suggests was occupied by nursing sisters. I received a complaint from a sister who worked in the cardiac department of the hospital that someone had stolen her electric toothbrush. It was obvious it was one of the other nurses but I never detected the crime. After an affair which lasted some months with the sister it all went 'pear-shaped' one night when she caught me with another woman in a city centre pub. I never knew nursing sisters knew such language!

To the young constable trying to get on in the service the accolade of the time was a 'chief constables commendation' Minor 'pats on the back' from sergeants and inspectors were all very well, but commendations from headquarters were the thing. It was always suggested that they helped towards promotion, although I know of many senior officers who made their ranks without such awards, again suggesting it was not always the best who were rewarded. I soon was to realize that the way some arrest was written-up and described could also have a bearing on being recognized as worthy of commendation. I also learned very quickly that certain unscrupulous officers were quite prepared to steal an arrest from you and take the plaudits themselves.

About 1.30am one morning I was returning to West Bar station along the dark side streets. I passed an alleyway off Bank Street when, as I glanced down, I saw two figures climbing over a wall which led to the rear of lock-up shops. Allowing my eyes to become accustomed to the darkness I froze against the wall wondering what my next move should be. I was too far away from the station to summon assistance so I began to creep towards where the figures had gone over the wall. As I stood in the lane I could hear them smash a window of the shops and realized that they had to come back over the wall the same way. I drew my baton and waited. Just at that time one of my colleagues passed the top of the alleyway. He was a much older constable than I and was also en-route back to the station. I flashed my torch towards him and he quietly joined me. After some ten minutes the two youths climbed back over the wall without seeing us. They had two large sacks and began to walk down the alleyway away from where we were hidden.

Naturally the most senior constable decided a plan of action but I was a little 'pissed-off' when he told me run all around the building to prevent their escape from the bottom of the lane. However I did as I was told, only to reach the bottom of the lane to find 'my' prisoners, complete with two sacks, being pushed inside the main door of the station by the older officer. I entered the station office to find my colleague displaying two sacks of stolen cigarettes from the café they had broken into and enjoying the congratulations of the station sergeant. I listened to his story of the arrest and I was staggered when I never got a mention. I went up the canteen feeling very cheated indeed. My older colleague was not very well-liked on the shift and when some other officers found out the truth of the incident they reported the facts to the station sergeant who allowed me to process the prisoner with the help of the night detective. A commendation for me from the chief constable followed this arrest.

In total I received seven commendations all for arrests.

Commendations were also awarded when officers discovered fires at properties on their beats. I know I was not alone in wondering why such an award should be made to an officer for simply doing his job. I discovered several fires during my service all extinguished by the fire brigade and not one leading to a commendation. Perhaps I did not write the report correctly.

My keenness knew no bounds at that stage in my career.

I persuaded my Mother to keep a look-out for a local youth whose details had been circulated throughout the country after he absconded from an East Coast prison. We had known him all his life because his family lived on a street adjacent to ours. A warning accompanied the circulation that the youth was believed to be in possession of a firearm stolen from one of the house-breaking offences he had committed whilst on the 'run'.

One morning I had gone to bed at home following a tour of night duty when I was woken by Mother shortly before lunch-time. The wanted youth had just walked past our house.

Hastily donning a pair of trousers and a pullover to cover my pyjamas I ran almost half a mile until I caught up with him. We had one almighty 'punch-up' before again members of the public came to assist me and telephoned the police. Squad cars arrived and the youth was arrested and taken to Attercliffe divisional police headquarters near to where I lived. He was interviewed at length and admitted offences all over the country committed during his time on the 'run' from prison. In the heat of the moment I had never even thought about the fact that he could have been armed and I was lucky because the shot-gun he had stolen had been thrown away some days earlier.

A chief constables commendation did come my way in respect of that arrest.

I mentioned earlier that if you missed the last bus home and were obliged to walk home you could get a 'pull' from a keen police officer. The law on stopping people 'on suspicion' has never been very clear and many lies were told by officers to justify having detained someone simply because 'they did not look right'.

This was the case one bright Sunday morning as I patrolled near to the infamous Park Hill high-rise flats in the city. In view of the day and time there were very few people about when I saw two youths approaching on the opposite side of the road. Many observers say that to be a good copper you need luck on your side at times and this arrest illustrates that

151

point. I don't know why I was drawn to the youths but I stopped them and on finding they were Scottish asked them to account for their movements. I herded them into a nearby yard so that neither could escape easily and both gave different accounts of how they had reached the area. I arrested them for no particular offence other than telling me lies. They were taken to the local C.I.D. headquarters where they admitted numerous offences of burglary committed all over the North of England.

Another chief constables commendation followed.

I have been lucky in other ways as well…...

About 3am one morning, I was alone patrolling one of the outlying beats where most of the houses were about to be pulled down leaving them in a state of dereliction. Infirmary Road ran through the centre of the beat leading towards the Sheffield Wednesday football ground. Walking towards me was a tall guy dressed very smartly in an expensive overcoat plus collar and tie. He made no intention to avoid me and as we met he said 'Good-morning' in a heavy foreign accent. I naturally asked him what he was doing in the area at that time of the night and he explained that he had 'pulled' a nurse earlier that evening and had just left her at the nurse's lodgings about a mile away. He was en-route into the city to take a taxi home. We had a laugh about how he had 'scored' with the nurse and then I was joined by a much older constable on motor cycle patrol. The man spoke perfect English claiming to be from Hungary and we really had no reason to suspect him of anything. He confirmed his name with documents in his possession and we allowed him to go. I did record his details in my pocket-book out of habit. Remember we did not have access to radios in those days. It was perhaps some days later when the older motor cycle officer drew my attention to a circulation and picture in the Police Gazette which was issued by Scotland Yard giving details of persons wanted and suspected all over the country. There was a good picture of our Hungarian 'friend' who was wanted for all types of crimes throughout the country and...... *carried a revolver at all times which it is thought he will use to avoid arrest.* 'I call that lucky!

Perhaps one of my finest arrests whilst a young copper (and one that certainly gained me a transfer into the C.I.D.) was that of 'Friday Night Fred' as the press had named him.

It was summertime and people persisted in leaving windows open during the night which of course made it so easy for burglars to carry out their trade. This guy 'Friday Night Fred' as the name suggested broke into numerous houses during Friday nights stealing whatever he found. It was reported that he had even stolen a set of false teeth that had been left on the sink in a glass of water. The local press had begun to ask questions of the police why he had not been detained. Numerous observations were set-up involving uniformed and C.I.D. officers but there was no real pattern to the 'break-ins' other than Friday night.

I myself had been seconded one night to the special observations, joining a very old and experienced detective

153

who was not at all happy being stuck in an unmarked C.I.D. car behind some houses in the hope that 'Fred' would come along. After a couple of boring hours on the observations he took me to his local pub where I got completely pissed.

So much so, that I was sick outside in the street and he took me home telling his Boss that I had been taken ill.

However back to my story - it was 2am in the morning and I was on an 'outlying' beat where Woodseats division joined West Bar. It was a Summers Friday night and for weeks 'Fred' had been doing his business without detection. I was tired having played cricket during the previous day and I sat down in a shop doorway, took off my helmet and wrapped my cape around me. It was so quiet that I was in danger of falling asleep when across the road I saw this man creeping from the rear of some houses. He sank into the shadows and disappeared from view. Sleep was suddenly forgotten as I hastened across the silent road in time to see the man climbing over a wall into a yard at the rear of some terrace houses. He was unaware that I had seen him, but before I tried to detain him my worry was how to get him to the nearest police box which was a mile and a half away. I had my truncheon but no handcuffs because as I said earlier they were far too heavy to carry on a regular basis. At this time, of course, I had no idea this was 'Friday Night Fred' that we had all been seeking. I crept into the yard and saw the man forcing open the kitchen window of the house. I did not need my torch because the street lighting was sufficient for me to size up my prey. He was not a tall man, but looked pretty

154

solid, so I drew my baton and moved towards him.

I obviously surprised him when I went to grab him but he did not utter a word. I took hold of his arm and almost 'shit' myself when I felt his powerful arms. Without even thinking of what would happen if he decided to resist I pulled him out of the yard and into the street where luck would have it there was a car passing driven by a newspaper worker who had just finished his shift. I stopped the car - bundled my prisoner in the back seat and asked the driver to take me to the nearest police box. I pushed the prisoner into the police box still with my baton in my hand. I asked the car driver to stay in the box with me because I really felt that I was going to have some trouble from my prisoner. Then it suddenly hit me.....the man had not spoken once and despite his obvious powerful build he had not made any attempt to escape. With the arrival of police transport he was taken to the C.I.D. headquarters where the night detective sergeant interviewed him.

It transpired that my prisoner was Hungarian and spoke no English.

The fact that I was in uniform meant that there was no way he would offer violence to me having been brought up in a country where to resist the uniform authority meant severe punishment or even death.

Later in the morning with the detective sergeant (later to become head of C.I.D. as detective chief superintendent) I searched a small bed-sit some 2 miles from where I had arrested 'Fred'. We found numerous items to connect him to housebreakings all over the city. He had been in the habit of stealing letters as well as other goods when he broke into houses so it was an easy task to trace many of his crimes.

Radios, watches jewellery and even the set of false teeth were recovered which must have made some poor person happy being able to eat properly again.

I received another chief constables commendation but the downside was that I had arranged to take my girl-friend away for the week-end and this had to be postponed because I remained on duty for over two days. Not a very good start to a romance.

The arrest culminated a successful period for me and brought my talents to the attention of the C.I.D. bosses who were over the moon that the infamous 'Friday Night Fred' had been captured. Many undetected crimes were laid at his door, the files being marked detected' although I am positive he had not committed all of them.

A few months after this arrest my dream came true - the 'Rhino Whip Case' had decimated the C.I.D. staff and I was posted to the department as a trainee detective.

The first six months of my attachment to the C.I.D. was closely monitored to ensure I was C.I.D. material but I passed with flying colours and achieved the position of detective constable. Perhaps it was a little harsh when writing earlier and describing my first days in C.I.D. as "being taught to take witness statements and then going out boozing and shagging" but without doubt this is where my problems started.

As I have been writing this chapter so many vivid recollections and memories have been stirred spanning the whole spectrum of C.I.D life. They range from broken marriages; affairs; drunkenness; violence to prisoners and perjury; the submission of false evidence to ensure the conviction of an accused and the tampering with forensic evidence to achieve the same result; the claiming of both false duty expenses and informants rewards.

All these aberrations, in my case, leading into a 'finale' of wholesale corruption and organized crime. I have already expressed my total remorse and write now 'the truth - the whole truth and nothing but the truth', but I close this chapter pointing out again that I reigned for some 25 years in a medium size police force and worked closely with officers, many of whom made it to the top. I am sure you will accept that I could not have possibly avoided suspicion for all that time unless many others were actively engaged in a strong supportive role.

Chapter 6 - 'Experience and results.'

"Always tell the truth - then you don't have to remember anything."

Samuel Langhorne Clemens, 1835 - 1910.

One of the first things impressed upon me when I joined the C.I.D. was that the promotion examinations to both sergeant and inspector had to be passed. This was more easily said than done because the working life of a detective in the 'sixties' was to say the least 'strange' and did not lend itself to concentrated 'home-study'.

In addition some of the subjects on the syllabus were so far removed from every-day policing that it was difficult to foster any interest in them. Imagine trying to consolidate detailed case law and regulations, knowing that you may never have need of them and if you did you could do what the lawyers do and reach for a text book. Many officers 'risked' that the examiners would not select a particular subject that year and so ignored them. The format of the examinations allowed a candidate to select questions from a list so it was worth a gamble. Two main areas of police work that I avoided in study were the Firearms Act and Liquor Licensing Laws (the latter being particularly ironic when I later headed the city centre Licensing Squad for a time after being promoted to sergeant.)

Today it would be difficult to imagine crimes more popular

than breaches of those regulations but to a young detective the legal supervision of 'pubs' was of little interest where 'real' crime mattered and in reality only the products they sold caused me any excitement. When you bear in mind that I worked in the Sheffield city centre, I did not expect to encounter many firearms; however at the police training school it was noticeable that officers from county forces paid much more attention to the firearms act. On a day to day basis on their 'patches' they would come across farmers, gamekeepers poachers and the like who were heavily involved with firearms so their interest was understandable Another point I noted was that county officers were much more interested in first aid than their city counterparts. This again was understandable when you consider in a city an ambulance can reach an incident in minutes whereas in the country it can take much longer and the officer on the scene needs to try and protect life.

I was still, to some extent really virtuous at this point in my career.

Several events during my uniformed career had left me in no doubt that the 'guardians of the peace' were not all as honest as they should be. Very early one morning I was patrolling High Street in the city centre where the council were erecting a new massive road scheme consisting of a roundabout with shops and toilets beneath. It was known informally as 'the hole in the road'. It was very quiet and I was making my way through the building works when I heard noises. Creeping silently towards the noises I found a uniformed officer from the adjoining beat busily packing the pocket of his regulation cape with small wall tiles. In other words, 'nicking' them. I was quite shocked, but seeing me did not seem to bother him at all. He explained that he had almost finished tiling his bathroom at home and just needed a few more to finish the job. I never told anyone and did not report him.

Whilst on night duty I was approached in the early hours one Spring morning by the divisional car patrol officers who asked if I wanted any free bedding plants. I turned them down, but with a list of plants required they then drove out of our division to Graves Park some four miles away in the Woodseats division where I understand they helped themselves to plants from the council greenhouse. Again I never told anyone and did not report them.

It was also not unusual for 'beat' officers during the night shift to steal radios from cars left open on garage forecourts. Hub caps or wing mirrors were also stolen to order.

One officer actually admitted to me that he loved to find shops or offices broken into on his beat. This would give him the opportunity to steal whatever he liked before reporting the crime.

I know of two officers who took money on a regular basis from a wealthy car dealer in the city because he was convinced that their efforts had saved him from prosecution for fraud.

Platinum and mercury were stolen from a safe in the city

centre one weekend and most of the haul was later recovered by metal squad detectives. Only a small amount of the stolen gear was returned to the lawful owners - the rest being sold to a 'bent ' scrap metal dealer' and the proceeds shared by the officers.

Why did I keep my mouth shut and not report these incidents?

Perhaps because I wanted to be 'one of the boys' as I did with my first 'piking' encounter.

The distressing point though, is that 'ALL' the officers mentioned here are still in the force and many are now senior officers.

Let me recall a massive indictment against the service from earlier where I described Detective Sergeant Lancashire and a constable from the regional crime squad charge keeping observations on their married Boss and making official notes of his illicit visits to a policewoman We are back to the freemason issue again where Sergeant Lancashire was a mason and due to that secured promotion at least three ranks higher than he should have been when he reached chief superintendent. This officer had entered the C.I.D. at the same time as me and as a direct result of vacancies that had arisen due to the 'Rhino Whip Affair'. Lancashire and I knew each other very well because we both worked on the same team. He did not like to take any chances and would run a mile from violent confrontation. I was not impressed with him in the early hours of one morning after we had arrested a

161

drunken Irishman for theft he left me to struggle alone with the prisoner as I tried to get him from the C.I.D. car and into the charge office.

A local insurance broker privately arranged for all police officers to get good rates when car insurance was required and in fact he was an ex school-friend of mine. Lancashire and I had only been in C.I.D. a few months when I received a telephone call from the broker one morning asking that we both visit his office almost adjacent to the Sheffield city cathedral. I assumed that he wanted to discuss motor car insurance rates. On attendance at his office the Broker came straight to the point saying...

"Your bosses have told me to have a word. If you two want to get on in the promotion stakes you've got to join a Lodge". Both Lancashire and I looked dumb.

"Freemason Lodge" explained the Broker seeing the uncertain looks on our faces…

"It's the only way to get on in the force and I can arrange things."

We talked for a little while longer and then left his office.

Lancashire was very keen to go down the freemason path, but I wanted to discuss the offer with my Father. My Father was quite clear saying…

"If you can't get on in the police without joining some secret organization then I wouldn't bother." Adding that my uncle had been a mason in the City of Hull where he ran a very successful fish business. My uncle had resigned due to the corruption and secrecy of the sect.

Promotion from then on simply became a matter of course for Lancashire, whereas mine stood still. We had both passed the examinations at the same time but the difference in our advancement was startling. After promotion through several 'non-descript' police departments such as 'Community Relations' etc., he finally reached chief superintendent. Many other officers took the same view as me that he was not worthy of the ranks that were coming his way and they had all been achieved through freemasonry.

So I passed the sergeants examination at my first attempt and the inspectors at the second, which shows the habit of studying waned as I got more and more engrossed in detective work. I was flying around like the proverbial 'blue-arsed fly', trying to gain C.I.D. experience and capturing villains here there and everywhere

It never crossed my mind that other officers, working 9am - 5pm - weekends off - were probably gaining as much recognition as I was. When I think of some of the tasks and departments occupied by fully qualified police officers - I am astounded.

Tasks that could easily have been undertaken by civilians.

There were two uniformed sergeants controlling the force wages department in headquarters.

One constable attended work each day in civilian clothes and went round the markets and other wholesalers purchasing produce for the headquarters and city centre divisional canteens.

One uniformed inspector was responsible (on the day shift, of course) for the licensing of Hackney Carriages (taxis) in the city.

One constable in my division was something of an artist so he was constantly being taken off patrol to paint posters and the like. Two other constables, before joining the force, were carpenters by trade and they too were often to be found repairing damaged wooden equipment at one of the police stations or making scenery for some police exhibition.

There was a designated constable who worked days only around the Sheffield town hall in the city centre. His duties were simply to ensure that local Counsellors and other civil servants found a parking place when attending meetings.

Another constable spent his days patrolling the wholesale fruit and vegetable market area. I am told that his Wife never needed to visit their local greengrocers shop.

Perhaps the best example though of 'misuse' of police resources was a uniformed constable attached to the mounted department, whose job among other minor tasks, was to drive a tractor and trailer full of horse manure. If you were a keen gardener and wanted manure you only had to ring the mounted department and some days later it was delivered free of charge. In my case the officer drove some twenty five miles round trip to drop of his precious cargo.

I admit some of these jobs are now being civilianized but it has taken many years for the 'merry-go-round' to stall.

So I put my heart and my head fully into being a good detective.

By now the nick-name 'Booper' was fully operational being used by all including senior officers. I am told that I had the 'gift of the gab' and a fair sense of humour confirmed by a detective superintendent addressing a murder conference. If a murder is not detected in the first 24 hours then the investigation can be in trouble. After a few days spirits begin to flag and I would try to instil some humour when the daily murder conferences were held.

The detective superintendent in this case said it was always pleasant to have me inject my sense of humour into the conference adding "that's all you're fucking good for".

I think he was joking.

I have only been involved in two 'Identification' parades in the whole of my service.

You will be aware it is a 'tool' used by the police to allow witnesses to view a suspect in a line-up of other similar people in the hope they can identify him or her. We had a long-standing arrangement with the local Salvation Army Hostel to recruit men to fill the parades but abandoned the idea when it became apparent that the 'dossers' used were so at home in the police station that the parade descended into a farce. As a young detective I soon learnt how the parade could be abused.

There were strict rules governing the conduct of the parade and officers so that the suspect was given a 'fair' chance. In my days there was no such thing

I had nothing to do 'officially' with the case I talk about, so I could go about my business, even in the vicinity of the parade, without challenge. The suspect had sold a large amount of stolen copper cable to a local scrap metal dealer. The outer covering of the cable had been removed by the thieves so the original owner at first was unknown. As the sale was going through a detective sergeant and detective constable from the regional crime squad visited the premises but left shortly afterwards not having realized that the suspect had been selling stolen metals. They had, however, noticed the thief himself.

Further enquiries led the police to the suspect who denied ever having been in the scrap metal dealers premises. The metal was subsequently identified as having been stolen from the Electricity Board. No help was forthcoming from the dealer who did not want his business to suffer by helping the police against the suspect.

It was therefore necessary for the crime squad officers to pick out the suspect on an identification parade. Of course they both identified the man without difficulty, perhaps helped by the fact that I had been told to occupy a position in an adjoining corridor to the parade. I noted the suspects clothing and position in the line-up, including the fact that he had recently shaved off his beard. I then passed all this information to the two police 'witnesses'.

Working as a 'junior' detective in a busy city centre C.I.D. office soon led to friendships and disputes when it became apparent who were prepared to take their fair share of the cities crimes and those who would disappear when most needed.

I mentioned earlier that I daily 'told lies on paper' and my tuition in that respect began as soon as I joined the department.

Remember I am recalling 'the sixties' and already things have changed in the amount of paper work required to log a simple crime.

One rule in my force was that a witness statement should be completed for 'every' reported crime whether it be the theft of a bottle of milk or a murder. In the case of a 'crime' so much paper would have already been spoilt before it reached the detective designated to investigate. A 'crime report' had to be submitted the same day with a supplementary report for further items stolen should that be necessary. Each day, the officer in the case was expected to endorse the report with all the enquiries he had made. This was part of the 'daily lies on paper' comment, because in reality it was impossible to carry out the enquiries expected and find time for anything else.

So, it was left to the end of the month where you would find the C.I.D office full of detectives busy typing all their lies on the reports so that the detective inspector was able to write them off as 'undetected' and file them.

False entries would include showing enquires made at local second-hand dealers, auctions markets and other sites for stolen property. Visits to metal dealers when metal had been stolen.

False meetings with informants or observations kept in the area. The report would be endorsed, quite falsely, that 'every'

167

prisoner arrested recently for such crimes had been interviewed.

What a load of 'bollocks' - but all this was condoned by senior officers who would not file the report until all the entries had been made.

Every year, H.M. Inspector of Constabulary would visit the force area generally selecting a sample of crime reports to see that they had been completed correctly. Obviously the scale of the crime dictated how many enquires were required to get it 'filed'. You would get away with a few entries for a stolen bottle of milk, but with a wounding offence or a serious house-breaking case more detailed 'lies' were required.

As I write steps are being taken to relieve officers of the 'paperwork burden' but I cannot see the 'lies on paper' culture coming to an end as officers face a rising crime rate.

Why am I pursuing this subject in so much detail when it is not going to bother me anymore? Perhaps as I sit here again today, alone and for another twenty three hours in my cell it is a good way to get it all out of my system. Perhaps it is because I am sick of the lies told by senior police officers and the government relative to the rising crime rate.

So, back to the C.I.D. business where I continued to work with many other detectives learning from them constantly. There were humorous incidents along with heartbreaking events. Just one C.I.D. team worked 'nights' at the Water Lane C.I.D. headquarters in the city centre and were responsible for persons arrested by other divisions. It was a good time often, to try and get paperwork completed and avoid the month-end chaos. In the headquarters building was the police-women's department which was never staffed on nights but if some female was arrested out of hours the suspect would be brought to the office to be processed. In the event of the female suspect having to be searched this would also take place in the downstairs police-women's department by one or two female officers. My team had realized that if we ran quickly upstairs - placing chairs against the office windows this allowed us to look directly into the ladies department. Some of the sights we saw made it a pleasure to be on nights but it all came to an end when a detective sergeant in his rush to climb onto the chair and see the girl undressed fell off and broke his ankle.

On the same theme - one of the officers kept a stethoscope in his desk, recovered from a thief who had ransacked a doctor's car at the local hospital. The stethoscope never got returned (similar to the rhino whip from earlier you will recall). On night duty and for a 'giggle' when some drunken female was brought into the office, it was not unusual for an officer posing as a doctor to dress in a white traffic coat and with the stethoscope round his neck carry out a detailed medical examination of the girl to ensure she was 'medically fit' to be detained. His colleagues secretly watched from an adjoining office.

All the time I was learning - and many events taught me to remember incidents so not to get caught out later in my career.

Imagine being the young detective sent with a detective sergeant and older detective constable to search the flat of a suspected thief who was in custody. Unknown to me the man had treated his female partner very badly and she had 'grassed' him up for stealing goods from where he worked. She had also made allegations of serious sexual abuse, including the act of sodomy committed against her wishes. Apparently during their 'love-making' it was customary for the man to use a torch as a 'sex-aid' to get her excited for the final act. Of course I was unaware of this, only being told that we were looking for a torch among other items as evidence. In those days we would never have dreamed of wearing gloves when searching the flat and my colleagues absolutely rolled about the floor with laughter when I found the torch and kept switching it on and off. Needless to say when they told me where it had been I dropped it like a red hot poker.

Whilst on the subject of 'sex-aids' I used to work with one detective who told me that he regularly used his wooden truncheon as a 'sex-aid' with his Wife. What about 'splinters'?

Other events taught me a very salutary lesson though, such as one mid-morning I was alone in a C.I.D. vehicle and driving passed some high-rise flats in Infirmary Road about 2 miles from Sheffield city centre. The flats were mainly occupied by young university students. I saw a small crowd of people on the footpath looking up towards the top of the flats. I glanced upwards just as a young man threw himself from the top and crashed onto the pavement below killing himself instantly. I steered the C.I.D. car swiftly across onto the footpath and jumped out alongside the body. It was apparent the boy was dead with his eye- balls having come out of their sockets even though his spectacles were still in place. A gruesome sight but experience had taught me just to get on with the job. I used the car radio to summon assistance and uniformed officers continued the investigation.

It was a classic case of some poor young student finding himself unable to cope with the pressure of his studies and taking the ultimate 'way -out'. What a waste of life.

I attended a small engineering firm in the city centre shortly after they had opened for business one Friday morning. One of three very old safes had been attacked by forcing open the back. Some £3.000 in cash had been stolen, but my 'instinct' and other facts made me unhappy. I pondered over the fact that it was the first time in many years that such a large amount of cash had ever been left in any of the safes and only the safe containing the cash had been attacked. Desks and cupboards being ignored. Entry to the premises had been made by breaking a window in the enclosed yard at the rear - but the pieces of broken glass were on the floor 'outside' the window and not 'inside'. The tools used to open the back of the safe were from the actual works and had not been brought by the thieve(s). No fingerprints or other forensic evidence were found at the scene.

I liked the old managing director of the company, despite him reminding me that he was a 'freemason' and knew most of the top brass in the force. My detective inspector became involved, perhaps due to the 'freemason' angle, and we were anxious to get a result.

I had taken an instant dislike to one of the young directors of the company during my initial enquiries and began to suspect him. He was very well known to one of my wife's friends and on checking with her I found that he was cheating on his wife (not a criminal offence I hear you say) but also up to his eyes in debt. Even the old managing director was unhappy with him as a worker and paid him no compliments.

I decided that he was responsible and arrested him.

He was interviewed at length and I did everything but slap him to gain a confession.

We had him in tears several times but he refused to admit the crime. During the interview my detective inspector had to constantly remind me that we were dealing with an educated man and not one of the 'low-life' that normally graced the cells. This in many ways restricted the interview. So the company director was released without charge and the crime report endorsed to the effect that 'I knew he had done it - but couldn't prove it'. How wrong could I have been?

Some months later I received a call from the Humberside Police. They had arrested two men for 'safe-breaking' offences and they had admitted the crime on my 'patch'.

Again learn from your mistakes in all life's events.

Violence to most prisoners to gain a confession was an every-day occurrence. Myself and another young detective were accused at Rotherham Quarter Sessions court of hitting a prisoner with a pool-cue to force him to make a statement admitting theft from the gas meter at his home. The jury found him guilty, accepting that police officers did not behave in that way but the tide is turning and it cannot be far away where more restrictions are imposed by the law authorities of the land to ensure prisoners are not abused when in police custody. There were many other occasions when it was alleged at court that I and other officers had assaulted prisoners to gain a confession to a crime. The allegations, naturally, were always denied.

There again some violence, in my opinion, can be justified. Take for example a youth living next door to the Doncaster Gate hospital in Rotherham. He was unemployed, a drunkard and a 'nasty piece of work'. Almost every week-end he would frequent the pubs in the town getting completely 'leg-less'. He would then feign an illness, such as a heart attack or seizure and the public would call an ambulance. The ambulance would take him to the 'Accident & Emergency Department' of the local hospital where he would discharge himself almost as soon as he arrived and walk home round the corner. The ambulance department and the Rotherham 'bobbies' were getting fed-up of him. Late one evening I was with a C.I.D. colleague leaving a low-class public house in the town centre when we found our 'friend' lying outside feigning his usual illness. Several well-meaning citizens were trying to help him and someone from the pub had called the usual ambulance. We intervened - arrested him and threw him into the back of the C.I.D. car parked nearby, but not before we had been verbally challenged by onlookers for our treatment of a 'sick' person. We drove him to the Rotherham police traffic department at Masborough, which was closed at that time of the night, dragged him out of the car and warned him that his little 'scam' at the expense of the ambulance and hospital staff was at an end. All we got was foul mouthed slurring keeping up his pretence of illness.

It was a bitterly cold winter's night and we thought that the large high pressure hose pipe used for cleaning police vehicles would be frozen. Luckily it wasn't...

We blasted him as he lay on the ground and even stuffed the jet into one of his ears.

The result was astounding. The man leapt up and ran dripping in water out of the station yard. We followed him at a distance as he ran almost a mile to our police station and threw himself through the front doors. He was absolutely wet through. Creeping into the office via the rear yard we heard him making a complaint to the night inspector that two detectives had assaulted him with a high pressure hose. The inspector, knowing all about the 'scam' with his false illnesses told him to 'piss-off' adding that none of his detectives would behave in such a way. The man continued to abuse the inspector so he was arrested for being 'drunk & disorderly' and thrown in the cells until the next morning. To my knowledge he never again tried feigning illness to get a cheap 'taxi-ride' home. You will recall that Rotherham town was where I first became interested in police work and also my female cousin whose Father was caretaker of the waterworks opposite!

I mentioned earlier that violence to most 'prisoners' was a matter of course, but as with the company director who had NOT 'screwed' the safe at his firm you always had to be careful if the suspect was of any intelligence. Any complaint later made by some 'educated' person could always have potential problems in that officers from the 'Rubber Heel Department' (official police department that investigated misdeeds by officers) had to take them more seriously than others. You may be aware that in most cases allegations against police officers are investigated by police officers and history dictates that the benefit of any doubt would go the officer's way. You will probably be saying right now that the system 'stinks' and you would be correct. However, consider where police officers have put their careers on the line trying to convict some 'scum' only to find that credence has been given to the accused and his allegations of assault or malpractice against the police have allowed him to be found 'Not Guilty'.

Before the allegations which have put me behind bars ever came to light I had been investigated by the force discipline department on so many occasions I cannot remember them all. As a detective sergeant I once appeared before the chief constable at a discipline hearing alleging that I had sworn at and threatened a motorist whilst driving a 'marked' police car. Brief circumstances being that we were working on a murder case in the Hillsborough division and we were not getting very far with our enquiries. It was not unusual to have access to a 'marked' police car on such enquiries to supplement the other vehicles being used. I was in the company of a very young detective from the same division at the time. We were very tired from the long hours already worked and circumstances were not helped by the fact that we had been drinking most of the afternoon in a public house frequented by the cities criminals. We left the pub in the 'marked' police car. I was driving when a car cut across me. I lost my temper and chased him with the Blue light of the police car flashing. I managed to stop him after about a mile and jumped from the car to remonstrate with him. He also jumped from his vehicle and began to argue with me. I gave him some right 'verbal'- using words that would have got anyone else 'locked- up'. He argued back but I had not noticed that the entire incident was being witnessed by several people in a bus queue and it did not help when he produced his warrant card to show that he was a police sergeant from the neighbouring Nottinghamshire force. He then made a complaint about my conduct.

A superintendent and detective inspector from the 'Rubber Heel squad' were deputed to investigate the complaint. The inspector, who was a pal of mine, tried every way to get the complaint 'shelved' including appealing personally to the sergeant - stressing that relations between our two forces could be seriously affected. All to no avail and so I went before the 'chief' one afternoon and pleaded 'Guilty' to discreditable conduct. Everyone thought I would get 'demoted' from the rank of sergeant but the 'chief' fined me instead.

During my time as detective sergeant things were not good at home. I had separated from my Wife and two children, moving in with a policewoman who had been divorced.

I did return home after a while but the damage was done so to try to ease the situation for everyone I thought it would be a good idea to get away from an environment that was doing me no favours at all. I applied to be seconded as a detective sergeant to the Royal Ulster Constabulary but was turned down due to having just recovered from a serious bout of Hepatitis. On reflection it was probably not the best route for someone like me to follow. The Ulster troubles were at their height and the way I was conducting myself as a copper in those days would have probably meant that I would have ended up being shot or 'tar and feathered' against a lamp post in County Derry or Belfast!

One Saturday evening whilst on duty, but drinking with another officer in the city, word reached us that my policewoman 'friend' and another female colleague, who worked in the Hillsborough police division had been seriously assaulted by some black youths whilst trying to detain a young girl reported missing by her parents. The parents of the girl strongly suspected that the girl was being abused sexually by the youths and were unable to control her. The two female officers found the 'gang' with the girl in a local park and tried to detain her. The black youths attacked them, knocking my policewoman friend over a wall and breaking the nose of her colleague. Both officers had to be taken to hospital where both were detained overnight. You will imagine that I was not best pleased. The other detective with me at the time in the pub was known as 'Big Pig' which tells you in two words the character of the officer. We found out that one of the black youths had been detained and was in the cells of a divisional station on the outskirts of the force area. We drove across the city to 'interview' him about crimes in our division. On arrival at the station I was pleased to see that the station sergeant was a very good friend of mine. His first words on seeing me and knowing my friendship with the policewoman were "Hello 'Boops'. - I wondered how long it would be before you turned up. Remember he's not marked (referring to their prisoner) so don't go overboard."

He then ordered the young office policewoman to go and make some tea, even though apparently she had just made some. The station sergeant gave us a big grin and opened the cell door. I slapped the youth as soon as we entered the cell but he did not even flinch. I was then pushed out of the way by 'Big Pig' shouting "Get out of the way, Booper. I'll teach him to knock women about." I simply stood in the corner of the cell whilst 'Big Pig' kicked and punched him all round the room. We checked to ensure he was not marked and then returned to our division. I visited my friend the policewoman in hospital just before midnight and then went home for the week-end.

The following Monday afternoon I reported for duty at 2pm to find a detective superintendent from the 'Rubber Heels department' waiting for me. He was investigating a complaint from a black youth who claimed to have been assaulted by two detectives whilst in the cells at another police station the previous Saturday evening. I was asked: "Did I know anything about it?" The superintendent added that the smaller of the detectives was nicknamed 'Booper' or 'Boomer' had distinctive white hair and was wearing a long leather coat. The other detective was, in the complainants words-'massive'-'evil' and the other officer called him 'Pig'. I told the investigating superintendent that I could not help him, adding that anyone attacking female police officers as the black youths had done were bound to attract hostility from 'any' officer. That was the last we heard of that matter.

As I said earlier when dealing with an 'educated' suspect it was better to follow the rules rather than risk a complaint.

This was the case, when as a young detective I became involved with a very experienced detective sergeant in a 'fraud' case that taught me how easy it was to 'con' multi-national companies and make easy money. We had received complaints from various companies including B.P. and I.C.I. that one of our Rotherham locals, who was unknown to us, was involved in systematic fraud by claiming to have attended interviews for jobs. He did not attend the arranged interview but submitted false rail/bus tickets/meal receipts to the company requesting payment pretending that he had. You would be amazed how many simply paid him without querying the claims! The man, who had graduated from university complete with degree, found the harsh cold world a difficult place to gain employment and hit on the fraud idea. He daily applied for positions of employment advertised in all the 'up-market' newspapers. More often than not he never even received a reply to his application, but in every case followed it up with a claim for expenses.

Most of the firms paid up without checking but a couple became suspicious and reported it to the police. When we searched his house the front room had been converted into an office where 'all' his claims, successful or otherwise, had been filed. There was even a printing machine to produce meal receipts and the like to perpetrate his fraud. It was a simple matter to trace all his crimes and prosecute him. Later in court he pleaded 'guilty' to several specimen charges and asked for hundreds of others to be taken into consideration by the court. A case, you will agree, where the actions of many large companies virtually encouraged the man to be dishonest.

Major fraud today is becoming rampant and steps are being taken by the authorities to contain the trend, but to an enterprising, dishonest intelligent individual there are still minor areas where a good living can be made.

'Little Bastard' was his nickname long before he joined my team as a C.I.D. aide, known throughout the force as 'L.B.' for politeness. When I first met him he was a uniformed dog handler and like all the others from that department thought he was invaluable in combating crime and preventing social unrest in the country. In reality, my experience of police dogs led me to believe that they were totally unreliable, uncontrollable unable to recognize friend from foe and were guaranteed to do something inexplicable at any time. Take for example on nights we were called to Rackhams department store in Sheffield due to the silent burglar alarm having activated in the police information room. A set of duplicate keys for the premises were kept in a safe at C.I.D. headquarters where many others for large city centre premises were also held and thus we were able to save time by surrounding the building and conducting a search before the 'reference' for the premises or even the caretaker in some cases had been called from his bed.

We sent the dog and handler in first, followed by other officers only to find that the dog had jumped on a large posh bed in the furniture department and 'shit' all over the place.

The dog handler tried to explain it was something the animal had eaten earlier in the day that caused his 'looseness'. I felt sorry for both officer and dog at the time but a few weeks later there was a repeat performance at Cole

181

Brothers department store in the middle of the night. This time the dog 'shit' all over the carpet in the perfume department prompting his handler to explain it was the 'aromatic smells' that caused such behaviour.

Another occasion on a 'newly-promoted' sergeant's course at police headquarters we all assembled in the West Bar divisional car park to see how a handler and his dog controlled crowd unrest. It was suggested by the handler that the thirty or so new sergeants should act as an 'unruly mob' surrounding the officer and his dog and he would demonstrate how to 'deal' with the situation. In view of my previous experience with police dogs I made sure I was at the back of the 'unruly mob' with an escape route through a fire door. Immediately there were problems when the handler, not realizing that the exercise had started, allowed too much rope around the dogs neck. A couple of daft sergeants at the front of the crowd decided to install some reality into the demonstration and began shouting and trying the kick the animal. Naturally the dog leapt at them and pulled the handler completely off his feet. The dog then sank his teeth into the 'bollocks' of one of the sergeants and after he was taken to hospital it was decided to call the whole exercise off.

But I digress because I want to go on about 'L.B.'

He was only small in size, full of humour, liked a drink and was completely averse to rules and regulations. I forget how many complaints of his dog having bitten prisoners, suspects and members of the public, were made, but in many ways, he got results.

Just before he joined my team in C.I.D. there was a rather amusing, but unseemly incident, involving 'L.B.' his dog and a station sergeant who was not particularly liked by anyone. The sergeant had no sense of humour but had an obsession with tidiness particularly on his desk. He had constantly told 'L.B.' not to leave his dog unattended in the office when going to the toilet or canteen. 'L.B.' replied that the dog had been in the back of a police van for most of the shift and needed a change of outlook. 'L.B.' took no notice of the sergeant's instructions and on many occasions when you entered the station office you would be confronted by one enormous smelly Alsatian dog taking up all the available floor space. Occasionally the dog would 'fart' so that we knew he was alive but generally he just lay there surveying everyone with a bored expression. The sergeant continued to berate 'L.B.' about the dog being in the office until it almost reached discipline action. One evening there was an almighty 'bust-up' between the sergeant and 'L.B.' about the dog. The sergeant tidied his desk and left the office warning 'L.B.' to remove the animal from the office. 'L.B's' reply to the departing sergeant was something on the lines of "I'll give you something to get fucking worked up about"..........The sergeant ignored him and left. 'L.B.' then got the dog to place both of his front paws on the sergeant's desk and 'L.B.' began to masturbate the dog. (I am told that dogs enjoy this behaviour and ejaculate very quickly). In any event as the sergeant returned after a few minutes he found his tidy desk and papers covered in dog sperm. He screamed at 'L.B.' to

183

get the dog out of the office, which was done in pretty quick time because even 'L.B.' realized that this time he had gone too far. As far as I know 'L.B.' never took his dog in the office again and it was retired on health grounds shortly afterwards. You read about Dog Handlers being distraught when they have to retire or lose their dogs. Not so in 'L.B's' case - he immediately sold the animal to a local working-mans club as a guard dog and to my knowledge never saw it again.

So the bosses needed somewhere to put 'L.B.' hoping it would keep him out of trouble and an attachment to C.I.D. as an 'aide' seemed as good a place as any! It was unusual for an officer with 'L.B's' 12 years service to be considered for C.I.D. but he was seconded to the team and spent most of the time with me, leaving my other two detective constables to work together. I knew there would be problems!

On the first week of night duty it was around midnight and I had not seen him since we came on duty at 10pm. At this time we worked in the Sheffield city centre West Bar division. A note in the diary showed him meeting an 'informant' but that was out of the question at that time of night. Either 'Boozing' or 'Shagging' were the bets or both in his case. It was about 4am in the morning when I was called by the station sergeant who was 'old school' and told to go to the rear entrance of the station. 'L.B.' was drunk and had tried to drive the C.I.D. car into the underground car park. Realising that he could not do it, he asked a uniformed constable to help him and then all the station knew about the event. The station sergeant was quite ready to forget about the incident and so 'L.B.' was taken home after being sick all over the bonnet of the car. He received one almighty 'bollocking' from me, basically for getting caught, as I took him home and the matter was forgotten. In fact he had been 'shagging' the bar-maid from the local C.I.D. boozer not knowing that many others had already been there. I enjoyed working with 'L.B.' for the six months of his C.I.D. attachment although I had been warned by my detective superintendent from the beginning, in his words- "L.B. will never fucking stay in C.I.D. as long as I've got a hole in my arse'. This statement proved to be true- that is 'L.B.' did not stay after his six months - not anything to do with superintendents rectum.

Shortly before Christmas 1981 the force held its annual carol service at the Sheffield Cathedral on a Friday afternoon. Being the sergeant I insisted that all the team should attend. I emphasized how good it would look on future promotion boards if we were seen at such an event. The two detective constables told me to 'bollocks' and went home. So after finishing duty at 2pm that afternoon only 'L.B.' and myself entered the beautiful cathedral in the centre of the city. It had snowed heavily that morning and we were dressed in heavy anoraks and hats. I removed my hat immediately on entering the church but 'L.B.' was way down the aisle before I caught him and reminded him where we were. He held a loud conversation with a police woman whom he had been 'shagging' for years before realizing that almost everyone in

185

the church were looking at us. By 'everyone' I mean all the 'shiny-arse brigade' from headquarters the police band and civic guests. So the service started and we each had a hymn sheet, which to be fair did encourage 'L.B.' to sing the Christmas carols at the top of his voice. At the end of the service we left the church and spent a pleasant afternoon drinking with a well-known 'D.J.' from Radio Sheffield. We left 'pissed' but were not due to return to duty until 10pm the following Monday evening.

We worked 'Night Duty' the following week and on the first evening were involved in an alleged 'armed robbery' where a youth who lived in flats close to West Bar station claimed that one of his mates had stolen his sheepskin coat whilst armed with a 'sawn-off' shotgun. We were not happy with the complaint but it required investigation and 'L.B.' and myself arrived at a house on the 'run-down' Manor estate about 2am in the morning. The so-called 'mate' who had stolen the sheepskin coat was supposed to be living there with his parents and with the help from two uniformed officers from that division we intended searching the house. En-route I had warned 'L.B.' not to do anything silly with the two uniformed men there. We did not know them and perhaps they would not take kindly to breaches of the 'Judges Rules' that I knew would probably happen. First of all I lost 'L.B.' whilst I was checking all round the house. One of the uniformed officers reported that he had seen him 'having a piss' against the front door of the house. That was a good start.

I sent 'L.B.' and one of the uniformed officers round to the back of the house, whilst I and the other constable bashed on the front door. Eventually lights came on inside the house and someone inside started 'fucking and blinding' - I don't think any of us had given much thought to what we would do if some 'twat' pointed a 'sawn-off' shotgun at us!

The Father of the suspect was shouting at us through the locked front door telling us to "fuck off". His son wasn't there he shouted and "There's no way you're coming in here without a fucking warrant". At that moment there was an almighty crash at the back of the house and 'L.B.' shouted that he was 'in'...

Leaving one officer at the front I ran round to the rear of the house to find the door hanging on its hinges and 'L.B' shouting about a "fucking warrant". He had the suspects Father laid across the kitchen table. 'L.B.' was shouting at the man "What do you think this fucker is?", waving a piece of paper in his face. The uniformed constable seemed way out of his depth and I told him to search upstairs and 'L.B.' and myself would follow. I dragged 'L.B.' off the Father who apparently had called him a "little c...t" which 'L.B' maintained gave him the right to kill him! We made a thorough search of the house and accepted that the suspect had not lived there for many years. I thanked the two uniformed officers for their assistance, leaving them to return to their division and no doubt report what 'evil' bastards we were in C.I.D.

It was whilst we were driving back to the city that I

remembered to ask 'L.B.' about 'The Search Warrant' he had produced - with a big grin on his face he waved the Hymn sheet from the previous weeks carol service in my face saying..........

"Ways and Means Act, Sarge. Fucking Ways and Means Act.".

I got injured on several occasions whilst in uniform and C.I.D.

One Christmas Eve I was in a C.I.D. car, actually 'on duty', but not having completed any real police work during the afternoon because we had been too busy boozing at the office party and then making private calls at other 'friendly' boozers. Myself and a colleague were making our way back to the office just before 10pm. We were passing the Bull and Mouth public house in Waingate, Sheffield to find the street blocked by a mob of fighting people. The scene was only yards away from the police central charge office round the corner in Bridge Street. As we sat in the middle of the road unable to pass we saw a police helmet thrown into the air and realized there was a uniformed constable somewhere among the fighters. We left our vehicle blocking the road and ran towards the crowd. We found a solitary constable trying to part several groups of fighting youths. He was using his truncheon but was in danger of being overwhelmed by the sheer numbers. We piled into the fracas hitting anyone we found with our fists. Neither myself nor my colleague were in possession of batons and bear in mind we were in plain clothes. We shouted that we were police officers which seemed to count for nothing. One youth smacked the uniformed constable in the face with his fist and I pounced on him. I hit the youth in the face and he fell against the police 'marked' car which we had only just noticed due to the number of people fighting. The youth and I struggled with each other-me hitting him and he hitting me. I took hold of him and dragged him towards the unmarked C.I.D. car and tried to push him inside. I think I told him he was under arrest for 'drunk and disorderly' but I wouldn't bank on it. He was in real danger of escaping and no assistance had arrived at that point. Things were turning really nasty. I dragged his head down and again tried to push him into the car. He was still struggling so I brought my knee sharply up into his face, which had the desired effect. I then pushed him onto the back seat of the car.

Certainly I never felt any pain in my leg due to the anaesthetized state I was in from the afternoon drinks. The youth was by then laid on the back seat of the car 'fucking and blinding' with blood pouring from his mouth. Assistance arrived and several youths were arrested and given a 'good hiding' in the time-established manner. With my colleague, I then drove my prisoner around the corner to the police charge office and dragged him inside. What a mess. The prisoner had blood pouring from his mouth and nose, was still 'fucking and blinding' and insisted showing everyone that his two front teeth were missing. Obviously he was drunk and I told the inspector I was charging him with 'assault on police' namely myself and 'drunk and disorderly'. I ignored a charge of assault on the uniformed officer because I thought it may complicate the case! We carried out the charging procedure and the youth was led off to a cell with one of the police staff giving him first aid. It was at this point that the inspector pointed to my right knee. I was quite shocked to see blood pouring through a tear in my trousers and also running onto the floor over my shoes. There was a severe laceration to my knee which at the time I could not really feel. I dropped my trousers to have a better look at the wound only to find the prisoners two front teeth stuck in my knee! The inspector insisted that I attend the hospital and was about to arrange an ambulance but I insisted that I went with my colleague.

The Casualty Doctor was naturally unfriendly bearing in mind the holiday celebrations had not yet really started and already 'piss-heads' like me were spoiling his Christmas.

He questioned me about the amount I had drunk that day, which I did not really think was any of his business and then sutured the wound, adding a tetanus injection. I returned to the C.I.D. office and quickly completed the 'arrest' report even under the influence of drink. It was by then the early hours of Christmas Day and I adjourned to my favourite nightclub Josephines. Very quickly I began to feel quite strange and whilst dancing with some female I realized that my right leg was not responding the way it should.

I managed to drive home, but two days later on Boxing Day I was admitted to the Royal Infirmary hospital where it was suggested that infection in the wound may require my leg to be amputated above the knee. Oh Boy! Merry Christmas!

After several weeks in hospital and concentrated medical treatment, I was discharged still in total possession of my right leg but with a warning of disablement in the future.

After a lengthy period of rehabilitation I returned to C.I.D. duty.

Oh yes! I almost forgot - The youth I had arrested for assaulting me pleaded 'Not Guilty' but at the magistrates' court was convicted and received a heavy fine. In the interim we had also charged him with damaging my trousers and so a charge of criminal damage was added which meant that he pay me compensation. I later received a minor payment from the 'Criminal Injuries Compensation Board' in respect of my physical injury, but 'all in all' it had been a bad Christmas.

Chapter 7 - Serious crime and more Corruption.

"The accomplice to all crime is frequently our own indifference."
Bess Myerson, b1924

So life in the C.I.D. continued until 1968 when two things occurred that stick vividly in my mind. The old Larceny Act.1916 was repealed and replaced by the Theft Act.1968 whereupon police officers, legal authorities and courts all had to return to school and learn again the new laws that replaced the old ones. The older C.I.D. officers thought at first it was going to be a little daunting but in fact the new Act was soon being used daily to put offenders before a court for theft and fraud. New offences had replaced the old 'simple' crimes that everyone understood and had been replaced with unknown descriptions of crimes such as 'False Accounting' and 'Obtaining goods by deception'. All the old offences committed to memory from the police training school were gone; signalling an era which the legal authorities claimed would be simpler for all concerned. I pass no comment on the changes because in my opinion and in reality nothing really altered.

The second thing to happen and stick in my mind was that Sheffield City Police -my city force -amalgamated with the adjacent and smaller Rotherham Borough Constabulary, which simply became another division of our force.

On 1st January.1968, together with one uniformed inspector I was transferred from the Sheffield city C.I.D I had served in for some 8 years and into the newly formed division of Rotherham. I was still a detective constable and from day one, the inspector and I were given the 'cold-shoulder' by our new Rotherham colleagues. They realised that from that moment they would be directed and controlled by Sheffield and did not like it one bit.

My new colleagues made it clear that I was 'persona non-grata' and it was only by representing the division at football that I finally managed to be accepted. The Rotherham borough force we had 'taken over' had operated for years as a small autonomous organization where nepotism was rife. As with every small town or borough in the country everyone knew everyone and to an outsider there was no way in.

This was the town that really persuaded me, as a young teenager to join the police after seeing the drunks being wheeled into the station on Friday and Saturday nights as I watched from my Uncles house opposite and getting caught in my cousin's bed.

Rotherham police force, for years had operated in its own way and they were extremely unhappy that government changes had forced them as a service to abandon a way of life that suited them, even if it was inefficient and not cost effective in any form.

I had been working in the C.I.D. for only a few weeks when an 'office incident' occurred though which made me think that the new division was not totally lacking in humour, only efficient work practices. Attached to C.I.D. was the tallest female police cadet that I had ever seen. As a local girl from the town she had joined the force with the intention of becoming a police officer and indeed she achieved that position. She was not the most attractive female in town but had a lovely disposition which was fully put to the test on her 18th birthday. She made the fatal mistake of telling some of the C.I.D. lads that it was her birthday. At lunchtime she was called to the C.I.D. office where the lads had bought her a cake and a small present. We held a little party and then she was told that she would have to be 'certified' as a member of the C.I.D. Without any more ado she was pulled across a desk - her skirt was pulled up and the Rotherham C.I.D. stamp applied in vivid blue to the 'chuckle' bit on her thigh. (The 'chuckle bit' to the uninitiated being the flesh between knicker leg and stocking top.) At first I thought she was going to scream the place down, but she burst into laughter and was accepted from then on as one of the 'boys'. What on earth her parents thought when she returned home that night with the office stamp on her 'arse' I cannot imagine.

The division did apparently have some other good points involving police procedure.

I had only been there a few weeks when someone told me about a group of drunks who had been arrested fighting in the town centre. They were all brought to the police station cell area and lined up. The old station sergeant brought a large cardboard box out of the cupboard and went down the line handing out coshes knuckledusters and other weapons to each prisoner. Apart from 'drunkenness' offences this allowed further charges of 'possessing offensive weapons' and also 'affray' ensuring that they all got some 'bird' when they appeared at court.

After a few months in the division I arrested a 'low-life' for stealing scrap metal from one of the hundreds of derelict council properties in the town. It was a straightforward case. I and a colleague had caught the thief en-route to the local scrap metal dealers with lead piping and copper boilers taken from deserted and unoccupied council houses.

He admitted the offence, was a well-known thief and pleaded 'Guilty' at the magistrates' court. I think he went to prison for a few weeks. On arresting him we had kept the stolen metal, as evidence, in the C.I.D. property store to be produced in court if he denied the charge. After the case, well-documented police procedure directed us to retain the 'evidence' for some three months in the event of an 'appeal' by the accused and then return it to the owners, in this case, the local council. A signature would be obtained from a council representative and attached to the stolen property ledger so that disbursement of the property was well accounted for and that would be that. Some few months after the case I remembered the metal still cluttering up the property store and suggested to my colleague that we should return it - he looked aghast at me… "What do mean return it? How are we going to pay for the fucking C.I.D. party at Christmas?" I was still very new to the division and started to

195

say that 'all' stolen property should be returned to the owners if they were known, but quickly realized that this was only what we had done in Sheffield C.I.D. with property stolen by shoplifters. So a false signature in the property book followed with the name of an official at the council and a good Christmas party was held later.

The detective chief inspector at that time apparently knew all about the 'scam'. A very strange man, who was unhappy with the amalgamation of the two police forces, appeared to take little interest in his work and took retirement. Apparently the only case files he ever took home were those of a sexual nature. He then joined a firm of solicitors in Sheffield city centre, but was often to be found in the 'Sex Cinema' most afternoons. Very strange.

The C.I.D. in the Rotherham division was staffed with most officers well past their 'sell-by dates'. Heavy lunchtime boozing was the norm and the detection of crime was something most of them had forgotten. One afternoon the station sergeant turned up for work so pissed that he was sent home but not before the duty inspector and he had swapped a few blows in the cells area.

There were some other good points to the division though. In the city I had left, Sheffield, you had to complete so much paperwork before the 'shiny-arse brigade' prosecution department would even try to get some prisoner remanded in custody. I often wondered if we were on different sides! In this division you could walk into the prosecution office staffed by a male inspector and policewoman. Verbally tell the inspector about the case. Give him a few notes on the back of a 'fag-packet' and your man would be remanded in custody by the town's magistrates without fail. Oh yes - apparently the inspector and policewoman had been 'at it' for years.

Like any police area though serious crime was becoming more rampant and a couple of murders come to mind that occurred whilst I was in Rotherham division.

All murders by definition are tragic, some more than others.

A young boy perhaps 10 or 11 years of age was travelling by car in France on holiday with his younger brother and parents. There was a road accident that killed both parents leaving the two boys orphans. The two youngsters eventually went to live with an Uncle and Aunt who lived in a middle class area of the division. One cannot imagine how the lives of the boys had changed overnight. The Uncle, apparently, was somewhat strict, worked for the Inland Revenue and whilst he and his Wife tried to give the boys a new and wholesome life there is little doubt that the boys were seriously affected by the tragic loss of their parents thinking the whole world was against them. One of the boys, then aged 14 was taking piano lessons being taught by a well-known music teacher in the town. There is no doubt the teacher was something of a disciplinarian with a habit of 'whacking' the fingers of pupils with a ruler if they made

197

mistakes. That is no reason to murder her, I hear you say and I agree but one can never understand the effect such chastisement would have on a boy who in his young life had personally suffered so much.

It was mid-afternoon when the call came into the C.I.D. that police had been called to a smart detached house in the Herringthorpe area of the town where an ambulance had been summoned. On arrival officers found the young boy covered in blood and the body of the lady music teacher lying in the front lounge near to her piano. Apparently the boy had made the '999' call alleging that he had disturbed another youth running out of the house. The boy claimed that he had called at the house for his normal music lesson to find another boy aged about 15 years of age ransacking the dwelling. The music teacher had been stabbed repeatedly and was dead. The boy had tried to detain the intruder but was attacked himself and the youth escaped.

Being the first C.I.D. officer on the scene it was pretty apparent to me that the young boy, even though he had called the ambulance, was to be regarded as a 'suspect'. Examination of the body of the lady showed that she had been stabbed all over, including her face and head with a large penknife which was on the floor. It later emerged that she had been stabbed thirty six times and the end of the knife had broken leaving a piece protruding from her head.

A full- scale murder enquiry started with senior officers and scenes of crime attending the house. Together with another officer I took the boy to the police station, not under arrest, and sat him down in the interview room. He was very pale faced polite and quite smart in his school uniform - despite the bloodstains. After searching through his clothing I looked inside his satchel. Among books, pencils and other items I found an maroon coloured exercise book. As the boy sat opposite me I flicked through the pages.........

In graphic and very detailed prose the boy had written what he intended doing to the teacher if she 'whacked' him again with the ruler whilst he was playing the piano.

If the lady did it again at the next lesson, so the boy had written, he would use his knife and stab her and stab her and stab her until she was dead. The words of a boy aged 14, who as I looked at him sitting at the table in front of me, I really could not believe he could have done such a thing. (Of course at this time I was completely unaware of his troubled background). Senior officers took over the questioning of the boy who admitted the crime and was later sent to a young offender's institution.

Not very often did I feel sorry for someone guilty of such a crime, but this was an exception and I could have wept for him. Many years afterwards I was told that the boy had served his sentence, coming back into society, where, with the help of his Foster parents became a model citizen.

Whilst in the same division, one morning I was in the C.I.D. office when the divisional chief superintendent came in and told me to get the keys for the C.I.D vehicle.

He really was a nice guy (too nice to be a Policeman with

his lecturer appearance and a degree in mathematics from some university). I knew him well because he had served in Sheffield whilst I was a uniformed and detective Constable there. He had been promoted and sent to the new division as the 'Boss' with clear instructions to bring the division and its officers into the 20th century. I understand even he faced some opposition from 'old-timers' as he introduced working practices that they did not like.

Back to the story - apparently there was a suspicious death on our 'patch' and he wanted to visit the scene, although to my knowledge he had no previous C.I.D. experience in his career. The other C.I.D. officers, particularly the detective sergeants were visibly 'gutted' that the Boss should take me to the scene instead of them. On arrival at the neatly-kept semi-detached house it was soon apparent that we were at the scene of a murder. (In fact, unknown to me at the time, my future partner Marion lived directly opposite)

The lady who lived there alone was aged almost 70 and lying on the kitchen floor in front of the fireplace. She had been savagely beaten across the face and body and a blood-stained poker was found alongside her. (I cannot help but notice, although I am sure government statistics will challenge me, that attacking old people in their homes or even in the street is on the increase. When society allows this trend to prosper then believe me we have lost it.) Immediately a well-practiced murder investigation operation swung into place with senior C.I.D. officers and scenes of crime men from Sheffield headquarters taking over the enquiry. The boss of the force C.I.D. a detective chief superintendent became the investigating officer and I became 'exhibits officer'. Again I knew the detective chief superintendent very well from my days in the city and held a lot of respect for him. He was 'old school' and many tales were told of the way he kept the streets clean of low-life as he worked his way through the ranks (No mathematics degree or freemasonry here I might add.)

On arrival he did what another old time C.I.D. chief used to do at the scene of a murder.

He cleared the kitchen of people, where the body of the murdered lady lay and then sat alone in the room with her for some 30 minutes or so digesting every facet of the scene that may become important when a suspect was arrested and interviewed.

We had noticed several full milk bottles outside the kitchen door when we first arrived, a clear indication of how long the ladies body had remained undiscovered. We emptied the bottles and I kept the silver foil tops after one of the local coppers at the scene had said that the town dairy printed bottling dates and times on the bottle tops. This could of course, help us to identify a time of death.

A detective sergeant from the scenes of crime department, who was 'useless' began a 'full' examination of the scene after the deceased had been removed to the local mortuary for a post mortem to be held. Local 'house to house' enquiries were started and within days we had our 'man'. A young R.A.F. man living a few doors away from the murdered lady had been on home leave for several days prior to the crime. Rumour had it that he was deep in debt and he had returned to his unit in the South of the country earlier than he should have done. A team of detectives immediately travelled South to interview him.

Everyone on the enquiry was satisfied that he had done it , but we still needed evidence.

The scenes of crime detective sergeant lived up to his reputation as useless...

Within a few hours he reported that his examination of the scene was complete and nothing of real interest had been found. You recall I described the detective chief superintendent as 'old school' and on hearing that the forensic search had been completed in a 'couple of hours' he went berserk. He contacted the detective inspector who ran the scenes of crime department and told him never to allow the detective sergeant a lead role in any major crime investigation again (in fact the sergeant went back into uniformed duties shortly after). The Boss also instructed the detective inspector to visit the crime scene personally and conduct a more thorough forensic search. Within hours the D.I. announced that he had found a 'beautiful' palm print above the fireplace, probably left when the ladies attacker had reached down to pick up the heavy poker he had used to kill her.

The R.A.F. soldier was arrested and brought back to our force area despite denying the offence. The palm print was identified as his and he was charged with murder.

Right up to his trial the soldier denied the offence and we became heavily involved in preparing a water-tight case against him. Several meetings were held with the detective chief superintendent assessing the case and ensuring that we were able to produce every conceivable piece of evidence to secure a conviction...... Yes - Those bleeding milk bottle tops!!!! You know the ones that could assist in proving the time of death etc.

Guess who, as 'Exhibits Officer' had thrown them away? - Oh what a bollocking I got from the Boss, the most minor criticism of me being that I was 'fucking useless'. The Boss told me to 'sort-it' and I knew what I had to do. Within hours of the bollocking, I had been to the local Rotherham dairy and collected enough milk bottles tops to prove any crime that the Boss wanted to prove in the force area!!!!!!!I was saved, but do admit to a sigh of relief when the accused soldier pleaded 'Guilty' and exhibits were not required. On a lighter note we used all the spare milk bottle tops to make Christmas decorations for the divisional canteen.

After some time I was seconded to the Number 3 regional crime squad as a detective constable.

On paper the idea of regional crime squads, located at various points across the country, was a good idea in tackling serious crime. Detective officers from adjoining forces were seconded onto the squad so that there was a nucleus of personnel able to be mobilized and sent to any part of the region. No.3 R.C.S. comprised of detectives from South

Yorkshire, West Yorkshire, Nottinghamshire and Derbyshire constabularies. None of the crime squad officers had experienced the freedom that came with the secondment, so together with overtime and other 'extra' payments it was a move worth making. The only 'down' side was that there were several useless officers in the squad like detective sergeants Howard and Lancashire, both later promoted and mentioned earlier in the book!

The concept of the crime squad was that as a 'ghost' outfit we would be able to infiltrate major crime without the day-to-day routine experienced in divisional C.I.D. offices.

A lot of money was spent on buying decent motor vehicles that did not resemble your normal C.I.D. cars. Private looking houses or warehouses even were bought as crime squad offices so that no-one knew where the squad were based. A fortune was spent equipping the cars with multi-channel radios often disguised behind the glove-box or under a seat. Devices, such as a secret button under the driving wheel console could be pushed allowing the driver to broadcast the conversation inside the vehicle without his passengers (villains?) knowing. Collars and ties were not expected to be worn although it was noticeable on the evening shift (5pm - 1am) most crime squad officers came to work in best suits and after-shave, which in reality indicated what most intended doing that evening.

The detective chief inspector running the squad at the time was my old detective sergeant who had 'borrowed' my pocket-book in juvenile court some years before. He approached me asking if I wanted to join the squad when a vacancy occurred and within weeks I was 'in'.

One of my first jobs was to try and officially 'bed' a middle-aged lady suspected of receiving stolen property from a spate of high-class housebreaking offences. I was considered for the part because she apparently had a penchant for young 'attractive' men who could sustain her appetite in bed. Why the hell I got the job I'll never know! She had become friendly over the years with a local Irish millionaire called Seamus Crehan who controlled a large construction business in West Yorkshire and there is no doubt that the millionaire had received a lot of expensive stolen property from the woman in the past. We were quite prepared to overlook that fact, probably because the detective sergeant I worked with at that time was very friendly with the man! In addition my sergeant was keen to involve us in the enquiries because it was his force area and a result would stand him in good staid when promotion was mentioned. We therefore set about out task with some relish and quickly established some significant clues. All the houses attacked were in wealthy areas and owned by active freemasons. In addition, every time a house was broken into it had been left unattended due to the occupants being at a masonry function that evening with their ladies. Then came a breakthrough when Seamus reported that the woman had offered him a very expensive but distinctive fur coat. We checked the details of the coat against the list of property stolen and undoubtedly it was from the most recent housebreaking

205

offence in the area. Again at a freemasons house. We checked out the lady concerned and would you believe she held a part-time job working as a secretary at a local chemists. It gets better - the chemist was an active freemason and engaged his secretary to type up all the forthcoming events in the mason calendar, including those when ladies were invited. Meaning, of course, that their houses would probably be unoccupied.

It was suggested that I be introduced to the lady by Seamus. My 'cover-story' being that I had recently come to work for the man as a director of his construction company. I was from out of town and 'available' for whatever she wanted. Would my 'charm' work on her? Seamus arranged to have a drink at his home with the lady and other friends one afternoon and I just happened to call. To be fair I did get on well immediately with the woman although she was much older than me, but quite well preserved. I made it clear I would like to see her again and we met a few days later, again at the home of Seamus, but only small talk prevailed. It had been decided that I would show interest in the fur coat as a buyer because Seamus had told me it was for sale. I asked the lady if she would sell it to me and it was immediately apparent that she was unhappy with Seamus for involving me. There was a row between the lady and Seamus in his kitchen, and hearing every word said, it was apparent that she did not know or trust me. She questioned if he had known me a long time and did he know my 'background'? The woman came back into the lounge, acknowledging that she was uncomfortable in dealing with me and asked what area the coat would end up in if I bought it. Unable to think of anywhere else I said - London.

We had obviously moved too quickly because she started to call off the idea saying that if Seamus did not want it there were other 'buyers' whom she knew and she would offer it to them. The evening finished and we parted with the woman saying that she would think about my offer. The following day she rang Seamus to see if he had checked me out thoroughly, adding that she did fancy a 'fling' with me, but was concerned that she did not know me enough and I could be a 'copper'. We waited a few more days then Seamus made contact with her to confirm that his enquiries had shown me to be trustworthy and the deal was on. The woman still insisted that Seamus be present when I bought the fur coat and so we arranged to meet at the Woodhall Service area on the M1 motorway.

My crime squad bosses were not that keen on the proposed operation due to a recent very complex 'case-decision' where an undercover police officer had bought stolen property in the same manner as we intended, only for the case to be dismissed at court.

The defence had argued in court apparently, that when the property passed to the undercover officer it no longer remained 'stolen goods' and therefore there was nothing illegal in the action. (I have kept this simple as I write because in all honesty I don't think any of us really understood the case decision). Still we decided to go ahead with the operation and meet the woman because we were anxious to arrest her and hopefully the actual housebreakers as well. So the plan was that Seamus and I would meet her on the service station, ensure the stolen coat was in her car and then call off the deal for whatever reason we could think of. Crime Squad vehicles would follow the woman until they could arrange for a Traffic car to stop her and she would be arrested. So a few days after Christmas, together with Seamus in his expensive Range Rover I waited on the Woodhall service station car park until the lady arrived in a Mini motor car. As suspected a man was driving the car, whom we assumed was one the actual burglars and Seamus and I walked towards them. On the back seat of the car was a suitcase which she opened and showed us the fur coat. Seamus said he did not think the deal should go ahead because he had been 'turned over' by the police that morning and was afraid that he was being watched. At this point, being satisfied that the stolen goods were in the Mini I gave an arranged signal to the watching surveillance cars by placing my hand on top of the Mini car. Obviously she was unhappy with us reneging on the deal asking the obvious question of Seamus - "Why the fuck didn't you ring me this morning and cancel the meet"? Seamus tried to appease her but we received more offensive comments………

"I don't fucking like this" she shouted and pointing at me………

"I don't trust that little 'c…t' either"

The man also swore at us and then drove quickly towards

the exit. Crime squad cars immediately set off in pursuit of the Mini, intending to keep the vehicle under observation until the Traffic car could be radioed to stop it. Seamus and I retired to a pub nearer his home to await news. Yes- you've guessed it.

The Mini got away together with the only evidence we had 'the fur coat'. Our Boss came to the pub to try to explain and apologise to Seamus but he was having none of it.

Ranting and raving that we were 'fucking useless' and he would never try to help the police again. I just sat there deep in thought ....

a) we had lost stolen property that was under our noses.

b) we had lost the chance to 'nick' at least the receiver and possibly one of the actual thieves

c) and I had lost the chance to 'get my leg over'

In the event my sergeant and I did keep close to Seamus for the remainder of our time on the crime squad enjoying his company, free meals, free turkeys at Christmas, trips to the races with £50 each thrown in to allow us to 'enjoy' ourselves, but the 'fur-coat' adventure was never mentioned again.

So we moved on to investigate other crime and perhaps one of the best arrests we made on the crime squad involved a youth named Danny Wilson who subsequently received 7 years imprisonment for burglary firearms and many other offences.

The detective sergeant I worked with at the time knew

Wilson very well and took a personal interest when it came to our knowledge that he was wanted for a variety of crimes in the Barnsley division of the West Yorkshire Police. Things took a more severe turn when Danny stole a Mini Cooper motor car and hid the vehicle in a lock-up garage on waste land near to Barnsley town centre. Two Traffic officers suspected that the stolen vehicle was being kept in the garage and decided to investigate (I know - unusual for Traffic officers to take such an interest in real crime). They approached the garage on foot unaware that Wilson was sitting inside with the engine running. As they opened the garage doors Danny drove the stolen vehicle out of the garage into the two officers injuring them. My sergeant and I made extensive enquiries and received information that Wilson had fled the area and was believed to be living on the outskirts of Manchester. We liaised with the No1 regional crime squad based in Manchester spending days in their area trying to locate Wilson. We even lived for some time as 'dossers' in a low-class lodging house in Manchester until our 'break' came and we thought we identified him returning to a flat shortly after breakfast one morning. Danny was living there with a Nurse from the city hospital. We were lucky in that my sergeant could positively identify the suspect and a operation was planned to arrest him, bearing in mind that he had already injured two officers and was then strongly believed to be armed.

To be certain that it was Danny, my sergeant and I kept observations for many hours from a house opposite until shortly after breakfast one morning we saw Wilson enter the flat. We were positive that we had our man. No.1 Regional crime squad officers, accompanied by uniformed dog handlers smashed their way into the house. Wilson was in bed and tried to reach a firearm under the bed but was bitten by a police dog and one of his arms was 'accidentally' broken in the struggle. The firearm and other antiques were recovered from the flat, later being identified as having come from a burglary offence at the home of the chairmen of the magistrates in Cheshire.

A chief constables commendation followed for the sergeant and myself.

Many other tales emanate from my time in the regional crime squad not all to do with the detection of crime. The misuse of police vehicles was appalling.

I mentioned earlier about squad vehicles being used by officers to take wives shopping or even visit pitch and putt courses whilst on duty.

The squad took possession of an Austin Maxi motor car *'with reclining seats'* which became the most popular vehicle in the squad and there was always a fight on afternoon duty to grab it. We also had access to the dirtiest, oldest decrepit looking van to keep observations. Complete with 'pee' hole in the rear floor to be used by male and female officers. My team once used it to keep observations on the M1 Motorway service area where numerous thefts from lorries were occurring. To add a little reality to the appearance of the

211

vehicle we loaded the rear of the van with old railway sleepers not realizing the weight which promptly 'knackered' the van forever. However this was not before the van had been used 'on duty' for shifting a variety of domestic goods for one of the detective inspectors. Furniture was always being moved in the van and even a friendly licensee used it to set-up an 'outside bar' at the local village hall. A whole squad team spent one day clearing a sergeant's garden with tools and equipment shifted in the van.

Apart from the 'misuse' of the crime squad observation van, there were other 'scams' taking place.

Two squad officers managed to get hold of an electric device that could be attached to the gas and electric meters installed by local councils to their properties. The device was able to turn back the meter reading so that when the gas or electric bill arrived it was much cheaper than it should have been. They made a small charge for the service and it proved quite lucrative.

The motto on the squad as far as criminals were concerned was to 'hurt' them in any way possible. We were having little success trying to capture a well-known villain in my city who was suspected of receiving expensive stolen goods from across the county and a host of other crimes. We kept observations on him and tried to encourage informants to 'grass' him up but everyone was frightened of his reputation and we got nowhere. Whenever we saw him in a pub or nightclub he and his mates always tried to 'rev' us up hoping that we would take some form of action against him that would lead to disciplinary problems for us. So we decided to fight back - setting a trap on a local rubbish tip and catching two rats. We took them back to the crime squad office and kept them in the boiler house for two days until they were starving. After we had taken a few drinks and in the early hours one morning we went to the house of the suspect and pushed the rats through his letter-box. We knew there were no children in the house. I am told that the rats caused a right mess on the ground floor even chewing the carpets and furniture. I understand that he always suspected us but could never prove it.

Another way of 'smartening up' a villain was to secretly attach chains to the back of his motor car when he was at some pub. The chains were then fastened to a wall or secure fence. We would then go into the pub and have a drink upsetting him by our presence.

When he left the pub we would follow him out and watch as he set off wrenching the 'arse-end 'off his car.

Information had been received that a local warehouse owner was in possession of several stolen television sets but he was always one step ahead of the police. We were loath to get a warrant to search his house or warehouses because we were unsure just where the stolen goods were being stored and for us not to find them at the first attempt would have blown the investigation completely. With officers sitting outside every building he owned we arranged for an officer to ring him posing as a friend and warn him that the police may be en-route to search the premises. The villain came running out of one of his warehouses, with his employees, each carrying a stolen television set, right into our waiting arms.

On my return to C.I.D. duties from uniformed sergeant I was attached again to the West Bar division in Sheffield city centre where my detective inspector was the guy who had tried to get me off the discreditable conduct charge involving the police sergeant from Nottinghamshire.

It was Saturday morning and the detective inspector had decided that he would accompany me to a house in Cemetery Road to arrest a black female named Lolanda for 'obtaining goods by deception'. The house was actually in the adjoining Woodseats division but the 'crime' had been committed in our division where Lolanda had given false details to the local gas company shop in her application to obtain a top of the range cooker. Her application had been successful and the new cooker installed at her home She had later been found out by the gas company and they wanted her prosecuting for fraud and their new cooker seized. It was not our 'patch' so we asked for uniform assistance from the division itself. We arrived at the house in our C.I.D. car to be met by a male and female uniformed officer in a 'Panda Car' and two British Gas engineers in their van.

What a farce………….

We all (that is six of us) went up the passage at the side of the house into an enclosed yard. As we pushed open the yard gate the kitchen door was open and there was one almighty scream from a black woman inside as she saw us. This was my first meeting with Lolanda. She came running out of the house with a large kitchen knife in her hand screaming that we were "fucking rass-clarts" (a slang word used by Jamaican and West Indian low-life). The biggest black man I had ever seen in my life dressed in a white vest and trousers was behind her. Lolanda was only slim but her attack took us all by surprise and panic erupted as six of us tried to go back through the yard gate together.

I am afraid to say the coppers were through the gate well ahead of the gas engineers.

So we re-grouped on the footpath at the front of the house, told the gas men to wait there until we called them and the D.I. myself and the two uniformed coppers went up the passage again. As we got to the gate Lolanda was there again with her bloke behind her, but this time she was carrying a large pan of almost boiling water. We were not quick enough and the water was thrown all over us.

We all dived into the yard and tried to grab the black man. We struggled with him, wrestling him to the ground and called for handcuffs which no-one had got.

What a scene: Four Policemen, no handcuffs and a black man who I am sure would have given Mike Tyson a run for his money. A clothes line was hanging across the yard so we untied it and wrapped it round the black man preventing him from moving. We then fastened him to the clothes pole as you would your dog outside some shops. Lolanda was at the door with another pan of hot water. Two kids were screaming inside the kitchen as she threw the water all over the inspector and I. The two of us pushed her into the kitchen which turned out to be a bad move because she picked the kitchen knife up again. She began slashing out at us with the knife and in fact both the inspector and I received knife wounds to our hands as we grappled with her. The wounds were not that serious but 'enough was enough' so I kicked Lolanda in the stomach and smacked her across the face as hard as I could. She dropped the knife and the three of us ended up rolling all over the kitchen floor as we tried to restrain her. In the meantime and for good measure we were being kicked and punched by two young black kids no older than 8 or 9 years of age. We finally managed to subdue her but it meant holding her on the floor for ages until further assistance arrived and she was then thrown into a police van.

The man was handcuffed and taken away by car. The gas men went into the house and disconnected the cooker in record time. Other officers had arrived and I travelled back to the station with a policewoman and Lolanda in the back of the police van.

What a despicable piece of 'shit' Lolanda was. Apparently she was a prostitute in her spare time and was screaming and shouting that she had been 'shagged' on a regular basis by uniformed 'beat' officers. Several officers were named which the policewoman and I instinctively forgot. We had not handcuffed her, which was probably another mistake, because it allowed her to pull her skirt up exposing her private parts. She was not wearing any knickers and kept pushing her fingers inside herself and screaming – "that's what the fucking coppers want from me" and "that's what I give your mates". We suffered this abuse all the way back to the station which I found entertaining as she ranted on about sexual exploits of the Woodseats coppers. I don't think the policewoman was that impressed because she worked with some of them. Both Lolanda and her man were taken to the city charge office and placed in custody. The two children were taken in to the care of the Social Services which caused another violent scene in the charge office when the Mother was told about it.

The detective inspector and I went to the local hospital for treatment to our knife wounds.

The inspector promptly fainted when he received a tetanus jab and was teased about it in the office for weeks afterwards. That Saturday evening I received a telephone call at home from the deputy chief constable enquiring about my injuries and praising us for the way we had acted that morning.

(No commendation in this case so perhaps the reports were not written correctly)

If I remember correctly Lolanda was sent to prison, having so many previous convictions.

However the tale does not end there as we will see in a later chapter where many years later I was involved in a murder enquiry in another part of the city and Lolanda and I crossed swords again.

A disturbing event occurred one day though which quite

possibly could have altered Policing in the seventies and eighties forever. Fortunately my colleague and I did not respond which, with hindsight, was undoubtedly a good move.

I was then a detective sergeant in the headquarters C.I.D. task force.

This task force consisted of a detective inspector, two detective sergeants and four detective constables available to attend any serious crime investigation in the force area.

The officers were all experienced men (although I use the term 'experienced' loosely in respect of some) and all were firearms trained.

By this time the Sheffield and Rotherham force had amalgamated with Doncaster and Barnsley divisions of the West Riding forces becoming South Yorkshire Police. My task force team had been seconded to Doncaster division where reliable information had been received that a post office in their town centre was to be attacked by armed criminals early one morning as the staff arrived at work. Each officer drew a Smith and Wesson handgun and ammunition from the force armoury and we mounted observations in unmarked police vehicles in the town. We were dressed in casual gear with our firearms contained in a holster beneath the armpit. I have lost count of the times that 'reliable information ' has come to nothing and it was the case here. Before lunchtime we were all 'stood down' with the C.I.D. task force officers involved in the operation returning to our base in Sheffield.

Myself and a detective constable named Richard were in an unmarked C.I.D. motor car travelling through the East end of Sheffield passing the massive manufacturing works Hadfields. The city and indeed the whole country was in a state of political unrest with workers encouraged by unions to go on strike and there was much unease in the big manufacturing sites covered by our force. Unknown to us there was a large scale demonstration outside one of the works we had to pass. Uniformed officers were in attendance but were grossly outnumbered due to the unions arranging for protestors from other parts of the country to demonstrate with the local workers. The striking workforce had just been addressed by a militant union official in a nearby car park and were making their way back to the Hadfields works full of enthusiasm for more violent disorder. Richard the detective constable was driving and I sat in the passenger seat of the car following some other vehicles when we found the road blocked by protestors.

The cars in front of us had stopped and we all found ourselves surrounded by a horde of protestors screaming and waving placards. One youth smashed his placard onto the roof of our plain clothes police vehicle. We could see uniform police helmets in the distance but they were too far away to help. In front of us was a small car driven by a lady with children in the rear seat. We could see that she and the children were petrified as the mob swirled around her car banging on the windows and rocking the vehicle from side to side. Then it was our turn. Snarling faces at the window of the car. Screaming obscenities and hitting the windscreen with placards. Rocking our vehicle from side to side until there was a real danger that it would turn over. We dare not use the police radio in case the protestors saw us …..

We were armed police officers…………………… What should we do?

We sat tight, trying to look as unconcerned as we could and trying not to look like policemen. It was only a few minutes, although it seemed like hours, and the crowd had passed allowing the lady in front to drive forward and for us to follow. Richard drove in complete silence for a short distance and then stopped the car.

"Why the fuck didn't we get out of the car and shoot one of the bastards. That would have smartened them up?" he said……… I made no reply!

Chapter 8 - Violence and Death.

"You know what I think about violence. For me it is profoundly moral - more moral than compromises and transactions."

Benito Mussolini, 1883 - 1945.

It would be impossible to describe any police force or any policeman without reference to Violence and Death. Certainly my police Life was full of it.

But in reality just what is the difference between the two? To the 'man in the street' - 'Attempted murder' is just short of 'Murder' although numerous legal textbooks on the subject will so confuse you that you may wonder how people are successfully prosecuted for this crime.

I really would be surprised to hear of any police officer in this century who has not been involved, to some extent, in violence and death ranging from murder to some simple domestic argument that never ever goes to court, but which drastically changes some-ones' life.

Why has life become so cheap that police forces throughout the country on Friday and Saturday night expect a life will be lost? More and more people going to their deaths publicly in pubs, night clubs, football grounds and other venues.

A policeman can never forget his first death be it natural or suspicious

In my case I was 19 years of age and had been on the beat for only a few months.

It was 10.50pm and I had telephoned the station from Pitsmoor police box to officially complete my tour of duty. This gave me ten minutes to walk to a designated road junction and finish at 11pm until the next day. I opened the police box door to be confronted by a very old man dressed only in shirt and trousers although it was a winters night.

He was in tears and almost unable to speak. He lived opposite the police box and managed to explain that his Wife had died and would I assist him. Together we went to his small terrace type council house. They obviously were not wealthy and in real terms the dwelling was a mess. As I entered the smell was overpowering but I followed the man into the downstairs front room where his Wife was laying in bed and very much deceased.

In fact she had died some two or three days earlier and the husband had remained with her trying to come to terms with his loss. Her night clothing was filthy. Neither family nor neighbours had found the time to check on the couple in those few days! It was tragic; even though the lady was at an age where statistics of the time would say that she was due to leave this earth. I had never encountered death before except seeing my Grandfather in his coffin before cremation. I was only 19 years of age and admit I almost began to weep with the old man. His life had come to an end just as surely as that of his Wife. I pulled back the bed sheets and the stench was unbearable. The lady had used her bed as a toilet for days and had never been cleaned. Her clothing was heavily stained with urine and excrement. I almost vomited there and then. I returned to the police box and called the station. They sent an experienced officer out to help me and we arranged for a local Doctor to attend and certify death. The police Black Maria then came with what most officers called the 'Cricket Bag.' The 'cricket bag' was a leather hold-all with long straps and handles designed to carry corpses found in all different circumstances. How many corpses had this bag held I wondered as we took the lady to the old decaying public mortuary in Nursery Street, Sheffield, where in view of the time of day no-one was on duty. The public mortuary was a dreadful place and ready for demolition. (In fact a new Medico-legal Centre was later built which was the pride of Sheffield and the country in Forensic terms.)

Being the junior officer I was guided by my older colleague who first of all told me to "Put kettle on -you'll find milk in fridge"............The only refrigerators I could see were the ones containing other dead bodies and I did not expect to find milk in there, but as usual I was wrong and brought out a half-full bottle of milk which put me off a cup of tea immediately. Because it was my first time, the older copper suggested that I should remove the stained clothing from the old lady. We would leave her then until the morning staff arrived to carry out a post mortem if the Doctor certifying her death would not issue a 'cause of death certificate'. I had seen ladies without clothes before, but they were generally aged 16 years to 20 years on the back seat of my Dads car, so

223

I found really found it embarrassing to strip this old lady. After I had completed the task and placed an identification tag around one of her big toes we returned to the station completed the paperwork and I went home. It was strange telling my Mother the next morning of my first sudden death and my experience with 'lawful' nakedness.

So many episodes of violence and death come to mind as I sit writing in my cell.

Prison lends itself to violent confrontations between prisoners over any issue at all.

Some prisoner will have borrowed tobacco or drugs from another prisoner and the debt gains 'interest' until settled by payment or a good hiding. I did not smoke so I was on a good 'scam' purchasing an ounce of tobacco from the prison canteen each week with my allowance and selling it for five pounds cash to other prisoners. When Marion visited every two weeks she always went home with a few quid smuggled in my underpants into the visit and passed to her when no 'screw' was looking. The only problem though, was that most of the paper money had been smuggled into the prison by visitors with drugs in condoms. A prisoner would swallow the condom when the 'screws' were not paying attention. After every visit the prison toilets had large amounts of paper stuffed down them to catch the bowel movements of the prisoner which normally included the condom.

Sometimes the condom got past without the prisoner being able to catch it and it would then go floating down to the prison sewerage farm where two prison inmates worked.

They were two of the most popular men in prison in view of the cash or drugs they found, but often the condom had burst by then so that the only thing worth recovering was the paper money covered in 'you know what'. The cleaner on my wing would clean the paper money to the best of his ability with detergent but Marion could never understand why most of the notes were discoloured.

A disturbing aspect of violence in prison was brought home to me one day when a I was approached by Officer Blackman here in H.M.P. Highpoint. He was a 'screw' I had really got on well with as I worked in the prison library. The 'screw' pointed out an inmate aged about sixty sitting quietly reading in the corner of the room and simply whispered.....

"Fucking 'nonse'. Two and half year old little girl. You understand. I'll leave it with you" I knew exactly what he meant. 'Nonsense Offenders' or 'Nonse' being the slang word to describe a Sex Offender who normally would spend his time in solitary confinement or on 'Rule 43' which meant segregation from other Prisoners for his own safety. I started to say to Blackman that I did not want to get involved but he walked away. I never mentioned to anyone what had been said and some two days later I was again approached by the same officer He whispered to me "Why hasn't the fucking nonse been done over?" I tried to say again that I did not want to get involved but he simply walked away saying, "I thought you of all fucking people would want to sort the c...t out". Twenty four hours later the old man was found in a

225

communal bath area with serious head injuries. A sock containing a snooker ball was lying nearby. That night a guy who had made his name in the East end of London boxing halls was receiving plaudits from other inmates for the attack. I kept well away from it all.

(I only write this paragraph now some 25 years later from memory due to the fact that the prison authorities had access to my writings and obviously would not have taken kindly to such a revelation.)

Some years before as a young detective on 'night' duty I accompanied an old detective inspector to the scene of a very brutal murder. The inspector was ready for retirement and really was 'old school' starched white collars and trilby hat. A 'Captain Mannering' well past his 'sell by date'. En -route to the scene he made it quite clear that he was unhappy with taking on a murder investigation at his time of life hoping to have finished his career behind his desk! Before we reached the house the inspector had decided that come what may he would not attend any post mortem examination because he was past that sort of thing and I was to become 'exhibits officer'. Before we left the office he insisted that we find some extra strong mints. In fact it was perhaps one of the most interesting cases of my career.

We arrived at a small terrace type house in Pitsmooor, a working-class area where I had been knocked all over the place some years before by the half-naked drunken black woman.

The house apparently was occupied by a Pakistani male and a white female.

We entered the rear of the house to find the sad-faced Pakistani being detained in the kitchen by uniformed officers. With the inspector, whom I noticed was holding a spotless white handkerchief to his face all the time, I went up the narrow stairs to a small bedroom. The body of a white female was lying under the bedcovers on a double bed.

Two other uniformed officers were also in the room. At first the lady simply looked asleep, but as the inspector leaned over her body moving her head a little, there were obvious strangulation marks around her throat. The detective inspector straightened up, still with his handkerchief under his nose and in a pompous and experienced voice announced: "Seen many of these in my time. Husband's strangled her. Probably been putting it about as these girls do!" (You will notice that he did not swear.)

So the detective inspector arranged for the Home Office Pathologist to attend, but forgot to notify the head of C.I.D. The pathologist arrived very quickly by traffic car with blue lights blazing and after we had all stood patiently in the murder bedroom, the pathologist enquired how long it would take for the head of C.I.D. to arrive? The detective inspector nearly died realizing that he not called him, which was strictly against force policy and a phone call was soon made to get the Boss out of bed. A short time later the detective chief superintendent also arrived in a traffic car with blue lights blazing.

227

His first move was to 'bollock' the D.I. in front of everyone for not calling him first, adding that he would see him later about that! The detective inspector was embarrassed but tried to regain some respect by assuring the Boss.......

"Open and shut case, sir. Strangulation - no doubt about it. Paki downstairs came home early from work and caught her at it with another bloke - so he's done her in."

I noticed a wry smile on the face of the pathologist but he said nothing.

We all went upstairs to view the corpse and had the shock of our life.

So far the only people to have viewed the body in bed were two uniformed police officers, two ambulance men, myself and the inspector. The inspector was garbling on to the chief superintendent that I was the 'exhibits officer' and I would attend the post mortem whilst he tied things up at the scene.

The inspector pointed to the ladies throat saying "Strangled, sir. See the marks?"

We then saw a movement under the bed-clothes, which took us all by surprise.

On pulling back the sheets we found a small baby girl perhaps two years of age laid alongside the body of her Mother. The child being very much alive and everyone had missed her. We called for the ambulance men and the child was taken away by them.

The chief superintendent was asking "How the fuck, did all of you miss the child?"

No-one replied but to distract the Boss the inspector indicated the markings on the throat of the corpse again. "Strangled. See, sir?" The Boss noted the marks but asked the pathologist if we could look closer at her face. As we carefully lifted her head away from the pillow it was pretty obvious that the strangulation marks were nothing compared to the wounds on her skull where there was a large gaping hole. A hammer with a broken shaft was under the head. The detective inspector looked sick!

The pathologist commented that the throat markings were probably the least of her worries -which didn't help the inspector's case at all. The detective chief superintendent 'blew'... "What a fuck up. You forgot to get hold of me. You've been here hours (which we hadn't) and still missed the kiddie under the clothes. You've been going on all the time about she'd been strangled but half her fucking head is missing.

"Let's hope he 'coughs' it (admits the offence) or somebody will be back in fucking uniform."

The pathologist who was a personal friend of the chief superintendent lightened the situation. "I'll need my bag in a minute but does anyone have a knife?" he said.

As keen as ever I was like lighting producing an old penknife I always carried. I gave it to the pathologist who opened the legs of the deceased and cut her panties open around her private parts. He closed the knife returning it to me saying, "I should clean that, son, before you peel any more apples!"

The Pakistani who had come to this country seeking work and employed in the local steel-works was arrested and charged with the murder. He was later sentenced to Life imprisonment.

The pathologist was to become one of the most eminent forensic science advocators in the World, but always had time for the 'common man'. He was a well-built man, mad about cricket and rugby and loved a joke and a drink with all social classes. He was always well dressed in a pin-striped dark suit, university tie and white shirt. He was never seen without his 'trademark' bowler hat. It mattered not the rank of police officers at any scene of a crime because everyone present was addressed the same.

(He was in fact a 'legend' and credited later, along with the local coroner in creating the first 'Medico-legal Centre' in the country.)

I attended the old mortuary in Nursery Street, Sheffield, travelling in the Black Maria with the body of the murdered lady in the customary 'cricket bag'. Early morning light was filtering through the dirty old windows of the mortuary by the time the pathologist was ready to conduct the post mortem examination. The detective inspector had returned to the C.I.D. office leaving me with the packet of strong mints.

The pathologist totally involved me in the post mortem examination from the start explaining the medical nature of wounds at the back of the head and the marks to her throat. For a moment it was easy to forget where I was and felt quite at ease until one of the staff pushed aside the front of the ladies hair and then removed the top of her skull with a small electric saw. The front of the body had been sliced open by mortuary staff and the pathologist carefully removed organs from the stomach region carrying them to a small table. At this point I realized why the inspector had been so keen to bring the strong mints. The pathologist removed more organs from the body describing one as the placenta from the womb area and said if I was lucky I would witness something very rarely seen. He then carefully slit the placenta open and there was a small, but perfectly formed body of a male child, curled into a ball awaiting his entry to life.

The dead woman had been heavily pregnant when she met her violent death.

> *'Never before or again, was I to see at first hand*
> *a life finishing before it really started.'*

So many murders in the years I served in the force, but some with undertones never fully explained.

A homosexual who worked as a Car park attendant behind the Fiesta nightclub in Sheffield was found beaten to death one evening near to his unlocked kiosk. I was a uniformed sergeant then and on duty that night but took no part in the enquiries into his death. The murder was never detected but extensive enquiries revealed that several serving police officers, with a hatred of homosexuals, were not completely eliminated (Please note this does not refer to the detective sergeant I refer to later in Chapter 10).

A serving police sergeant in the force was arrested and found guilty of murdering his Wife. I had worked with him in C.I.D. although he was much older than me. He was a smashing guy who you would be more than happy to call a friend. I really did not know his background, but later found that whilst he was a young police officer he had been lodging in the Crookes are of the city later marrying his landlady. It was not a marriage made in heaven and her body was found washed up on a beach in the North of England.

Scotland Yard became involved in the investigation with a detective chief superintendent and his 'bag man' a detective sergeant from their famous murder squad travelling to our force area. It was not uncommon in those days for the Yard murder squad to be called in to take over an investigation if the local police chief thought the case might be difficult.

Of course with the Scotland Yard input this meant that any enquiries requiring their specialized knowledge such as fingerprinting or checking of records etc. would get priority. As a police force I think that's all we got in the shape of expertise from their involvement and I was not impressed as I chauffeured them around. The detective chief superintendent was a chain smoker and always pissed on whisky, whilst the sergeant looked about 15 years of age and homosexual.

The case was detected mainly due to two officers from a Northern force who recalled the sergeant, whilst off duty and in the middle of the night, had called on them to assist him to change a puncture on his car after colliding with a roundabout. The prosecution were later to claim that the dead body of the sergeants wife was actually in the back of the car as the two Northern coppers helped their colleague. A fact they were obviously unaware of! It was alleged that the sergeant then continued North to throw his wife's body in the sea.

Without doubt any C.I.D. officer working in the same area for many years would come across the same villains or members of their family.

You will remember the 'evil' black woman Lolanda who stabbed the inspector and myself when we tried to arrest her for obtaining a gas cooker by deception. It was perhaps seven or eight years later when I was a detective sergeant in the headquarters task force that Hillsborough division enlisted our help with a murder. You will be familiar with multiple council flat dwellings where every window and door looks alike and the occupants are encouraged and expected to make their property look vividly different! The fire brigade were called to such a flat dwelling early one morning where one flat was well ablaze. They extinguished the fire but tragically found the body of a middle-aged black woman inside. forensic officers attended together with a pathologist to find that the woman had been strangled before the fire was started. A murder enquiry commenced.

The enquiry team were so short of experienced C.I.D. officers that my normal colleague from our task force was allocated a 'rookie' officer to work with and the same applied to me. The first major happening of the enquiry was that I ended up on a disciplinary charge after falling out with the sergeant motorist I mentioned earlier. You will remember we had fallen out after I had chased and stopped him for cutting me up in a marked police car. The second was, that as I returned to headquarters one day to catch up on some paperwork I saw the 'sky-diver' student I mentioned earlier commit suicide by leaping off the top of some flats.

However enquiries into the murder continued, but at a very slow pace and in fact, to the best of my knowledge the crime has never been detected. From the start one 'suspect' came into the frame again and again. Guess who lived next door to the murdered woman- Lolanda the evil black gas-cooker woman! I brought this to the notice of the senior murder team and agreed with them that the last person that should interview her in view of our previous clash was me.

Further enquiries were made and she was arrested by other officers, taken to the murder headquarters and interviewed at length. I am told that Lolanda ' fucked and blinded' at the interviewing officers the whole of the time and they got absolutely nothing from her. With no other real suspect and the enquiry going no-where the investigators looked for other avenues to try and explore in an effort to crack the case. It was a long shot, but we decided to try and unsettle the black woman by letting her inadvertently meet me in the corridor of the station hoping that she would recognise me from our 'bust-up' over the gas cooker years before. I know it sounds 'far-fetched' but it was the only chance we had of maybe

234

causing her some concern about her position.

I walked down the corridor as Lolanda was being escorted from the interview room.

She looked straight at me but began to walk past. I said "Hi - you don't remember me"...........Lolanda stopped and I really took a good look at her and she at me. Time had not been good to her, despite only being in her early forties, she had developed an aged appearance well ahead of her time. She looked at me for a second, then screamed "You mother fucker. You fucking bastard. You took my fucking kids".

She lunged at me, but other officers restrained her and the idea to gain a confession by that means was forgotten.

Other serious violent crimes formed part of my working life.

The city centre where I had spent most of my time had suddenly come to life after 10.30pm in the evening with the introduction of licensed night-clubs open until 2am.

The Fiesta club, Scamps, Crazy Daisy, Wapentake, Hoffbrauhaus and the famous Josephines became 'must-visit' venues for 'clubbers' and particularly C.I.D. staff.

It was necessary for the city centre division to increase the night C.I.D. staff and also uniform patrols to combat the violence that was now being experienced well into the early hours of the morning. Glassings, stabbings, sexual assaults (fuelled by drink) and other types of assault were now being reported at a time of day when in the past people would be getting up to go to work. The authorities were realizing that a glassing or stabbing was only inches away from murder!

But elsewhere in Sheffield other happenings were taking place where people never dreamt or even considered that their actions could lead to murder and often did.

I was then a detective sergeant in the West Bar division of Sheffield city centre.

A new uniformed chief superintendent Carter had taken over command of the division.

He was a 'bastard'. He came from Doncaster, one of the old West Riding divisions amalgamated with our area to become South Yorkshire Police. He was big in stature and opinion of himself, which without doubt arose because he was out of his depth in the 'big city'. To make up for his deficiencies he bullied officers of all ranks, moved staff just to show he was the Boss and changed long-standing divisional working practices which, in the opinion of many, led to a lowering of standards.

Let me quickly explain how such a 'misfit' came to be in charge of Sheffield city centre division when he was blatantly out of his depth. Government had decided that police forces throughout the country should be amalgamated to produce larger but more efficient constabularies. The existing Sheffield and Rotherham Constabulary based in Sheffield city centre and being the major force became the headquarters for the newly formed South Yorkshire Police. I did not have a problem with that, but the new force then, overnight, enrolled officers of all ranks from other forces who were not in the same league as us.

I had already witnessed this when Sheffield had amalgamated with Rotherham as I explained earlier. To keep everyone happy, several senior officers from the amalgamated forces were given roles in the new organization, despite the fact that no-one knew of their pedigree. So in real terms I was serving then in a new police force with plenty of 'right plonkers'. Chief Superintendent Carter mentioned above was one of them and I fell out with him when he discovered I had left my Wife and was living with a divorced policewoman. In essence he told me that I had to move out. In those days affairs between male and female officers were tantamount to treason or murder - if you got caught or if you were of a junior rank Force standing orders dictated that the police authority had to approve where police officers lived and this gave senior officers like the 'bastard' I mentioned license to interfere in relationships between officers. I could understand that some control should be exercised when housing allowances were paid to individual officers and I accepted that police officers should not reside in licensed premises owned by their families, but in reality and with the World changing in respect of 'partnerships' the old 'ideals' were going out of the window. In any event in some circumstances it was necessary for a senior officer to 'vet' the accommodation before officers moved in.

To get round my problem, I 'borrowed' a flat owned by the widowed Mother of a C.I.D. colleague. Took my detective inspector to view it and confirmed that I was living there alone and paying the rent. Everyone knew it was a 'scam', but it satisfied my inspector and he confirmed it to the new Boss who accepted the situation grudgingly.

With Carter continuing to make enemies, the division failed to police itself in the accomplished manner of the past and I simply kept out of his way. Then one day I saw him in a different light.

Imagine a girl 14 years of age, living with her family in the Hyde Park high-rise flats on the outskirts of Sheffield city centre. Soon she will be leaving school to find employment in the 'big world'. She will probably have met a young man and the early flush of romance is starting. Life as this age is good - very good until...........

The young girl, 14 years of age, was walking to the local shopping centre in the flats complex when some 'bastard' threw a television set from the top landing which landed on her head killing her instantly. Life finished at 14 years of age. How desperately sad and why? Together with other C.I.D. officers I went immediately to the flats when the call came in. Ambulance staff and uniformed police officers were already at the scene, their demeanour telling all of us attending that a life had been lost under very tragic circumstances and there was nothing we could do about it, other than catch the 'swine' responsible. I arranged 'house to house 'or in this case 'flat to flat' enquiries on the top landing of the dwellings knowing that, without doubt, we would capture the culprit and he would pay. There had been several reports over the previous few weeks of items being thrown over the parapets including a double bed and a three piece suite so we had plenty to go on. No one had been injured before, but this brought a whole new meaning to 'anti-social' behaviour and stunned onlookers, including police officers, who were trying to come to terms with some persons complete recklessness. The girl's body was covered in ambulance blankets, whilst we all stood in small groups a respectful distance away, awaiting the arrival of senior officers and scenes of crime department staff.

I was suddenly aware of a big guy at the side of me and was surprised to see my 'favourite' Chief Superintendent Carter in full uniform at the scene.

He asked me what had happened and I described the tragedy to him.

He was looking at the blankets covering the girl all the time I was speaking to him and he never once looked at me. He said he would like to view the body' in situ' (that is where it lay) and suggested that we move all police officers away from the immediate scene.

I asked officers to move away and walked with the Boss towards the pile of ambulance blankets. I bent down and lifted the blankets away from the body exposing terrible head injuries to a young girl who had probably never harmed anyone in her life.

I thought over the years, and after witnessing some evil gruesome sights, I had developed a shield to protected me from showing any feelings at all to such tragedies. A few

239

whiskies would put things right and I could move on to the next outrage without any real feelings of compassion. I looked up at the chief superintendent to see massive tears rolling down his cheeks. He purposely faced the wall away from onlookers and continued to weep. I think I said something like "Tragedy, sir. A real tragedy" and I could feel my voice beginning to tremble, but he said nothing and together we digested what one stupid 'bastard' in society had done. It was only a few minutes, which seemed like hours at the time, before he composed himself, calling me by my first name, which really brought me back to earth and suggesting that certain actions should be taken.

No one else had seen the humility of Carter and I never mentioned it to anyone.

It is a fact of life that murders come and murders go. Some warrant National headlines and massive media exposure, whilst others make the front page of the local newspaper on two or maybe three occasions.

I said earlier that whilst seconded to the number 3 regional crime squad we were drafted into North Yorkshire to assist their force in the shooting of the Harrogate postmaster Donald Skepper by the infamous 'Black Panther'. We were way off our 'patch' but two reasons caused our involvement. One was that when the murder took place in Harrogate most of the North Yorkshire C.I.D. were engaged investigating the I.R.A. bomb blast on the M62 motorway. The second reason being that two 'target' criminals from our area had attracted some suspicion for the Harrogate crime and it was decided to mount 24 hour surveillance on them. Television series like 'The Sweeney' and others always make it look easy for police officers to trail suspects and invariably get a good result. Let me tell you, in real life nothing can be further from the truth.

The regional crime squad ran a local course on surveillance techniques and there was also a one week course at Tintagel House in London on the same subject. The local course was run by one of the detective inspectors on our squad (in fact the same officer who died some years later in the garage of his home when filling his lawn-mower with petrol prompting suicide theories!) In our exclusive crime squad vehicles we chased the 'target vehicle', another crime squad car, all round the country for a week, not really gaining any particular expertise but recognizing that if someone does not want to be followed then no-one can follow him successfully. In reality if you think you are being followed by one or more surveillance vehicles all you have to do is go round the first roundabout five or six times and I guarantee that will 'fuck-up' anyone following you. We had the assistance of a police motorcyclist, dressed appropriately as a 'hells angel', and this was one way that surveillance could be successful. Imagine following a suspect vehicle in the streets of London and you will realise that only a motor cyclist would have any chance of keeping up with the 'target vehicle.' One humorous point in respect of 'our' motor cyclist was that in real life he had very short hair but to portray a 'hells angel' or a 'wild biker'

241

he had fastened long pieces of hair to the inside rim of his crash helmet so that as he rode along his long unruly hair was blown all over the place. We often stopped at cafes and service stations for refreshments whilst on the course and you can imagine the looks of other diners when he removed his helmet!

So for a few days we tried to follow our 'target criminals' for the Harrogate murder as they went about their business. After about two days sitting in a crime squad vehicle parked on a pub car park opposite the house of one of the suspects it had become farcical.

Particularly when the 'suspects' approached the crime squad officers and set out their travel plans for the day saying it would suit them and 'us' if everyone knew where everyone was. I am led to believe that on one occasion the 'undercover officers' actually took one of the suspects in their squad car to keep an appointment with his probation officer so that he wouldn't be late. The surveillance operation had become a 'farce' and it was soon terminated allowing us for the remainder of the enquiry to engage in checking farmers and gamekeepers in North Yorkshire who possessed firearms. It was not the most effective way of conducting a murder enquiry but there were very few clues for the murder team to pursue. Each day en-route to the murder headquarters. I was to pass the police training college at Pannal Ash, Harrogate where it had all started for me so many years before. No-one more than our team were elated at the capture of the 'Black Panther' which allowed us to return to normal crime investigation.

Whilst a detective sergeant in the city I recall being involved in a most unusual set of circumstances arising from death. Massive building development was being carried out in the centre of Sheffield and at one time it seemed every day all the bloody streets were closed and traffic diverted to facilitate a new office or shop. One morning we were called to a building site, adjacent to the Sheffield Cathedral and in a very old part of the city where one could still find old cobbled streets and the offices of the city's legal profession.

Workmen had found several skeletons whilst excavating and thought it suspicious!

In fact they had uncovered an old burial ground, confirmed by the council records and the problem then arose what to do with the skeletons and assorted bones.

'Internment' was the answer and it fell to me and a young detective constable called Martin to arrange things through the council. The builders were excellent, having collected all the bones they could find and placing them in a large black wooden box resembling a coffin. They had even included rope handles to assist us. The council completed all the paperwork, and arranged for a Vicar to re-inter the remains. In a marked police van one afternoon we collected the coffin and made our way to Wardsend cemetery. It was one of the oldest burial grounds in the city situated on a steep hillside overlooking the Sheffield Wednesday football ground. We had arranged to meet the local Vicar at the graveside who would inter the remains and apparently a communal grave had already been prepared. Martin and I called at a friendly pub on the way, just for a quick pint, leaving our 'friends' the deceased outside in the police van. We then drove to the cemetery as the rain started to lash down and the wind began to blow. We arrived and started to carry the coffin up the hillside, not knowing just where the grave had been dug. In our normal shoes we were slipping and sliding all over the place The Vicar appeared, wrapped in an enormous cape and Wellington boots, obviously having experienced burials in the cemetery on days like this. We were absolutely pissing wet through, sliding about in the mud and the box was getting heavier and heavier. The Vicar appeared unsure just where the new grave had been dug but arriving at an open hole with soil piled alongside, we all agreed that was it and the weather further dictated that the coffin was going in that hole come what may. You've guessed it.

The hole was not big enough to put the box in. Martin said something like "What the fuck do we do now?" which I thought would upset the Vicar but he seemed pissed off as well. The rain continued to lash down as we all stared at the hole and the coffin. The Vicar said "I can't stay too long because I have another funeral to conduct." I think I said, "Can we leave it here and come back tomorrow" which was so unchristian that I was immediately ashamed for even thinking it.

Then over the top of the hill, through the mist and driving rain a figure appeared.

He was dressed in dark clothing with a hood over his face and a spade across his shoulder. I am not kidding it was a perfect setting for a horror film. He approached us, shouting "I thought you'd have done it by now. I've come to fill it in."

Martin did not swear this time but simply said "Hole's not big enough".

The grave-digger looked at our box, then the hole and said "Biggest fucking coffin I've ever seen pal. They just said dig a grave and that's what I've done."

We realized then that he was pissed and for a moment I had visions of having to take the coffin back to the police station and return the next day. The Vicar intervened and asked the grave-digger to make the hole bigger, which after much complaining he agreed.

Finally, with rain still pouring down we slid the box into the hole that was filling quickly with water and two of us jumped on the top to push it down. The Vicar read a few passages from his Bible and perhaps was going to read more but the grave-digger began to fill in the grave and we all left. When we returned to the station and enthralled everyone with details of our afternoon- no-one believed us, but I assure you it is absolutely true.

It was late one afternoon and I was a detective sergeant in the Sheffield city centre C.I.D. when we received a call that an ambulance was in attendance at council flat dwellings behind West Bar police station. An old man had been found in the house with serious chest and head injuries by a social worker making a regular check on the Husband and Wife who were the actual council tenants. The old man was rushed to the Hallamshire Hospital, Sheffield where first reports indicated that his injuries might prove fatal and that they must have been caused at least 24 hours earlier.

I attended at the scene with other officers and found the flat to be a place of absolute squalor. All the rooms were filthy with wallpaper hanging from the walls. There was a distinct urine smell throughout the building. Crockery and cooking utensils in the sink had not been washed for weeks and what carpets existed were threadbare and stained.

The Husband was a serial alcoholic and gambler. His Wife was of low intellect and a pitiful excuse for a female. Hence the visit by the social worker. It also transpired that the old man was living there illegally just 'bunging' the Husband a few quid a week for a bed. I took them both to the station and spoke to them separately. Both gave the same story that they had found the old man the previous day suffering from his injuries but he had refused to go to hospital. Both agreed the injuries had been caused by him falling down whilst drunk. Their explanation was total nonsense!

I visited the hospital but was unable to speak to the old man at that stage due to the serious nature of his injuries. It had been further established, however, that one of his ribs had punctured his lungs and murder was looking imminent. I went back to the station convinced that the Husband had caused the injuries and anxious to gain a confession before the suspects started asking for a solicitor. I interviewed the

Husband again, who was about 40 years of age and one of 'life's-losers'. He denied having assaulted the old man, sticking to his story of having found him injured the previous day. I spoke to the Wife again but she was terrified of her Husband and there was no way she was going to change her story. So I had to wait to see if the old man would recover before being totally certain of what had occurred.

In view of the fact that the Husband and Wife were not under arrest we were detaining them in the C.I.D. office. There was a partition in the centre of the office which allowed us to seat them separately although in the same room. I was desperate to get to the truth as quickly as I could and came up with an idea that might just jog things along.

I arranged for a female detective to phone me from another office pretending to be my Wife. The Husband and Wife heard one of my colleagues shout that my Wife was on the phone and I took the call in the corner of the office but with my back to both of them.

My 'Wife' and I made small talk about one of my kids had come home early from school having been ill and then I said "Oh no, I won't be home for tea, in fact I may be here all night 'cos we've just started a murder enquiry. I'll ring you later love." I put the phone down just as the Husband fainted -falling from his chair clutching his throat. The Wife screamed so loudly that the inspector came rushing in thinking we'd killed them both. One of my colleagues picked the Husband up and put him back on his chair.

The man was crying and saying "I'm sorry. It was me. Dirty bastard asked for it."

One of the female detectives speedily took the Wife into another room, returning almost at once to say that the woman had admitted that her Husband had assaulted the old man the previous day. It transpired that the Wife and the old man had been in alone the previous day whilst the Husband was at the pub. The Old man got his 'pecker' out and suggested that the woman play with it. Whether or not she did I don't know, but apparently she told her Husband when he came home and he smashed the old man to pieces. The Husband admitted the offence in the form of a statement under caution.

The Old man recovered from his injuries thus allowing a lesser charge than murder to be put to the Husband who went to prison.

Okay, so I broke the rules on many occasions, but look at the environment we worked in.

Whole families devastated due to some persons recklessness. For the victims, life can never again hold the attraction it once did.

Consider the young girl who was killed by the falling television set and her family - you tell me how life has been fair to them? You tell me how they will ever get over the loss of a loved one and then criticise me for bending the rules to put such 'scum' away.

I am reminded of politicians, government officials local council leaders and the judiciary who arrive at decisions that

248

in their mind will benefit others without a clue of what they are talking about and as long as it does not impact their lifestyle. When council officials approve a site for 'travellers' or 'pikeys' in the future can I suggest they built it next door to their homes and let's see how they enjoy freedom in society.

Chapter 9 - Sex in society.

'Sex is one of the nine reasons for re-incarnation
- the other eight are unimportant.'
Henry Miller 1891- 1980.

He was the biggest copper I have ever seen in my life. A man-mountain. Yet he was also the most gentle, amiable person you would ever meet - Oh! and his 'nick-name' was 'Tits'. You would never guess in a million years how he came by that name and despite the affable picture I have painted of him I do not recall many people actually calling him that to his face. 'Tits' was a strong Catholic man patrolling his beat in the dead of night past Sheffield's Jessops Hospital. The maternity unit was situated on the ground-floor and 'Tits' was able to see easily into almost every ground-floor room where new Mothers were breast-feeding their babies. The officer thought it was wrong and offensive, so he submitted a report to the station sergeant asking for contact to be made with the hospital and the practice stopped. I don't know if any action was ever taken by the station sergeant but from that day to this, my friend, the walking giant was called 'Tits'. I found it so embarrassing to patrol with him simply due to his colossal size.

One tea-time we were both due to go on traffic duty, where in the morning and evening rush-hours, certain road junctions would be manned by an officer dressed in a white coat and gloves. We collected our coats from the local police box and walked to the road junctions. It was pouring down with rain meaning that we had to wear the bigger waterproof coats that made me look a right 'pillock'. 'Tits' and I walked past a stationary bus full of workers heading home. We could see they found it hilarious the difference in size between 'Tits' and myself, so to make me feel even more humiliated he put one of his massive arms around me and completely lifted me up in the air. The crowds on the bus loved it. (While on the subject of 'Tits' there is a male in prison here with me who has a fine pair and I'm told is very 'popular' with those serving long sentences.)

Other beat officers though found time to pursue past-times with a sexual link.

We talked earlier about 'piking' which obviously 'excited' several police officers and caused them to act in a way that would have got them the sack if they had been caught.

In the Attercliffe division of the city a nightly 'ritual' used to take place some 50 yards away from one of the beat police boxes. A young, very well-endowed female, lived in a small terrace type house with her parents just round the corner from the police box. Her family were well-known to the police for all the wrong reasons. She was in the habit of bringing her boy-friend home after the pub and they enjoyed sex in the living-room with the light on, although the curtains were always tightly closed. Their nightly sexual activity was

251

apparently well-known to the local coppers who never missed a chance of a 'pike'.

The closed curtains did not cause a problem because almost every evening the officer on the beat, knowing that the couple had returned home, would collect the wooden stool from the police box and carry it across the road to their house. By standing on the stool at the front door he was able to look through the 'fan-light' window above and enjoy the 'show'. How no police officer ever got caught astounds me, but I am assured the couple unknowingly performed for many officers in this way for many years until the girl finally married her boy-friend.

Conversations about sex in the police canteen were no different to those in working men's clubs, factory canteens and the like.

One young beat constable allowed his sexual leanings to get him dismissed from the force. It was well known to many officers that if one crept into the darkened yard at the rear of a gymnasium situated on The Moor, Sheffield it was possible to peer through gaps in the outer door which led directly into the ladies changing room. The officer in question apparently was enjoying the sight of a very attractive young lady dressing before leaving the gym. As she left he noted the registration number of her motor car - checked the owner details on the police national computer and then anonymously telephoned her at home describing in vast detail the colour of her underwear and other intimate personal facts. When she complained it did not take a

Sherlock Holmes to identify the officer concerned and he subsequently left the force.

Sex, to my mind, has always been a great 'leveller' and it matters not the upbringing or otherwise of a male or female when lust takes over. Different people have different fetishes, some totally illegal and some downright weird.

Certainly we, as the police, were privy to secrets not available to the public.

It was only a few months before my trial that I had a drink with a friend of mine who was a member of the Scotland Yard Flying Squad - 'The Sweeney'. He was an ex- C.I.D. officer from my force, who had married and transferred to the Metropolitan police force. He was a good guy and had made his way into the famous 'Sweeney'. I kept in touch with him and met him occasionally when he returned North or when I went down to 'The Smoke' (London). It was during one of our conversations that the subject got round to children being sexually abused and how it seemed on the increase. Apparently he was aware of a paedophile enquiry conducted by the Metropolitan police that had led right to the door of a Home Secretary, but was then quietly forgotten. I am sure you are not surprised by this statement.

I cannot though, for the life of me understand why 'nonses' (sex offenders) are imprisoned, other than to physically protect our children. One regularly sees reformed gamblers, drug users, alcoholics but never 'nonses'. To my mind they are medically and not criminally 'sick' and absolutely no useful purpose is gained by locking them up.

Certainly the prisons I have served time in appear to have no means nor desire to re-habilitate them. Unnecessary manpower is wasted by the prison service in having to protect them and not all receive the protection they are due as I wrote earlier when a 'screw' encouraged the 'beating-up' of one of them.

The most memorable case I dealt with involving a sex-offender was one of those cases, as a copper, you never forget the details.

It was shortly after tea-time one summer evening when a Mother telephoned '999' to say that her seven year old daughter had been attacked by a man. I went to the house with other officers and met them. They were 'working-class' folk living in a terrace type house on the outskirts of Sheffield city centre near to the Hallamshire hospital. Many of the surrounding houses were derelict awaiting demolition and then, no doubt, the inevitable high-rise new flat dwellings would occupy their location.

The girls Father was a long-distance lorry driver and away from home at the time. Her Mother explained that when her little daughter had come home from school that afternoon she had sent her to the local shop to fetch a bottle of 'Hendersons Relish' sauce to complement their tea-time meal. (To the uninitiated - you have not lived until you have tasted this sauce with a meal. Sheffield made in the 1800's with the recipe unchanged for many years it is served all over the World). The little girl collected the sauce bottle and was returning home past some derelict houses when she was grabbed by a man who dragged her into one of the buildings. The little girl dropped the bottle which smashed and was later recovered by the police indicating exactly where the attack had taken place. When dragging the girl into the empty house the man had placed his hand around her mouth to silence her, but one of his fingers had gone inside her mouth causing a substantial wound at the side of her tongue. The little girl had struggled and broke away from the man, running home screaming.

I obviously needed a description of the man and spoke to the very distressed little girl with the help of a policewoman. Description-wise the one and really only point that the little girl insisted on, was that her attacker looked like a 'monkey'. I could not get any more helpful details from her. I was determined to try and solve the crime because the last thing we needed in the city was public panic at the thought of some loose 'sex-offender' attacking children. I went through all the local known sex-offenders and showed the little girl many photographs without result. I made enquiries at the shop where the girl had been and also at the few houses that were still occupied and I visited all the pubs in the area, many of the landlords knew me and agreed that in this type of case they would assist if they heard anything. I also called at the local Salvation Army hostel but without result.

All the time during my enquiries I was pushing the description from the little girl that her attacker resembled a 'monkey-man', although in my heart I would have loved a more detailed picture of the man.

It was evening time mid-week, some days after the attack on the little girl, when I received a telephone call from one of the pubs I had visited during my enquiries.

The wife of the landlord knew me personally and rang to say, "The man you want, who looks like a monkey. He's in my pub now." With another C.I.D. man I raced to the pub only to find our friend 'the monkey' had left, but was believed to be staying at the nearby Salvation Army hostel. I thanked the landlady and went to the hostel with my colleague.

I was a little annoyed that the hostel staff had not been as keen as my landlady friend to identify the suspect. We asked the door-keeper if anyone resembling a 'monkey' was in residence and he actually confirmed the room occupied by our suspect. No-one likes sex offenders and I was in no mood to abide by the judges rules or any other 'fuckers' rules but my own. I kicked the door open and there laying on the single bed was the 'monkey'.

The little girl had been so exact because I have never seen a male whose facial appearance was so much that of a 'monkey'. We arrested him and took him to the C.I.D. office. He denied doing anything wrong from the outset and it was only when we checked his record that he got the first of many 'good-hidings'. The 'monkey' had only been released from prison three days earlier after serving five years for sexual offences against small girls. He had a string of sex crimes recorded against him and had spent most of his adult life in prison. I repeat what I said earlier, how had prison re-habilitated a man like him'? Once a 'nonse' always a 'nonse'. Again the system failed, because South Yorkshire Police had no idea that he had come to live among us and so children were at risk as soon as they opened the prison gates for him.

I kicked him all over the station. I even hit him with a metal chair and did what no interviewing copper should ever do - I caused a wound to his head. I was desperate for an admission so that I could lock him up and safe-guard our children and the public.

It is not totally unusual for prisoners sometimes to make an admission to a crime in the form of a written statement under caution and then refuse to sign it. They may have fallen out with the interviewing officer or perhaps have been told that they would not get bail so they withdraw their co-operation with the police. It was not good practice, but there were previous cases that had gone to court in such circumstances, and the police had been allowed to introduce the statement of admission by the accused, if a senior officer at the time had endorsed it to the effect that the accused had admitted the crime but had refused to sign it. (I have simplified here a rather complex legal issue which I'm sure you really have no interest in!).

I wrote out the statement for the 'monkey' totally admitting the attack on the little girl and blaming it on 'sexual urges'. I told him to sign it but he refused. He got another 'good hiding', but by then I was realizing that in his 'criminal' life-time he had suffered more good hidings than Mike Tyson's opponents.

The only senior officer at the station that night was a uniformed 'shift' inspector.

I had worked with him as a constable and knew of the many 'scrapes' he had got himself into. I was confident that he would endorse the statement to the effect that the prisoner had agreed that the contents and admission to attacking the girl were true, but would not sign it when he was refused bail. The inspector refused and again I was in the position of falling out with a senior officer when I was only doing my job and trying to protect the public. He instructed me to bail the prisoner, even though he was of no fixed abode and we all knew there was no way he would return voluntarily to the police station.

I 'fucked and blinded' at the inspector, reminding him of his own children and letting him know that when the 'monkey' attacked his next child victim (as he most certainly would) it would be on 'his' conscience - not mine. I think my last words to the senior officer were "If he (the prisoner) kills a kid next - I'll never let you fucking forget it"

I bailed the 'monkey' for three weeks on the condition that he would return to the police station at a certain time and date, knowing full well that he would not keep the appointment. I then released him.

I was so incensed by his release I was determined to try and keep some sort of track on him and I returned to the Salvation Army hostel the very next day to try and persuade the staff there to keep me informed on his movements. He had left already and no-one knew of his whereabouts. Needless to say he failed to answer his bail conditions three weeks later and his details were then circulated in the 'Police Review' magazine across the country. In many ways this was a wasted exercise, because I did not have any further evidence against him and if he did show up I could not have charged him with attacking the little girl. Some four months later I received a telephone call from the Braintree police in Essex saying that my friend the 'monkey' was in custody and they had seen my' Police Review' circulation. Apparently he had been trying to entice two small children from a play area into some woods when the Mothers had seen him. They attacked him and it was only the arrival of the police that prevented the man from being seriously injured. I was not hopeful of obtaining a confession to the crime in my area, but I still travelled down to see him. I was alone as I entered the cell where the 'monkey' was being detained. The whole scene was a 're-run' of the time I arrested him in the Sheffield Salvation Army hostel room with him laying on the low bunk resembling a 'monkey'. The Mothers had done a good job though when they caught him and his face was bruised and scratched.

I said I was alone as I went into the cell, so I picked up a metal chair from the corridor outside and took it in with me. His eyes registered alarm as he obviously recognized me and thought he was going to get 'belted' again with the chair. He jumped up from the bunk saying, "All-right all-right I admit it. That little girl who dropped the sauce bottle"

I took a statement from him where he fully admitted the crime and I returned home.

He later appeared before court and pleaded Guilty to the offences in Essex. He asked for the Sheffield offence involving my little girl to be 'taken into consideration'. He was again sent to prison, this time for ten years, knowing that with parole he would soon be out to continue his 'nonse' activities despite the judge describing him as a very dangerous man.

There were other cases during my time in C.I.D. where elements of a sexual nature were present.

This ranged from a case I dealt with where a man was arrested and convicted of 'bestiality' - that it is sexual intercourse with his dog. It was about 7pm one evening when I was called to the front desk of Rotherham police station to be met by a Mother and teenage daughter both in floods of tears. They had arrived home early that evening in the Eastwood area of the town and as they walked up the passageway at the side of the house they could hear their pet collie barking as if in distress. They rushed into the lounge to find the husband having sex with the animal. I can't even try to think how they felt at such a sight. They ran out of the house and came to the police station to report the incident. Together with another C.I.D. officer I returned to the house and interviewed the husband who readily admitted the offence appearing to be totally ashamed of himself.

The collie dog was examined by a vet and later went to live with another family.

I arranged for our scenes of crime department to take a photograph of the collie dog which I submitted to the magistrates' court with the prosecution file. The photograph was not really required as evidential value, but I was hoping the magistrates were 'dog lovers' and would react accordingly when sentencing the man.

Other events taught me that life is strange but no more strange than where sex is involved.

In the same town Rotherham, was a dirty horrible tramp called 'Cocky Smith'

He was homeless and one of the local firms allowed him out of kindness to sleep in their warehouse. Where did he get the name 'Cocky'?... Yes you're right, he was once caught as a young man trying to have sex with a cockerel!

Another regional crime squad 'target criminal' was arrested in the early hours one morning on a farm on the Pennine moors miles away from the city.

The farmer who detained him was positive the man was trying to have sex with his cows. Officers were delighted with this information hoping to embarrass the villain on the next occasion he came into police hands.

I mentioned earlier about the man arrested for theft from work who was also accused of 'buggery' with his girl-friend which is a criminal offence. Apparently in the force training school one day the lecture was 'Sexual Offences' and during

261

the lesson, reference was made to 'Sodomy' and 'Buggery' and its illegality. I got this tale actually from the training inspector who was asked by a constable in the class if such conduct was illegal between husband and wife? When told it was, the constable went quite pale later explaining in confidence to the inspector that he had always understood it was the 'done thing' between partners when the female monthly menstrual cycle occurred.

'Ignorance of the law is no Defence'?

One murder I worked on also had sexual undertones.

It was the one I mentioned earlier where the detective superintendent leading the hunt, thanked me for instilling some humour into the daily conference briefings but also described me as 'fucking useless'

The body of a married lady in her thirties was found strangled on a nature reserve in a police division some way from the city centre. The body had lain undiscovered for a couple of days and was found, as most corpses seem to be found, by a man walking his dog. A murder investigation started and we, as the C.I.D. task force team, were assigned to the enquiry. I've said before if a murder is not detected within twenty four hours then the investigators have problems and this was the case here. The scene was examined with great care as all murder scenes were (apart from the one where the old lady had been bludgeoned to death earlier in Rotherham) No damning forensic evidence was found.

It was generally accepted by the investigators that the lady had gone to the nature reserve by vehicle but where she had been killed was uncertain. It did not take long for the police to strongly suspect the Husband. The 'sex issue' had raised its head again with the Husband suspecting his wife of being unfaithful and relations between them deteriorated.

We established that the married couple, despite their unhappiness with each other, had been to a national sports event together in the days before her body was discovered.

The Husband claimed that on their return home an argument had taken place and the Wife had walked out. He had not seen her since. Numerous police enquiries were made but the crime remained unsolved. Perhaps another death in society directly attributed to a member of the human race failing to control sexual desire?

'Woman with skirt up runs faster than man with trousers down'

Perhaps is the attitude of many police officers to the crime of Rape!

There are, no doubt, cases where a woman will scream 'Rape' when it is unjustified.

However, a genuine case of rape to my mind is just as serious as murder or attempted murder and the law recognizes that fact by providing a maximum life sentence.

Detective training schools and also local instructors paid much attention to the Sexual Offences Act and associated crimes.

As with a murder scene, much vital evidence can be found at the scene of a rape or sexual attack to prove, or in some cases disprove, the allegation and efforts were made by all the Instructors to ensure we had a good working knowledge of the law.

I did not become involved in many rape investigations during my twenty-five years, provoking the thought that many such heinous crimes go unreported and questioning the amount of time spent digesting the law on this subject.

One case though, I need to write about in some detail to demonstrate the horror of such sexual behaviour.

In the East end of the city a young lady had been found wandering in the street during the early hours of the morning, close to her home, extremely distressed and in a state of undress. We can call her Alice. She complained to the officers who found her that she had been raped a short time previously by her brother-in-law.

I was the night detective and called to the scene, ironically a few hundred yards away from where I had been born. This allegation was acutely distasteful because Alice was accusing her brother-in-law of attacking her. A disturbing 'family matter' you may think.

The facts were simple.

The husband of the victim had gone out drinking locally one night with his older brother and friends leaving his Wife Alice at their home. At the end of normal licensing hours all the boys had caught a bus into Sheffield and continued their drinking in a late-night disco.

After a short time in the disco the brother-in-law left the party and went back to his brother's house, knowing that Alice would be alone. He was very much under the influence of drink. He then raped his brother's Wife. No detailed description needed here from me. The man simply forced himself on his sister-in-law and sexual intercourse took place, undoubtedly without her consent. Any doubts I might have had regarding the authenticity of the complaint were dispelled when I later saw the victim Alice at Attercliffe police station with a blanket around her shoulders and unable to hold a cup of tea without spilling it. My heart went out to her.

Alice was obviously not the most confident female I had ever met and when I researched her background I found that basically the family of her Husband were in reality the only family she had ever known. It was obvious that she was going to be subjected to immense family pressure to drop the complaint and had no-one to turn to. In view of the serious nature of the allegation I was joined by a detective inspector, who was not really my type but on this case we worked well together and put forward a decent case warranting prosecution. We interviewed the suspect brother-in-law who put forward the only 'defence' he could, namely that his brother's Wife had 'led him on' and really had 'asked for it'. The case was visibly lacking evidence.

Forensic evidence did not really come into it, because it was agreed by all that sex had taken place. The real issue in law was 'Consent' and anyone seeing the attacked girl that night would have agreed with the investigation team that this was definitely Rape.

The file was completed at speed to try and resolve the situation which was involving families, relatives and friends of the victim. It was necessary to send the file to the D.P.P. for his agreement to prosecute the suspect or not. In fact, in practice if the D.P.P. thought fit to continue with the prosecution his office would lead the case throughout. The D.P.P. quite rightly agreed for a prosecution to commence and we arrived at the local magistrates' court for 'committal proceedings'. I do not intend to get into the realms of court procedure and bore the 'arse' off you, but I need to quickly outline how the system works.

In a serious case like this, the accused first goes to the magistrates' court where procedures are in place to 'send' the case to the crown court without any evidence being heard.

Any fight by the accused against the allegations can take place later in the splendour of a crown court. However, the law allows for a challenge to be made by the defence at the lower magistrates' court that the allegation or charge against the accused is not proven and should be disbanded at this stage. Witnesses that would be later called at the crown court can be summoned at this early stage and 'interrogated' by the defence to try and get the case thrown out. In practice most magistrates' courts would send a case to the crown court simply because they had not got the legal knowledge, or 'bollocks' to kick it out, so we were pretty confident that we would get past this stage.

The only problem was our 'star witness' - the victim Alice.

I had been in contact with her on several occasions and knew the family pressure she was under. She kept insisting that the case be dropped to save her any further grief and I was running out of excuses why she should stand by her allegations and get her attacker put behind bars. I later found out that each time I made contact with her, the Husband gave her more hassle suggesting that she dropped the case. Her husband, being younger than his accused brother was dominated by him and it really was becoming a nightmare for the victim. The idea of appearing as a witness in court, giving evidence of a sexual nature against a member of the family, was quite rightly a massive challenge.

As I entered the magistrates' court that morning with the detective inspector and a representative from the office of the D.P.P. for 'committal proceedings' to begin, I knew we had lost and I could have willingly, at that moment gone looking for the accused and killed the 'bastard'.

Alice was sitting quietly and alone in the public area. Her face was deathly white, her hair was untidy and it looked as if she had not slept for a week. No other members of the family were with her, but her broken arm encased in heavy plaster and bandages said it all.........She explained that she had fallen at home earlier in the week, but she knew as we all did that no-one believed a word of it. I took Alice into a private police room and sat holding her hand for some time trying to convince her that she could not allow this to happen, but to no avail. The woman's life had only really started

267

when she met her Husband and his family and she could not throw that away, even if it meant risking a similar attack from her brother-in-law again. The case was dismissed.

To me, it meant that in my police career the only 'genuine' prosecution for rape that came my way was sacrificed by evilness. The courts, politicians, perhaps clergy and others will argue that, 'it is better that a guilty man escapes the consequences of his unlawful actions than an innocent man suffer' In this case I found that maxim difficult to swallow!

On a side note, I must by that time in my career have started to show signs of being out of control, because after the case was dismissed I was approached by the head of C.I.D. and warned not to approach the brother-in-law to see 'Summary Justice' done!

Still with sex, but a more outlandish way for a guy to get a thrill, was when a uniformed policewoman I know stopped a local villain driving his car through the city centre.

She was quite a good copper, attractive and buxom, but known to be quite arrogant and headstrong at times. She insisted that he took a breathalyser test and prepared the kit.

The motorist was still sitting in his car with the window down and she instructed him how to blow into the device. Whilst she was concentrating on the procedure and holding the equipment to his lips the villain leaned out of his car and put his hand right up her skirt. His conviction for driving under the influence and indecent assault being reported in the local press made him a hero!

Incest is another crime on the books that screams to me of 'mental illness.'

I never personally was involved in a case of Incest and from memory it was crime that did not get reported often. I wonder why? When we amalgamated with the Rotherham police force I mentioned earlier there were several mining villages and towns adjacent to this police area. It was often rumoured that the crime of Incest was rife and had been in these communities since the middle ages. Having two daughters of my own I cannot for the life of me understand how any Father could behave in such a way to his own.

I mentioned earlier 'weirdos' and I certainly came across one who I arrested for shoplifting again in Rotherham. He was an Irishman well turned fifty years of age and had been detained by a store detective for stealing ladies panties. We searched his bed-sit and came away with the largest collection of pornographic pictures I had ever seen.

In addition he had a collection of 'dildoes' or 'sex aids' made from rubber, cork, wood, metal and plastic. I had never seen such a collection and all were painted or decorated in some way. The Irishman treasured them like one would antiques or paintings.

Small plastic containers were also found with pubic hairs inside which the man freely admitted had come from his lady-friends over the years. He was gutted when we confiscated the lot and burnt them in a local works furnace.

One of the last cases before I was suspended involved a civilian radio operator from the force control room.

On my team, at the time was a young police constable who was serving his attachment to C.I.D. He was older in service than the average attachment constable and had just finished a spell with the Vice squad. He had potential, having used his time on the Vice squad to form 'honest' relationships with several of the girls, whom he hoped to use as informants in the future. Following a phone call he received one evening I went with the constable to meet one of his prostitute contacts who had a rather bizarre story to tell us.

She was frank about her 'work' and during that afternoon had met a 'client' in the red-light area of the city. The man said he could only afford a 'hand-job,' which in sexual terms is self-explanatory and they went back to her flat where she 'relieved' him sexually and of his cash. The man then put a proposition to her. He required her to partially undress and carry out the same sexual act (hand-job) on him but wanted her to talk to him about the pleasure of having sex with dogs. He wanted her to speak about masturbation with dogs and other actions, that I will not go into here, as though these things were an everyday occurrence. The girl agreed reluctantly, quoting a price of nearly £100 thinking that would put him off. The man accepted the price and together they went to a local cash point and drew out the money. They returned to the flat, the man gave the girl the money and she undressed.

She then tried to think of sexual phrases and actions with

270

dogs to speak to the man about as she masturbated him. According to the prostitute it was the man who was doing most of the talking and she just kept uttering an odd 'oh' and 'ah' when she thought it relevant........ *Picture it - please picture it.........*

After some time the girl lost interest and told her 'punter' to finish off. The man became annoyed saying that he had not received value for money and this led to a disturbance in the flat. Unknown to the 'punter' the girls 'pimp' was also in the flat and obviously came to her rescue threatening to throw the client out of the house.

At this point the 'punter' produced a police 'Warrant Card' from his wallet stating that he was a police officer and would arrest the girl for prostitution. The girls 'pimp' responded by threatening to expose the police officer as a pervert. After a short time the 'police officer' left the flat and the girl made contact with the ex-vice squad officer who took a witness statement outlining the strange events.

I liaised with senior officers at headquarters in view of the suspicion that the 'punter' was a serving police officer and then the discipline department (Rubber Heels squad) would take over the enquiry. It transpired very quickly that the punter was in fact a civilian radio operator employed by the force and responsible for broadcasting messages and the like to patrol cars in addition to administrating '999' calls. He carried an authorisation card, similar to a warrant card, allowing him access to police headquarters and obviously was totally out of order using the card in the way that was

271

alleged by the prostitute. I was told to interview the man and then submit a report. I interviewed him at police headquarters with the ex-vice squad officer and we were both amazed when he readily admitted the allegations made by the girl. He explained that he was a dog owner and confessed to sexual behaviour with his own dog as if every pet-lover acted in the same way. He was suspended from his duties and I took him home, enquiring on the way how he would explain his early departure from work. The man said he would confess all to his Wife and asked if I would be gracious enough to be present when he told her. I declined and left him at the garden gate! I never did find out the final outcome of the case because I was suspended from duty shortly afterwards. I do know that the union NALGO took up the mans' case alleging 'wrongful suspension' from work and the like. The union officials were obviously not pet-lovers!

Like the ex-vice squad constable I mentioned earlier, I cultivated prostitutes as 'snouts' and often received invaluable information relative to crimes committed in the city. What a 'Jekyll and Hyde' existence a lot of prostitutes lead. One of the girls I knew, was actually working full-time in a care home and only went on the 'batter' in her off-duty time to supplement her income. Another girl came from a very well-off family and simply became a 'working girl' to get sexual excitement. However most of the girls were low-class thieves and drug users controlled in the main by black pimps who made their lives a misery demanding more and more cash. I got really close to one girl though who was as ugly as sin but knew more about the cities 'low-life' than anyone.

I will call her 'Glenys' and she was as hard as any man I have met. She had the most horrible looking teeth and wore the shortest skirts I have ever seen. Many is the time I have been to her council flat drinking cheap lager from cans whilst heavy rock music visibly shook the thin flat walls causing her neighbours untold misery.

I had been living with Marion, my partner, only a short time when we were approached in the city centre one morning by Glenys asking for some money. She was wearing a very expensive light green suede Jacket and skirt that left nothing to the imagination. Marion was quite taken aback when I readily handed over a few pounds and the girl went off to pay her council rent.

The problem though with informants, is that they begin to think they are beyond the reach of the law and untouchable, so they commit crime in the belief that their police friends will excuse and be able to cover-up their actions. In some cases 'yes', but in others 'no'.

The day of reckoning for my police informant Glenys arrived in the following way.

It was nearly midnight one Sunday evening, when a guy I knew quite well from the city came to the front desk of West Bar station asking for me by name. He was, to my knowledge a small-time car dealer who was always in the money.

I always thought that he was a homosexual and to this day I

273

am sure that he 'batted for both sides'. It was not unknown!

In his car earlier that evening he had toured the 'red-light' area of Sheffield looking for a prostitute to do business with. In fact he found two girls, one was young and I learnt later that she had only been 'on the game' for a few weeks. The other girl, undoubtedly from the description given by the victim, was my friend Glenys. The man agreed financial terms with the younger girl and all three had gone to Glenys' council flat.

At the house the younger girl and the man went into the bedroom and undressed.

The man paid the girl 'up front' and then foolishly left his trousers on the floor near to the bedroom door. In one pocket of his trousers was £200 in cash. On at least two occasions whilst he was engaged in sex with the younger girl, the older girl Glenys entered the room asking if they 'wanted a cup of tea'. It must have been like a Brian Rix farce but I am assured it was true. When the man had finished with the young girl she was up like lightning, dressed and left the bedroom. The man dressed and discovered, of course, that the £200 was missing from his trousers. He heard the two girls whispering in the kitchen and a distinctive West Indian male voice. He ran into the kitchen but only found the two girls there. He demanded the return of his money but they told politely him to "Fuck off".

The man then came to the police station to make the complaint and offered to take us back to identify the flat. I told him that would not be necessary, because I knew only

274

too well that the older prostitute was Glenys and it was her flat where the theft had taken place.

After taking a statement of complaint from the victim, in case he changed his mind in the cold light of day next morning, I went to the flat with another officer. It was in darkness and the time was then about 2am. However, I knew exactly where to find Glenys at that time of night. I particularly sought the assistance of an older detective constable who was the night detective in the adjoining Attercliffe division. I knew where we were going to find Glenys was almost certain to lead to some friction and unrest.

How right I was.............

I said earlier that the theft had taken place around midnight on a Sunday evening.

The city centre was notoriously quiet at that time due to the night clubs being closed and pubs turning out about 11pm. People were on their way home, anxious to find sleep before work the next morning, but for those who were not restricted by such a tedious chore as work there were one or two illegal drinking dens that proved attractive.

One very low-class drinking den in particular was to be found on the first floor above a block of shops in Spital Hill, Burngreave. It broke every rule in the safety manual regarding fire environmental and health regulations. It was also the exclusive domain of West Indians with very few white people ever crossing the doorstep. It was known locally as 'Donkey-mans'. The time I report here was shortly after the Toxteth riots and other racial unrest in the country which

275

prompted police chief's to look the other way rather than cause similar unrest in their cities by instigating police action against such unlawful and illegal 'drinking-dens'. Many of my colleagues took the same view as me, that if some white person operated in this way they would have been closed down very swiftly. The illegal drinking club should have been hit with everything the police had.

You will have gathered by now that I was not the sort of copper who 'thinks things through' before action, but I did on this occasion, recognizing the potential trouble for myself, my C.I.D. colleague and also the force. I knew I would be allowed access by the management because they knew me a little and were happy that I was not the type of copper to give them trouble without due cause. However, I intended arresting Glenys, hopefully the other prostitute and maybe their West Indian 'pimp' so serious confrontation was imminent.

I discussed my plans with the duty uniformed inspector on duty, but he did not want to get involved, only allowing us the assistance of a Panda Car and one uniformed officer.

He made it clear if things went wrong it was my fault.(Ironically the same inspector who had refused to assist me to lock the 'monkey man' up earlier.)

With my colleague I entered the downstairs entrance to the club, and climbed the stairs to the first floor, leaving the Panda car and officer on view outside with instructions to summon the 'cavalry' if things got out of hand.

As we walked into the dance area of the den it was almost

impossible to see anything.

There were small lights above the DJ's area and we stumbled over glass bottles and even couples as we searched for Glenys and her mate. The Reggae music was deafening and the air was charged with cannabis sweetness and West Indian perspiration. I found Glenys at the rear of the room and my colleague and I sat with her for a short time drinking the bottle of beer the management had thrust into our hands.

I told her I wanted to see her outside, but did not tell her about the complaint of theft.

She was very drunk and it was some time before she agreed to move nearer the door where there was more light. I then realised that she was heavily pregnant, although the complainant punter had not mentioned this to us when describing the girls who had 'rolled' him. We were then outside the toilets when a young white girl came out who was obviously the other prostitute we were looking for. I took my chance and told them they were both under arrest for theft. Things went dramatically downhill from then.

Some black youths had been crowding us whilst we were talking to the girls and started to intervene. We were at the top of the steep stairs. Suddenly the lights were switched off plunging the area into almost complete darkness. People began to scream and push into us. A glass bottle smashed on the wall at the side of my head and I crouched to the floor.

I felt around the doorway and found the light switch giving us some brightness at the top of the stairs, but the crowd were in danger of pushing us down the stairs and only Glenys was still there. The younger girl had disappeared.

The black youths were becoming aggressive threatening us with bottles and pool cues.

They had been joined by an older black guy, well over 6 ft tall, who I recognised as Glenys' pimp. He knew me a little and asked why I wanted to arrest his girl.

I told him briefly about the complaint and dropped a real 'clanger' when I mentioned the stolen £200 realising immediately that Glenys had 'short-changed' him. He was not well-pleased. My colleague was trying to hold Glenys by the arm and protect her from the pimp who was trying to grab her hair. Next minute the pimp smacked Glenys in the face and I turned in time to see my colleague hurtling full length down the stairs landing at the bottom with Glenys on top of him. Glenys was screaming that she was "fucking pregnant". Others in the club were screaming the favourite West Indian abuse "fucking rass-clarts" and then the lights were switched off again. I ran downstairs, grabbed Glenys and with the D.C. dragged her outside and tossed her into the back of the police Panda Car. We all dived in and the car sped away with Glenys screaming at the top of her voice. On arrival at the station I took Glenys into the charge room only then to notice that she was clutching several bank notes in her hand. She refused to hand them over and it took three male officers to hold her on the floor and prise them from her. There was £80.

My next course of action was to get the uniform duty inspector to organise a van full of coppers to return to the club, arrest the young prostitute and also dish out 'Summary

Justice'. He refused and there was one almighty row between us again where I accused him of having no 'bottle' and allowing the 'scum' in society to dictate police policy. He countered by saying that he was not risking a racial situation simply because a 'punter' had been 'rolled by two hookers'. He threatened me with disciplinary action, but I told him to "fuck off" and left. Constantly, in my opinion, the police service is found to be lacking in credibility by their actions, or inactivity. Detectives had been abused in this case, assaulted, threatened and thrown down stairs by people occupying premises that were being run totally illegally. With no action being taken is there any wonder that the 'low-life' in the drinking den thought they could do what they liked.

Just to complete this part of the tale, when I arrived at work the next afternoon I was seen by the divisional superintendent and complimented for the way in which I had handled the previous night's events. I started to argue, saying that we should have returned to the club immediately and smashed it to bits, but I got nowhere.

Here was another senior officer (freemason) who would have died if he had been in the club with us the previous night and faced the abuse and threats that we did.

I told him, in no uncertain terms, that we, 'the police', were losing the War.

His reply: "Booper, now you know why you'll never get inspector rank. The force does not want senior officers like you causing racial trouble. It's all about politics these days and you'd better get used to it." I think I said something like, "It's blokes like you with no fucking bottle -looking for the next rank or waiting for the next lodge meeting while the public gets fucked." I then walked out of his office.

So back to Glenys, she admitted stealing the £200 from the punter and the £80 was her share. I arrested the younger prostitute the next day and she admitted the offence but needless to say I recovered no cash from her. Both girls went to court and pleaded 'Guilty'. Both were fined. The 'punter' got £80 of his £200 back perhaps wishing that the he'd kept his 'pecker' and his cash in his pocket.

In the police canteen it was not unusual for officers to openly discuss what sort of behaviour gave different men different sexual thrills?

I have never understood what sexual pleasure one gets from asphyxia or hanging but I once came across a man who did, although in the state we found him he was unable to tell anyone again just what turned him on.

The information from an outside division was that the body of a female had been found inside a land-drain on some waste land at Hackenthorpe and they were treating it as murder. The C.I.D. task force was asked to assist and my team rendezvoused with other officers at a temporary murder headquarters in a bowling alley some three hundred yards away from the actual land-drain. We could see the scene of the crime quite clearly from the bowling alley but other officers and scene of crime investigators were actually in the land drain and therefore we had no reason to enter. Within a short time photographs of the scene and the deceased female were available to all the murder investigators.

They showed the normal round concrete tunnel entering a larger enclosed area.

Entry from the outside was gained by walking down a steep embankment - opening a heavy unlocked metal door which led into the drain. The body of a female dressed in a white bra and pink silk slip was leaning against the wall. There was a rope around her neck. The body was badly decomposed and the bottom half of the trunk was missing. The normal murder enquiries started, but not before the new chief constable arrived with the press to ensure the evening edition of the 'Star' newspaper carried a photograph of him leading the hunt for the killer. Chief Constable Blakey was only very small. Many thought under 5' 8" and therefore not tall enough to be a police officer. However, he was Ex-Army, so that fact alone guaranteed he would make a good chief constable. We pissed ourselves with laughter when he arrived in his customary bowler hat, expensive dark overcoat complete with shiny new Wellington boots. He declined the offer of overalls from the scenes of crime team, I assume thinking that would diminish his dapper appearance in the eyes of the public and walked towards the entrance to the drain.

The press were happily snapping away with their cameras when the chief slipped going down the embankment, landing in the mud outside the metal door to the drain.

His overcoat was covered in mud and his bowler hat rolled into the stream.

My team and I were crying with laughter some distance away, but ensuring the chief did not recognise us.

We were some hours into the enquiry when it was abruptly called off.

Whilst in the drain, the body had apparently been eaten away up to the waist by rats.

When the pathologist fully examined the corpse of the female it was found to be in fact a male. Further tests confirmed that the man, who lived locally, apparently gained a sexual thrill from dressing in ladies clothes and applying severe pressure to the neck.

Not that uncommon you will agree, but one mistake and your family have funeral arrangements to make and face the 'whispering' of friends and neighbours for years to come.

Chapter 10 - The Demon Drink.

"The inn keeper loves a drunkard but not for a son-in-law."

Jewish Proverb.

It has been difficult for me to write all this account of my life in the police without recognizing the influence of 'drink'.

Drink formed part of a policeman's life in the sixties in so many ways.

I mentioned previously that there were characters in the force, none more so than a Scotsman, Detective Sergeant McIntosh. Funny how 'nick-names' were all the rage but I suppose that was the same in the Fire service, the Army on building sites and in other occupational environments.

The sergeant here was nick-named 'T.D.' short for 'town drunk' and boy did he live up to his title. I first new him when I was a young constable attached to the city centre division and he was what was called 'the reserve man'. He stayed around the office, collecting and delivering post to the various police boxes and other duties.

He went into the C.I.D. as a detective constable after many years in uniform and shortly after became detective sergeant. There was an 'unwritten' force policy at the time that all new sergeants from C.I.D. should return to uniform for at least 12 months but in the case of 'T.D.' that was overlooked. He teamed up with another Scottish detective in the force and together they attempted to drink every pub in the city dry.

But 'T.D.' was a good copper. He nurtured several informants, making some spectacular arrests which allowed his drinking to be overlooked by the bosses. When the force set up two C.I.D. task force teams 'T.D.' was 'tailor made' to lead one. I later joined his team and with two other detective constables daily fought crime almost always under the influence of drink.

There was a young constable in one of the outer Divisions who was very effeminate and undoubtedly homosexual. He did not last long on the force and left to become a shop assistant in the city centre. 'T.D.' and I were leaving a pub one evening in The Wicker, Sheffield when we saw the ex-constable entering the public toilets opposite. The toilet was part of the 'gay-run' or 'cottage run' where homosexuals visited each public toilet along several roads in the city centre hoping to enjoy sexual activity of their particular brand. 'T.D.' hated the practice and all homosexuals. The sergeant insisted that we visit the toilet and I knew what was going to happen. The gay was standing facing the stalls with his penis in his hand and turned round smiling until he realized who we were. 'T.D.' simply walked up to him and in his heavy Scottish accent snarled "You fucking poofter" smacking him at the side of the head. The gay boy squealed backing away and trying to defend himself, but 'T.D.' was going to have another go at him. 'T.D.' rushed across the urinal but slipped on the wet floor and fell into the pot stalls. The ex-copper rushed out of the toilet screaming, with myself making no effort to stop him, whilst my sergeant was 'fucking and blinding' with his knees in the piss. 'T.D.' was not happy and insisted that we go looking for the gay to give him another good hiding. I persuaded him that it was better he went home and changed his trousers as they were to stinking of urine.

The bosses were realizing that 'T.D.' was becoming something of a liability and he still had some time to serve before reaching retirement age. Things came to a head one afternoon when my colleague and I received a telephone call in the task force office from the station sergeant in the West Bar division. He told us to get down quickly to Shalesmoor where 'T.D.' and a Scottish pal of his were in danger of being arrested for drunkenness. 'T.D.' was officially on duty. We shot down the road to find a police panda car and Black Maria van stationary outside a low-class pub. 'T.D.' and his pal were laying blind drunk on the footpath, having been thrown out of the pub by the landlord who was insisting they were arrested even though he knew 'T.D.' was a cop. The uniformed coppers were unsure what to do with a drunken police sergeant. My colleague and I had a quick word with the landlord, apologized and told him we would deal with it. We took both drunks home in the police van and no paperwork was ever completed regarding the incident. 'T.D.' came to work the next day as though nothing had happened but moves were already afoot to limit his working freedom and he was moved to a desk job in the crime intelligence department within days.

I may appear a little critical of 'T.D.' but in reality most of the C.I.D. officers I worked with all my service could have fallen foul of the law in relation to drink driving.

I said earlier that I was fast gaining a reputation for being a detective with knowledge of most of the major criminals in the city and quite often I would receive a telephone call from other officers asking where they might locate a certain villain.

Such an enquiry was received early one evening from the Nottinghamshire force who were looking for two of our major criminals to eliminate them from their enquiries into a particularly nasty robbery that had taken place that afternoon. I knew both suspects very well indeed (in fact one was Brendan, who later became my informant) so if anyone could find them you would think it was me.

It meant some decent overtime pay, plus expenses because our enquiries would undoubtedly take us into the Sheffield pubs clubs and drinking dens. I set off in an unmarked C.I.D. car with my colleague, detective constable Martin driving. Martin had assisted me to 'intern' the bones at the Wardsend cemetery some months before when the rain had poured down and the coffin would not go in the hole. I knew him well and could trust him, so any scrapes we might get into should not present a problem.

We visited virtually every drinking place in the city, buying drinks in some places but being treated by the management in others. As the evening wore on I began to notice that Martin was beginning to drive more and more erratic and he was showing signs of being 'pissed'. Now I know that you will take offence to this statement - but having spent years illegally 'drinking and driving' if you follow certain rules you are as safe as the next driver. Concentration is the key - 'mind over matter'- absolutely ignore everything and simply concentrate on your driving and you will not have a problem. I'm not going any further into this because I don't expect any of you to agree with me but that's my opinion.

Anyway back to the story -my driver detective constable Martin was beginning to think he was the world's number one racing driver and I was getting worried. I told him to slow down on so many occasions that eventually I 'blew' and said I would drive, but I was too late. It was about 2am in the morning and by then we had been drinking continually since about 8pm the previous evening. We were returning to the C.I.D. office not having traced our 'suspects' and were in our own division. My colleague was speeding along Charter Row a dual-carriageway in the city centre and approaching a set of traffic lights.

I could see a taxi stationary just before the lights and although they were at green I had a premonition that the taxi was going to do a 'U' turn in the road. I shouted a warning to Martin, but too late, the taxi driver without any consideration at all for other traffic turned across the road and we hit him. Both vehicles stopped and there was a few seconds when I suppose the World stood still for everyone involved.

The taxi driver was a Pakistani, but there again tell me one that isn't nowadays.

The initial and inevitable outburst from Martin driving was something like. "fucking hell I'm pissed what happens now?" I had left the C.I.D. car and was dragging the taxi driver out of his cab telling him that he wasn't fit to be on the road until I realized that there was an 'official' path, we as coppers, had to follow. I said to Martin "I've got to ask for an inspector to attend and deal with the accident because he is the next rank up from me."

The D.C. knowing that he was probably 3 or 4 times over the limit said, "I'm going to run away - pretend you don't know who was driving" which even he recognized was the daftest statement ever. Martin sat in the C.I.D. car with the door open and his head in his hands waiting for the certain breath-test that would cause his undoubted suspension from duty. Martin, however, did not know who the duty inspector was that night and I did. The duty inspector attended, a brilliant uniformed copper who called 'a spade a spade' and put the word 'fucking' into virtually everything he said.

"Now then 'Boops' what the fuck's happened here?" said the inspector on his arrival.

I laid the blame for the collision fairly and squarely on the Pakistani taxi driver, not knowing the inspector hated the Pakistani race. By then members of the public had gathered and Martin was looking more and more sick. The inspector made a big show of telling everyone in earshot that he would breathalyse both drivers The Pakistani taxi driver just shrugged his shoulders whilst my colleague almost shit himself and I thought he was going to faint. The taxi driver was first and passed the test with no problems.

The inspector went through the procedure with detective constable Martin.

The inspector lifted Martin's breath sample high into the night air to gain a good view of the result and as a trophy to the onlookers before declaring "Negative" whereupon he then threw the sample straight down the drain and that was the end of that

Having been promoted sergeant whilst a detective constable I followed the recognized route of ex- detectives and went into uniform for at least 12 months. It was not a good move for me or the force. I was too long a plain clothes man and wearing the uniform seriously restricted my working life. My main problem was that as a uniform sergeant I was posted back into West Bar division in the centre of Sheffield where I knew virtually every landlord and club owner in the district. This meant visiting public houses on 'official' licensing visits and always finding the need to check the cellars where there would be one or two free pints laid on.

Many years before as a very young constable I had visited a small back-street public house with my sergeant. He was well over six feet tall and heavy built. We were both wearing our regulation capes because of the rain. The pub was quite full and we moved through the tap-room, which had gone deathly quiet as we entered, looking for any breaches of the licensing laws. The inevitable happened in that the sergeant's cape caught a full pint glass of beer on one of the tables sending it crashing to the floor.

Silence reigned for a few seconds and then the comments started……..

"Fucking hell. I hope you're gonna pay for that?"

"That were fucking deliberate. Bleeding coppers"

The sergeant apologized and made for the door, leaving one very annoyed drinker indeed.

Outside the sergeant said, "When I start buying beer for 'wankers' like that - I'll retire - fuck-em" The lesson from that was that I never wore my cape when visiting pubs in an 'official' capacity.

I used to enjoy visiting the low class pubs in the city centre when in uniform until one summers evening. It was stifling hot and both the constable and I were in shirt sleeves order as we entered the Bull and Mouth public house in Ladysbridge, Sheffield. It was very busy in the pub and we pushed through the mainly male drinkers, several of whom I recognized. Suddenly a pint of beer was thrown all over me, all down the back of my helmet and shirt. I turned and grabbed the first guy I could see with any empty glass, kicking and punching him towards the door. The rest of the crowd were laughing and shouting that we had got the wrong man and outside the pub I quickly realized that was true. I released the man and told him to clear off. We returned to the pub, because as I had forced the innocent guy out of the doors I had seen a well-known villain laughing among the crowd. I was certain then it was him but knew there was little I could do. I had arrested him on several occasions whilst in C.I.D. and he had appeared at court on numerous occasions for theft or assault. With the constable, I went up to him and we stood facing each other in the centre of the pub tap room –"Well" he said, "It wasn't me and you can't prove it was". I replied quite loudly nodding in the direction of his friends - "Do they know you're a fucking 'nonse'? Kept that quiet haven't you?"

I then left the pub with the guy screaming after us that he was not a 'nonse' and shouting he was going to report me which he did later that night. The duty inspector, knowing that I had been drenched in ale told him to "fuck off" or he would lock him up.

Every Friday and Saturday night on completion of the afternoon shift at 11pm one sergeant and several constables on the group were selected by the inspector to work four hours overtime until 3am.When it was my duty the inspector always allowed me to 'hand-pick' my team. I said earlier with the advent of longer licensing hours and the arrival of 'night clubs' public disorder in Sheffield had become a problem into the 'wee' small hours and the police had to respond to it.

My favourite night was Friday and the 'Booper Sweeney' team was formed.

In my team I had one constable who always drove the police riot van - he later was transferred into the traffic division. I swear he could turn a Ford Transit van on two wheels and so with blue lights and horns we used to arrive at incidents in seconds.

Another constable was nick-named 'Lurch'. He was six feet eight inches tall and as ugly as sin, but always handy to have around when the trouble started.

The next constable was smaller, but still well over six foot and for years held the title of British Police Judo Champion.(In fact he was the officer mentioned at the beginning of the book. An accredited air pilot who flew several villains about but never faced any disciplinary action)

The other constable was the 'scribe' whose duty it was on the following Sunday afternoon to write up all the arrest reports. Not one grain of truth ever was put on paper, the officer simply made things up to suit whoever we had arrested and charged, mainly with drunkenness offences.

The Friday night ritual though always started at Whitbread's local brewery in Bridge Street, Sheffield where we were allowed access into the mess room which had a tap direct from the beer vats. Two or three pints, free of charge of course, and we were ready to challenge the city. The little brewery 'perk' unfortunately came to an end when one constable spent nearly all the night shift in the brewery mess-room leaving about 5am in the morning. An early-morning worker reported seeing a uniformed constable walking up the main street in the city urinating from beneath his cape. The constable then proceeded to hit passing cars with his truncheon until the duty inspector and a sergeant attended whereupon the drunken constable smacked the inspector and was locked up. I am told that by 11am next morning he was in front of the chief constable and dismissed from the force.

Even I got 'goosed' once though by a couple of young constables who had joined the 'Booper Sweeney' team one Friday evening because my usual members were away for one reason or another. It was a warm summers evening and we were sitting outside a pub in the city centre at closing time. Two young constables were chatting to a couple of pretty girls and asked if we could give them a lift to the Cavendish night club in another part of the city. I saw no reason to say no and the girls climbed in the back of the van with the two coppers. We drove to a quiet back street near to the night club and I waited with the driver for the back doors to open and the girls climb out. Nothing happened, only some disturbing sounds from the rear of the van. I waited a while longer and still no appearance from the girls and the coppers, so I left the front of the van and opened the back doors. The street lights showed two young ladies with next to nothing on and two coppers minus their trousers. Diplomacy dictated that I told them they had five minutes and then they were out.

Perhaps one of the best times of my career as a uniformed sergeant started on a Friday afternoon with a radio message for me to attend the divisional headquarters to see the superintendent. If only he had known that at the time of the call I was enjoying a pint in full uniform with a friendly landlord just off The Moor. We were in the garden of the pub where no-one could see us.

I went to D.H.Q. and saw the Boss.

He smiled as I entered his office and told me to sit down. I really liked him and had got on well with him since I was a police cadet at headquarters many years before and where he was one of the only good guys in the Prosecutions department. He was quite an authority on the licensing regulations and Oh by the way, he was definitely not a freemason. He asked me how the uniform sergeant business was going and how long before my twelve months was up. I said there was still several months to go and he nodded in agreement when I said I was looking to get back into plain clothes as soon as possible. Another smile and then he said. "I'm probably making the biggest fucking mistake in my career, but I want you to take over the divisional licensing department for a time." Even I saw the funny side of that but answered with a straight face "love to, sir".

West Bar division being in the centre of Sheffield had a specialized licensing department due to the many and varied problems arising from the regulations. Staffed by a sergeant and three constables it was their duty to regulate pubs, clubs, betting shops, dog tracks and keep a watching brief on all types of betting and gaming whether that be in a William Hills Betting establishment or the raffle at the local church hall.

The officers worked in plain clothes, which obviously suited me, and we picked the hours we worked with Friday and Saturday evenings being a must for all the team.

I said earlier that from police training school throughout my career I had avoided any serious study of the licensing regulations only being concerned with what I could drink in pubs and clubs, but I was fortunate because in the department at the time were two bright academic constables who were destined for higher rank and knew most of the regulations to the letter.

The very next evening at 5pm I met the team, spending about thirty minutes in digesting the various reports and office procedures. By 5.30pm we were entering the Three Cranes pub in Bank Street opposite the station as it opened, with my new team looking a little apprehensive, never having worked with a sergeant before who was drinking when the shift started and probably at the end as well That first Saturday evening my team claimed the record for prosecuting 'under-age drinkers. After a few beers in the local pub, we hit the cities clubs and pubs where we knew the young frequented simply pulling them outside, checking their identity and reporting them for the offence. We were successful in beating all previous records because I split the team into two so that double more offenders were reported that night than previously. Apparently all my predecessors had insisted that the whole team stick together in view of being in licensed premises where anything could 'kick off.'. I dispensed with that idea because we were then in possession of personal radios that worked sometimes, but were a re-assurance of sorts, should things go wrong.

About this time a recent Court of Appeal decision had presented the management of night clubs with a 'legal nightmare'. The case 'Carter v Bradbeer' remains in my mind and affected how drinks were served to customers after normal licensing hours had finished and clubs mainly were operating under late night licenses. I do not intend to dwell on the legislation any further really, because it was a stupid law which caused different venues to serve drinks to customers in different ways some by having staff stand in front of the bar and handing drinks to customers or simply waiter service only. Anyway it cost the clubs a lot of money in trying to abide by the legal decision and we as the licensing squad were supposed to enforce a law that nobody really understood or liked. By not enforcing this new rule fiercely though, I did gain some credit from the night clubs that was to stand me in good staid later when I returned to C.I.D. duties.

One incident though, in the licensing department brought me into conflict with one of the best known licensees in the city. He was a 'larger than life' character known to a lot of policemen, but in my opinion he got more from us than we got from him and I did not like him. The fact that one of the divisional detectives was 'giving his wife one' did not really come into the matter. The publican was very successful in the trade and his city centre pub was always busy with the concert room showing local acts. Word reached us that his Friday lunchtime shows were getting out of hand with female strippers going further than was decent. In plain clothes I visited the pub with one of my colleagues on a very wet and cold Friday lunchtime. The weather had played a part in enhancing his trade because there were loads of scaffolders in the audience who had been 'rained off' and had decided to enjoy the last working day of the week in the pub. The concert room was packed with the windows all steamed up from the wet clothing of the audience or maybe it was the antics of the strippers. My colleague and I stood at the bar with a drink watching the girls undress and noting the lewd comments of the males in the audience, and I might add several females. With more and more beer consumed, the comments became louder and lewder from the audience and things were getting out of hand.

The landlord, who was present, did not seem interested in trying to control events simply letting guys paw the girls as they danced near to the edge of the stage and the girls occasionally getting to grips with the guys. Then an occurrence that, in the opinion of my colleague and I, placed the publican in breach of his Music, Singing and Dancing Licence. The licence, granted by the local authority included several 'do's and 'don'ts' including the prohibition of any offensiveness in the premises in relation to the acts.

Imagine two steeplejacks, pissed out of their brains, in scruffy working gear and muddy boots using a couple of the large metal spanners that steeplejacks carry in the belt around their waist as 'sex aids'. Two of the strippers, still with some clothes on I might add, allowed the men to push the spanners between their thighs, to the absolute delight of the crowd. This was another occasion when 'Booper' put brains before brawn and we made no effort to stop the performance, quietly leaving the concert room. When the afternoon show had finished and all the audience gone, we returned to the pub and reported the landlord for the breach of his Music, Singing and Dancing Licence. A report of the event was then sent to the local authority. He was not pleased, recognizing immediately the effect it would have on his trade. In the end, with his contacts in the local authority, the publican settled for a caution and promised to be more aware when future events took place. The matter was closed but the incident led to any similar 'lewd' shows being curtailed.

The divisional superintendent seemed happy with the way I was running the licensing department and arranged for me to accompany him one evening on a 'Rubber Heel' job.

I mentioned earlier that there was a force discipline and complaints department responsible for investigating complaints against officers, nick-named the 'Rubber Heels department'. Sometimes they could not cope with the number of complaints made by the public or others and farmed out investigations to superintendents and above. A complaint had been made against a serving uniformed officer by a family in the Barnsley police division. An incident had taken place in a working men's club where the constable and his family had become involved in a heated argument with another family. This led to a brawl inside the club, finally being sorted out by the committee. No-one was seriously hurt and the only reason the family made a complaint was because a policeman was involved and they hoped he would be further punished by the force.

How wrong they were with this superintendent....

My Boss had already interviewed the family making the allegation of discreditable conduct against the officer, who had apparently sworn at them when the fracas took place.

The superintendent had already made his mind up and just needed a couple of witness statements from the committee to finalise his report suggesting no further action.

Now the police are extremely wary of becoming involved in anything to do with working men's clubs. In many ways the club, and particularly the committee, are a law unto themselves (like the freemasons). Police have no power to enter these clubs, without a warrant, and they are notorious for their unlawful conduct. The committee are selected from the membership by the membership fostering all the problems you will imagine with that sort of election process. Committee men were well known for obtaining free ale and a cut from the fees paid to artists performing in the club. Their 'expenses' obtained by manipulating the one-armed bandits and other machines in the club was legendary. So it was no surprise when we attended the club in plain clothes to meet the committee, we sensed hostility.

We had travelled to the club in the superintendent's car and the idea was that after the enquiries he would drop me back at our city centre divisional headquarters some 15 miles away. We needed witnesses to the incident, but were going down the path, even at that stage, of deciding the officer complained about had no case to answer. The superintendent kicked the night off by buying all the committee a drink which led to the first of many.

It was pretty obvious that the family making the complaint were not well liked in the club and yet the officer and his Father before him had been members for years without any undue hassle. Most club members knew he was a police officer and accepted the fact.

During our evening in the club more drinks were taken and the superintendent was pissed out of his brains but happy that his enquiries would undoubtedly lead to the complaint being dismissed. We left the club and the Boss drove out of the club car park straight down a one-way street almost hitting a vehicle coming in the opposite direction. Our car ended up with the engine stalled on the footpath. I suggested that I drove and took the Boss home leaving his car there and arranging for a lift back into the city.

The complaint against the officer was dismissed.

So many police 'boozy' tales come to mind such as the Rotherham division station sergeant who always needed a 'good' drink before going home from work in the evening or after the morning shift. He would visit a pub close to the station, down as many pints as he could before closing time and then drive home, obviously well over the drink-drive limit. One night he crashed his car and the duty inspector was called to the scene whereupon the sergeant knocked him over the wall into a front garden. The sergeant later appeared in court charged with driving under the influence, but the inspector forgot about the assault. (It is a sobering thought as I write this that both those officers are now deceased.)

Licensed premises were the pick of a West Indian burglar we can call Lewis.

It was the early hours of Sunday morning and I was the detective sergeant on the 6pm - 2am shift which I loved. About 2am I was in Josephines my favourite night club where I was always welcome having gone to school many years before with the owner.

An urgent telephone call was made by my division to the club asking me to attend a city centre public house where a man had been shot. The public house being the Museum on Leopold Street, Sheffield where we had almost got caught 'piking' many years before and in fact was only 100 yards away from the night club. I walked round the corner to find the place swarming with uniformed coppers. An ambulance was also present.

The landlord and his wife were only young and it was the first pub they had managed.

They were quite keen on the licensing regulations making sure they had closed at 11pm, cleared the premises and were ready to go out for a late supper. They had thoroughly checked the pub before leaving and the premises were secure. They returned shortly before 1am and went to bed. The landlord was a member of a local gun club and kept two shotguns quite legally in a bedroom cupboard. About 1.30am loud noises downstairs in the bar area awoke the Wife who roused her sleeping Husband. He grabbed one of his shotguns, loaded it and crept downstairs into the main bar

301

area where he found a window smashed and assumed that the intruder was still on the premises. He shouted upstairs for his Wife to telephone the police and continued his search of his pub. The Wife got out of bed, went onto the landing area and began dialling '999' when to her horror she saw the lounge door slowly opening and the black face of Lewis peering round the corner. She screamed at the top of her voice and Lewis turned back into the lounge. Her husband alerted by the screams came running to the foot of the stairs when there was a crash of glass from the upstairs lounge indicating that Lewis was trying to escape via that route. The Husband, still in possession of his trusty shotgun realized the intruder was hoping to escape that way, ran out into the rear yard (the same yard where the two 'fucking perverts' almost got caught. 'piking' many years before!). Lewis was then on the slated roof outside the upstairs lounge window and the landlord jumped onto a small wall to get a better view. Bear in mind the yard was no lighter than many years before and Lewis had the distinct advantage of being black. Lewis was trying to negotiate a drop from the slates into the yard but the landlord was determined he should not escape. He pointed the shotgun in the direction of Lewis and fired. Now this is where it gets humorous, although not at that moment for the Landlord, his Wife or even Lewis. The recoil of the firearm caused the landlord to fall backwards over the wall breaking his leg. The pellets from the gun hit Lewis in his left eye, causing him to fall from the slates and land on the other side of the wall to the landlord.

Both men lay on the ground screaming in pain.......

Uniformed officers were quickly on the scene and both men taken to hospital, in separate ambulances. I attended at the pub, taking a statement from the Wife and possession of both shotguns. Later at the hospital I found Lewis detained in a side-ward minus the sight of his left eye. Would you believe he denied breaking into pub saying that he had gone into the yard for a 'piss'? He had no explanation why he had fallen from the off-shot roof in the yard. When I later checked his record I found that he had several previous convictions for burglary and theft offences mainly in licensed premises. He went to prison again for this offence. The Landlord was in hospital for some time with a serious leg fracture. I submitted a report to the D.P.P. suggesting that no useful purpose would be served and that it was not in the public interest to prosecute the landlord for wounding Lewis. The D.P.P. agreed, although his firearms certificate was revoked and he lost his two shotguns.

Some 18 months later our friend Lewis, the now 'one-eyed black burglar' was at it again. He visited the Crazy Daisy club on High Street, Sheffield, which opened at night and also lunchtime and hid in the toilets when they closed for the afternoon period.

He emerged from the toilets when he thought it was safe stealing money and cigarettes.

When I attended the scene later that day and asked if any 'low-life' had been in the pub during the lunchtime period the licensee mentioned a black youth with one eye - Lewis!

I arrested him but he denied the offence. Again he was unlucky, because shortly before he had hidden in the pub toilets a cleaner had washed all the floor. There was a beautiful 'foot-print' matching his trainers. So Lewis went back to court - to prison and I assume he is still looking, with his one good eye, at pubs and clubs as an easy source of income!

Finally for this chapter back to the 'underworld' of the city and the sort of situations that the public could never envisage. I'll call him Derek, one of the hardest men in Sheffield and district.

The tales of his past were legendary - 'bare-knuckle' fighting and illegal fights with gypsies and the like. He was always in the money and for some considerable time drove a blue Rolls Royce motor car which in any northern city in the Sixties and Seventies meant villain or millionaire. I tried to get close to him hoping that he would make a good informant because of his links and we did have a good rapport but I never got anything worthwhile from him. Many of his 'business' ventures failed, but the police sat up and took notice when he opened a public house in the Attercliffe area of the city. There were no dwellings in the vicinity of the pub, only warehouses and factories fast becoming derelict like the workers who used to toil in them. It was amazing that he was granted a licence for the pub in view of his police record and privately views were expressed that people in authority had been bribed to allow such a thing to happen.

The criminal intelligence unit opened a file on the pub anticipating all sorts of heinous crimes.

Without doubt Derek was careful not to blatantly breach licensing regulations, opening when the law said he could and closing at the declared time, normally 11pm at night.

Information was constantly being ferried to the local police station that 'drinking after time' was rife and without doubt the pub would have been raided if it had not gone out business shortly after it opened.

Derek rang me one morning in the task force and suggested we had lunch at Tuckwoods, Surrey Street, Sheffield, a small inexpensive restaurant. He said he had a 'problem' he wished to discuss. So I duly met him in a restaurant normally occupied by the cities bankers and solicitors at lunchtime and where old ladies interrupted their shopping for a meal. Alcohol was not served and in fact it was a place I had visited on several occasions with my Mother and Father. I expressed surprise at the venue when I met Derek and secretly smiled when he said that he was a regular customer there with his Mother. It did not fit his image at all.

Derek did not come straight to the point about his 'problem' so we had lunch and then went to a couple of pubs in the city centre where one or two of the drinkers seemed surprised to see Derek in the close company of a copper. After the pubs Derek asked if I would go with him to see his Mother in Hospital, who was seriously ill. Although by then we had drunk quite a lot and were well over the limit to drive, I was in the C.I.D. task force unmarked car so that did not present any problems. At the hospital Derek introduced me to his Mother as a business associate and it was apparent that the old lady was very near death (in fact she died the next day). By then it was past 3pm and the pubs had officially closed until tea-time. Derek shed a few tears about his Mother, making me swear that no-one ever got to hear about them and suggested we went to his pub where we could have another drink. The pub was officially closed and we had to go round the back where a special knock on the door allowed us access. Inside at the bar were the finest collection of local villains I had ever seen and the atmosphere changed as soon as we walked in. I must admit that I did feel a little anxious with the office only knowing that I was meeting Derek, and them having no idea where we were going. Still I took comfort that no-one would have the bottle to offend Derek in public or would they?

We had a couple of drinks before the comments started...

"Fucking hell, Derek. What you doing with the filth?"

"Is he joining our side Derek? Could do with a copper 'smartened up'?" (Bribed)

Derek laughed it off and went into the rear of the pub, I assume to see the staff.

He was gone some time and I stood alone. I tried to make conversation with the drinkers in Derek's absence but got no-where and I could feel the atmosphere becoming tense.

Suddenly one very powerful guy came over and gently pushed me back to the bar.

I knew him from the city but not his name. He was holding

a camera in his hand.

"What a fucking picture it would make" he said, waving the camera at me, "If we held a C.I.D. sergeant bollock naked on bar with a beer bottle stuffed up his arse."

The other villains laughed nervously and I seriously wondered if the guy was pissed enough to try it. I laughed nervously as well but the guy walked away from me as Derek came back into the room. We went to sit at a table away from the other drinkers but even Derek had sensed the atmosphere. He asked me if everything was all right. I said it was, but excused myself by going to the gents. I stayed in the gents longer than normal just to gather my thoughts hoping that the atmosphere would have changed when I went back to the bar. On my return things had gone very quiet and I noticed that the camera-man had left. I sat down with Derek and finally found out his 'problem' was in respect of his Irish bar manager who had run off the previous day with a load of cash from the safe.

Apparently he had been falsifying invoices to show that the brewery had been paid for deliveries of beer and spirits when in fact the money had gone into his own pocket.

A very brave man, I quietly thought, knowing what Derek would do if he caught him.

There was no real formal accounting system at the pub and Derek had no idea how much had been stolen. Basically Derek was saying to me, you catch him before I do or he's dead meat. I knew he meant it.

I took a few details and explained that maybe the brewery

could supply me with details of the cash they should have received thus giving me an idea of how much had been stolen. I said I would circulate details of the bar manager to try and catch him before he returned to Ireland. Over the next few days I made contact with the brewery but found that their system was no better than Derek's and it would mean hours and hours of work sifting through delivery notes to calculate a figure the bar manager could have stolen.

Some weeks after my brush with the beer bottle thug in Derek's pub I received a telephone call asking me to meet the assistant chief constable (crime) on Bacon Lane bridge over the canal in the East end of the city where he was convinced that the missing Irish bar manager had been found. I attended as instructed (although to this day I never did find out why the A.C.C. was there) and found police vehicles, fire brigade and ambulances all blocking the small road over the canal bridge. It was about two miles away from Derek's pub. The A.C.C. asked me to describe the Irish bar manager and pointed to the water below the bridge. It was possible to see a male body standing upright in the water with the top of his head just below the surface of the water. The head of the man was almost ripped off. Apparently barges had gone over the corpse for some days causing serious injuries when the bottom of the boats had scraped on the man's head. The A.C.C. was convinced that it was the man I was seeking, but when police frogmen fully recovered the body it was obvious that it was not. In fact it was a murder victim. Apparently a few nights before, three youths had left another local pub and started to fight on the canal bridge. Two youths ganged up on the third and after beating him up they threw him into the canal where he went straight into the water and his body remained upright due to the feet and legs being trapped in the heavy mud. Barges passing to and fro had really messed up his head. Two youths later pleaded 'guilty' to Manslaughter at court. I never did find the missing bar manager and suspect that he found his way back to Ireland, looking over his shoulder all the time in case Derek located him.(The Bacon Lane canal bridge later achieved fame featuring in scenes from the film 'The Full Monty'.)

It was many months after this incident I arrested a guy for theft who had been among the villains in Derek's pub when the 'heavy' threatened to 'disembowel' me with the beer bottle. He told me what had happened at the pub in my absence that afternoon.

You will recall that shortly after that incident I went to the toilets and remained there for a time. Unknown to me Derek had been listening to the conversation whilst in the rear of the pub and had witnessed the guy threatening to stick the beer bottle up my 'arse.'

In my absence Derek had lifted the guy who had threatened me from his stool. Head -butted him and threw him out of the front door with the warning that: "No-one insults any friend I bring in my fucking pub, copper or not".

The Demon Drink. Oh, how boring our lives would be without it.

Chapter 11 - The Big One.

"Man can climb to the highest summits, but he cannot remain there too long."
George Bernard Shaw, 1856 - 1950.

The 'Big One' is a term used alike by criminals and detectives to indicate entirely different achievements.

Remember, as I write here in 1985 some things remain unchanged ....

Expressions such a 'nonses', 'poofters' and 'the big one' will no doubt outlive the users.

Every villain dreams of pulling off a major crime that will reward him so successfully that he can retire. Most of my fellow inmates here in prison talk daily of 'the big one' they are planning for when they are released. Criminal activities that will bring them the life they see on television of big houses, cars and exotic holidays abroad. They dream of villas abroad and untold wealth, a far cry from their D.H.S.S. benefits and small time criminal activities. Detectives similarly look to the day of the 'big one' when they arrest someone who has evaded capture nationwide for some time or the arrest of a target criminal. Without doubt 'the big one' exists in the minds of 'baddies' and 'goodies'.

In my case 'the big one' was the recovery, through an informant, of stolen diamonds conservatively estimated at ½ million pounds. The trail leading to their recovery was long and at times a little dangerous, but after many 'twist and turns' I experienced the euphoria of holding diamonds worth ½ million pounds in my hands. Unfortunately the 'twist and turns' also indirectly led to my arrest and conviction for corruption and other criminal offences.

When I first thought of writing this book it was simply to expose everything and everyone involved in the police 'system'. Get it out of my system and occupy my time 'inside'. Particularly, I wanted to get at those other corrupt officers who played major roles or simply enjoyed 'walking-on-parts' in the criminality of my enterprises.

The investigating team that prosecuted me know very well who those officers are.

Their names have been put to me so many times during interviews and even as I write here in prison I am awaiting a further interview by senior officers, anxious, or on the face of it, apparently anxious, to capture them. Veiled threats regarding an appeal I have pending and early parole have already been made when no other witnesses were present.

So far I have resisted their efforts to tell all and my conscience has no stomach currently to be labelled a 'grass'. The investigators could have allowed some mitigating credit in my case and I would have responded favourably towards that, but I now hold the tag of a villain and after some months here in prison I can only act and react offensively towards authority. The investigators used the old business man as a witness against me, promising him the earth and I amazed

311

that his basic intelligence did not tell him that he was being used. What a shock he must have had when the judge said 'Seven Years'

In all honesty I fully expected my informant pal Brendan to turn 'queens evidence' when the shit hit the fan and he did. 'No honour among thieves'. How true!

Let me tell you more about Brendan.

A violent career criminal, armed robber, regional crime squad target criminal and police informant. The 'lowest of the low' some might think, but I was the sort of detective prepared to take the risks and mix with him and others like him. Brendan lead me to my downfall but also to the 'the big one'.

I was quietly doing paperwork in the West Bar C.I.D. office Sheffield as a detective sergeant one morning when the telephone rang and it was Brendan wanting to meet with me. The alarm bells started to ring. Why did he want to meet me? He was known to be an informant for detective sergeant McIntosh or 'town drunk' to coin his nickname and only the week before had assisted that officer in recovering stolen jade value £90.000. Apparently a burglary had taken place in the North East of England and with Brendan's efforts police stopped a car speeding down the A1 motor way, arresting the occupants and recovering the stolen goods.

Brendan had intimated that he had some information for the police and my Bosses agreed that the meet should take place but every effort should be made to protect me in case he tried to set me up in some way - offering me money or seeking to gain information valuable to himself or others. We opted for me to wear a hidden microphone so that other supporting officers could hear the conversation in case things went wrong.

We approached the regional crime squad for the 'loan' of a microphone because they had that sort of equipment, but they refused because at that time I was not a member of the squad. Were we on the same side I hear you ask? So the regional crime squad offered to have an undercover officer in the pub where I was to meet Brendan which was better than nothing. (In any event I had doubts about the microphone because I thought Brendan was cute enough to invite me to the toilets in the pub and frisk me before he said anything.)

I entered the Red Lion pub, London Road Sheffield just after lunchtime and went into the tap room. Brendan was there already but the expected request to ensure I was not 'wired-up' did not arise, meaning that he was not intending trying to trap me and wanted to deal in some other way. Brendan and I did know each other a little, but we were certainly not on speaking terms and it was some time since I had seen him because he had only just been released from prison a few days earlier. In the corner of the tap room was a big scruffy looking guy sitting quietly with a pie, a pint and a copy of the Sun newspaper. I did not know him but he turned out to be the undercover crime squad detective.

Brendan made a point of indicating the scruffy bloke in the corner and said …..

"I suppose he's one of yours- watching your back?"

I said "no" but just then a crowd of girls came into the pub and two of them said "hello" to me. They were in fact friends of my Wife but to Brendan they were coppers as well,

"Bloody hell, you're not taking any chances are you?" he said.

I tried to reassure him that they were not with the police but I think to this day he did not believe me. I asked Brendan why he was speaking to me and not detective sergeant McIntosh whom he normally dealt with. He explained that he could not rely on the officer any more who was getting worse day by day with the drink. I mentioned the officer's nick-name of 'town drunk' which Brendan thought funny, but true. Satisfied, I listened to Brendan's tale.

It was immediately apparent that Brendan had picked up some information whilst in prison which he thought could lead to a nice 'earner' for himself. Brendan gave me details of a crime which he wanted me to identify and then notify him of any reward offered. He stressed it was unlikely that the offence had been committed in my force area. It was a particularly nasty crime where four or five villains, wearing masks had broken into a mansion or similar property. Certainly the property housed servants or staff and the old lady occupier had been attacked and tied up. A key had been found which opened a safe and a haul of diamonds had been stolen. Brendan was able to describe some of the property in detail, suggesting that he may have already seen the goods. There was a diamond tiara, which could not be recovered having already been disposed of. There was a diamond necklace, ear-rings, brooches and several single diamonds. Brendan added that the goods may have Royal connections. He was not prepared to say more at the first meeting, but asked me to identify the crime and we would meet again. (On leaving the pub Brendan assaulted the taxi driver previously explained in Chapter 3)

I liaised with senior officers at police headquarters in view of the nature of the information received. I made contact with every criminal intelligence unit in England, Wales and Scotland but could not identify the crime. I made contact with Scotland Yard in view of the 'Royal' angle suggested by Brendan, but to no avail. It looked at one point that Scotland Yard had identified the crime having taken place at 'Broadlands', home of the late Lord Mountbatten. I spoke on several occasions to the Private Secretary of Mountbatten and also to Lord Brabourne (son in law) but they were unable to help.

(Like many others I was shocked some time later when the I.R.A executed Mountbatten on his boat. I am not a Royalist but one has to register outrage when murdering cowardly bastards like the I.R.A. commit such wickedness.)

I met with Brendan again telling him that I had failed to locate the crime. He then added that following the incident there had been massive press and media coverage and a police mobile unit had been set-up outside the mansion for some days. I then sent a message to all police forces in the country setting out the details Brendan had supplied and asking for suggestions of where the crime may have been committed. Within hours we had a reply, ironically from the adjacent West Yorkshire Police, detailing an offence that had taken place in the city of Wakefield only some 25 miles away from our force area. Immediately a meeting was held with senior detectives from both forces to discuss the crime, the goods stolen and more important the reward on offer!

The details of the crime were that an elderly lady, divorced and living alone in a wealthy area of Wakefield was cared for by three of four 'staff' in view of her frail almost senile condition. Her ex-husband was a retired colonel and chairman of the local magistrates. (His surname was the same as the informant Brendan, which I found amusing.) It had been some months since masked raiders had broken into her home and taken property from the safe. The stolen diamonds had been in the family for years and years and no-one could really describe them in any detail. In view of this, the crime had been 'logged' as only £30.00 stolen. A mobile police unit was set-up outside the detached house and the press reported the case in some detail although I understand they were aware that valuable property had in reality been stolen.

A further meeting was held involving the ex-husband colonel our informant and senior officers from both forces. In law the ex-husband apparently still had good 'title' to goods in his wife's safe-keeping despite their divorce. In view of her medical condition we knew it would be impossible to use her as a witness, and in fact she sadly died before the end of the case. Again the irony of the situation could not escape me

316

with Brendan, an accomplished and committed major criminal, sitting down with an ex-colonel cum senior magistrate to discuss 'business'. We all met at lunchtime in the Three Owls public house outside Wakefield. Yours truly, being the lowest in rank, paid for the drinks.

The meeting was brief, with Brendan describing in as much detail to the magistrate the stolen diamonds he hoped to recover. The ex-colonel agreed that the property was probably his, although frankly admitting that it was years since anyone had opened the safe to look at the jewellery. The 'Royal connection' was explained by the colonel and it did involve the Mountbatten family. Apparently many years before, the colonel's ancestors bought the jewellery from the Mountbatten family who were a little 'down on their luck' at the time. The diamond tiara was one item he recalled.

An agreement was struck between the magistrate and Brendan. It was a simple deal with both men shaking hands. If Brendan was to recover the jewellery, the colonel would give him £5.000 cash. After the trial Brendan would select four diamonds for himself and the remainder would be returned to the colonel. Not a bad deal, you may think, but would you take the risks?

The operation could then begin in earnest......

I made frequent trips with Brendan and a detective inspector from the West Yorkshire Police up the M62 motorway into Lancashire and the small village of Rawtenstall where we believed the stolen goods were held. They were in the possession of a wealthy antique dealer who

317

had just served a prison sentence for receiving stolen goods. He had been in the same 'nick' as Brendan. We made a thorough check of Rawtenstall village and surrounding area trying to devise a plan to seize the stolen goods, not knowing for certain if they were being stored in that area. Brendan had intimated that the dealer was very cautious in dealing with anyone and in respect of this amount of stolen property he would not take any risks.

Brendan made contact with the dealer telling him that he had managed to get his hands on plenty of cash and would make a deal for some of the gems. A time and date for their meeting was arranged. We then involved the Number 1 regional crime squad based in Lancashire who would make the arrest and obtained permission from an assistant chief constable in their force for Brendan to wear a secret microphone. (It later transpired that the A.C.C. did not have the authority to permit such action but he said it should go ahead with so much at stake.) - Compare that with the refusal of our crime squad initially for me to wear one of 'their' microphones!

So on the day I collected Brendan from his home and we drove over to Lancashire where we met senior officers from West Yorkshire where the robbery had been committed and the Lancashire regional crime squad officers. Since early morning a female undercover crime squad officer had been keeping the dealer's house under observations from the bedroom window of a friendly neighbour. It was imperative that Brendan be afforded some degree of protection. If the

318

dealer were to find out that officers from other forces were involved he could, by simple deduction work out who had 'grassed' him up and he was a very nasty piece of work. The plan was simple - Brendan would go to the house of the dealer on foot - explaining that he had left his car on the other side of the village for security reasons. We hoped and prayed that the dealer was keeping the stolen gems at his house, but if not undercover officers would try to follow the dealer wherever he went to get them. Brendan would examine the diamonds and make an offer for some or even all of them with a view to returning in a few days with the cash and the deal would be complete. Brendan would leave, perhaps taking the dealer for a quick drink and then walk to his car leaving the dealer to return home.

The Lancashire regional crime squad officers were in possession of a magistrates Search Warrant allowing them to search the dealers house for jewellery stolen when a shop was broken into in Preston some days before. The plan was that with the return of the dealer, the officers would enter his house and make a search under the terms of their warrant, hopefully knowing exactly where the stolen diamonds were being stored having been told by Brendan. Plain clothes vehicles were hidden all around the small village and we were blessed with perfect radio reception.

The 'big one' or 'My big one' was about to start…………

Brendan approached the dealers house and rang the door-bell and was admitted.

The radio allowed us access to everything that was said,

even to the noise of Brendan sipping a cup of tea. The dealer was heard to say he would fetch the gems and the watching policewoman saw him leave the main house and go into an outbuilding, returning with a small dark coloured parcel. The dealer and Brendan gloated over the gems, expressing pleasure at their appearance and quality. After half an hour it was apparent that the two men had 'halved' the stones with Brendan agreeing to pay the sum of £20.000 for his share. They shook hands on the deal and the dealer agreed to go for a drink with Brendan who made a time and date the following week when he would return with the cash. The watching policewoman reported the dealer revisiting the outbuilding to secrete the parcel and then both men visited a small pub nearby.

We could still hear the conversation between Brendan and the dealer in the pub with the dealer congratulating Brendan for leaving his vehicle on the other side of town.

Inside the pub, Brendan excused himself from the dealer, entering the gents toilets he spoke into the microphone confirming that the diamonds were just as anticipated and shortly after said goodbye to the dealer and walked into town. Again the watching policewoman reported the dealer returning home.

The crime squad officers allowed some time to pass before raiding the dealers house in true 'Sweeney' style with unmarked cars pulling up to the back and front.

Three of the senior detectives, Brendan and I went for a pub lunch that developed into one almighty 'piss-up' as we awaited the news. We did not anticipate a long wait,. All my dreams had come true. From the day that Brendan offered me the information I had lived and breathed the outcome as successful and it was about to become real. Many worries though still tortured me. Would there be any 'hitches' with the operation?

Would the colonel be able to identify the diamonds after so many years, to the satisfaction of the law?

Would Brendan be exposed as the 'grass' in the eyes of the dealer, although I admit to reducing that worry low on my list. Brendan had explained that his policy of 'personal insurance' was that another person had also viewed the goods with a view to purchase, so the dealer could never be 100% sure it was Brendan who 'grassed' him up.

We all estimated that within the hour we would be getting even more 'pissed' with the diamonds recovered, the dealer arrested and we could all go home. After some two hours we were getting worried with no acknowledged result. It was then past 3pm and the pub was closing so we had to leave and wait on the car park.

We were joined by the senior crime squad officer after a short time who admitted they could not find the diamonds and he added, if their policewoman had not seen the goods being taken back into the outbuilding they would not have believed they were there.

They had sent for additional lighting and tools in his words to "tear the fucking building to pieces, because we know the gear is there".

Brendan and I sat alone in one of the police vehicles on the pub car park all afternoon.

We talked a little, but with the beer and Brendan's love of the police, I was subjected to many abusive diatribes in respect of police inefficiency. I told Brendan to "fuck off, because normally it would be you laughing at this police cock up and there's fuck all you can do about it anyway".

So we slept a little until 5.30pm when the pub opened for the evening session and we went back inside for more ale. Heavens knows what the landlord thought?

By now Brendan was becoming verbally abusive and offensive. I thought at one point that it would develop into a punch-up between us and whilst he was no doubt the stronger, with a violent criminal record, I had a beer bottle close to hand which I would have used - you bet! We stared into our drinks as only the time and no words passed between us when suddenly a crime squad vehicle came flying onto the pub car park with lights blazing and horns blaring, it was touch and go if he would stop before crashing into the tap room Brendan and I ran out of the pub. One of the senior officers was sitting in the front passenger seat of the vehicle and was holding a large tray on his lap with a towel over it. He pulled back the towel and there were the diamonds. Over half a million pounds on his lap. They glistened in the early evening sunlight like sparklers children hold or wave about on bonfire night. On their own, laying on a dirty towel, they did not excite nor provoke feelings of affluence or wealth but they were ours and the operation was a success.

We left the Lancashire regional crime squad officers to complete the 'paper-work' in respect of the dealer. They were over the moon, having captured 'bang to rights' one of their target criminals. I do not remember how we got home that night, but there were still many other problems to arise from my 'big one.'

Together with Brendan I met the colonel a few days later, after he had privately viewed the recovered diamonds. The colonel had immediately identified them as having been stolen from the safe at his ex-wife's home (can you blame him suddenly coming into a half a million pounds windfall?) and he gave Brendan the promised £5.000 cash. Needless to say the diamonds were kept by the police to be used as evidence against the dealer in due course when he was finally tried. This was not to be for some two years, which really was beyond the control of the police. Brendan became quite angry at the delays in seizing his 'reward' of four diamonds but from his personal experience he should have known that the law is a 'ponderous old fool' that rushes for no-one and particularly not a 'grass'.

It was to be expected that the arrested dealer was unhappy that the local regional crime squad just happened to search his home looking for the proceeds from a burglary offence in Preston and accidentally coming across such a high value 'find' from another police area. The interviewing officers warned us that the dealer had 'ear-marked' Brendan as the informant and he had assured them that solid retribution would follow. The dealer was undoubtedly 'putting two and two together' in relation to the visit of Brendan and was suspicious. Brendan tried to allay those suspicions by telephoning the wife of the dealer the following week confirming that he would visit to pay the £20.000 and finalise the deal, only to be told that her husband had been 'nicked'.

It would be nice to report that the process of the law in relation to the prosecution of the dealer went ahead as normal, but this was certainly not the case................

I was asleep at home around midnight some days after the operation when I received a telephone call from Brendan's wife. Brendan had gone into hiding because a black Rolls Royce motor car containing four 'heavies' was touring the Sheffield city centre looking for her husband. Even the most junior detective could work out what they wanted.

I telephoned the city centre division and asked them to keep a 'look-out' for the Rolls Royce whilst I went to collect Brendan from where he was hiding. Brendan and I toured the city centre in my Wife's Mini motor car but saw no sign of the Rolls.

The division also confirmed there had been no sightings of the distinctive motor car so, thinking it was safe, we decided to go for drink in Scamps night-club where we were both known and therefore would not be out of place. I dropped Brendan near to the club and he went in on his own which was our normal ritual. I parked my car and followed some time after to allay any suspicions that we were together. As I reached the club a black Rolls Royce motor car was pulling up at the front door. Two of the biggest men I have ever seen in my life got out of the Rolls Royce car followed by two smaller men who were local villains. This was obviously the 'hit team' organised by the dealer to have a word with Brendan. I was trying to think of some way of stopping them entering the club and perhaps 'murdering' Brendan. Suddenly I recognized one the 'gorillas' as a very well known heavy-weight professional boxer from West Yorkshire. I had seen him box on television occasionally and whilst he was not the best in the land he was quite 'handy'. I also recalled several regional crime squad circulations describing him as 'hired muscle' and one to be extremely wary of. I went up to the group and said 'hello' to the two local guys. I intimated that I knew the 'hard man' from his television appearances and asked what he was doing in town? I never got any further because a marked police patrol car came quietly round the corner stopping alongside us. Two officers got out of the car and asked if I was okay? One of the local guys, trying to appear 'hard' in front of the others said something about "Fucking coppers everywhere" whereupon they all got back into the Rolls Royce and drove away. I entered the club and relayed to Brendan how I had saved him from a right 'pasting'. A couple of years later I wished I hadn't bothered when he gave evidence against me!

Some months later I watched the boxer fighting in a title fight on television where he was easily beaten by a young and up and coming heavy-weight. Shortly after that the boxer appeared before court charged with robbery and was sent to prison for some years.

To my knowledge there were no further approaches to Brendan from the dealer.

So the months passed by with Brendan pining for the remainder of his reward.

For my part I was trying to fully utilise Brendan as an informant and gain further arrests through him. There had been some envious looks in my direction from senior detectives in my force when the full strength of the Lancashire job was made public and there was a commendation for me from the West Yorkshire Police where the crime had been committed. So, I think to keep up his own 'reputation' in the eyes of the police and to ensure that he kept us 'sweet' whilst waiting for his four diamonds, Brendan came up with another nice little arrest.

A divorced lady lived alone in a beautiful house in the Dore and Totley area of Sheffield. The area being recognised as perhaps the wealthiest in the city.

Her ex-Husband had left her well-off with substantial maintenance payments.

She had become involved with a local rogue, who despite his criminal side could charm ladies with ease and swept her off her dainty feet. He was many years younger than her and although he wore a wig he was a true 'ladies-man'.

Let me just digress a little to say that I knew the rogue very well from my Rotherham days. Early one morning in the Oasis Club, Wortley Road many years before, I had found it amusing when an off-duty detective constable, having been abused by the rogue, tried to throw him down the stairs by

326

grabbing his hair - which came off causing the youth severe embarrassment.

So back to the story…the affair blossomed, in the ladies eyes only, with the villainous boyfriend waiting for the moment when he could arrange for her house to be 'screwed' and expensive antiques and other property stolen. The villain arranged to take his lady-friend out one evening for dinner leaving the house unoccupied. On their return, 'surprise-surprise' the house had been burgled and antique furniture and other goods to the value of £10.000 had been stolen. The local C.I.D. suspected the villain when their enquiries revealed how close he was to the lady complainant, but they had no evidence to go on and he had the perfect alibi for the crime having been at dinner with the lady

The lady would not hear that her boy-friend had been involved (how many times have we heard that before.) The boy-friend approached Brendan to get rid of the stolen gear and guess what - Brendan suggested taking them to an antique dealer he knew living in a small Lancashire village called Rawtenstall (You have to admire the 'front' of Brendan suggesting the dealer with the diamonds knowing very well the man was then still remanded in custody.) The boy-friend did not fully trust Brendan or anyone really, so he suggested the two of them would drive in one car whilst a pal of his would follow in a Rover car with all the stolen goods. Brendan did manage to contact us before they set off and so we knew which car to stop, but it was disappointing in one way that we knew then we would never be able to implicate the boy-friend and his lady-friend would still think him innocent. It was something of an anti-climax when we stopped the Rover car on the M1 motorway outside Leeds and seized the stolen antiques.

Woodseats Division, Sheffield took over the case, but could not implicate the boy-friend and the poor Rover driver went to prison for receiving stolen goods. The boy-friend walked away scot-free. Shortly afterwards he ditched his lady-friend, which pleased me, because I could see him arranging to have all the antiques stolen again! Brendan received a small reward for that job, about £100 I recall, but he was waiting, not very patiently, for his four diamonds.

Some two years after the small Lancashire village Rawtenstall had surrendered the local antique dealer and his diamonds to us his case went to court. The antique dealer admitted 'receiving' the jewellery knowing it to be stolen and other serious offences from all over the country. He was sent to prison for many years.

Two days before Christmas a final meeting took place in the same Wakefield pub where it had all started. The colonel, senior officers from my force and the West Yorkshire Police where the crime was committed were also in attendance. Many rounds of drinks were ordered and Brendan finally took possession of his precious four diamonds (I did manage, however, to avoid paying for a round of drinks this time.)

My 'big one' was over, but I am sure Brendan's mind was leaning towards others.

Brendan refused to tell me how much he had sold the diamonds for, simply telling me to "fuck off" but he did buy the drinks in many meetings afterwards.

My relationship with Brendan became closer and closer, but not in a professional sense.

Through my contact with Brendan I was constantly able to supply crime intelligence to the force headquarters but it was of limited value. I still pushed him for more and more information and to get me off his back he suggested we raid the Sheffield home of one of his best friends where we recovered stolen emeralds from South Africa and some cannabis (villains have no scruples at all!). His friends, who were in show business, skipped bail and are still believed to be in the U.S.A.

I later introduced Brendan to the old Businessman we met at the beginning of the book.

A 'coalition' of businessman villain and police officer was formed, which at the time was exciting, but eventually led me to prison.

EPILOGUE

So, in my prison cell and with many regrets, I look back over almost 25 years fighting crime at the 'sharp-end'.

Again, I repeat how ashamed I am for my actions and have to seriously consider how I will earn a living on my release. It is now 1985 and I waited 20 years for 'the big one' but let my criminal actions dissipate the result and success.

Obviously there were times in my illegal travels where I thoroughly enjoyed myself, but that comment must be counterbalanced against what I lost and I do not recommend the path to young officers. At this moment there are corrupt practices flourishing in every police force in the country at the highest and lowest level and I'm sorry to say they always will. Many will never come to light, but do not expect as a matter of course those that are will be diligently exposed.

What does the future hold, in my humble opinion, for the millions of law-abiding people out there? People whose lives are dominated by the Sun newspaper and the happenings in Dallas and Dynasty.

Many will continue with the football pools hoping for a win that will alter their lives forever.

Lawyers will continue to make vast amounts of money from the misdeeds of others.

The likes of the 'monkey man' will continue to target small children every time they are released from prison.

Glenys will continue as a prostitute until her looks prohibit her from providing sexual favours even to a blind man.

Brendan will never perform an honest day's work in his life continually looking for an easy shilling.

Police forces will continue to encourage senior officers with academic skills and a complete lack of common sense.

Without doubt the public are to witness social changes on an unparalleled scale in the next few years.

Let me forecast three Legislation issues which, in my opinion, will affect the future.

Cannabis and Drugs: Drugs, including cannabis, will swamp society with all the various associated medical and criminal complications. Some will be legalised eventually leading to a tax benefit for the government but leaving drug dealers searching for a viable financial alternative.

Liquor Licensing Laws: The public will be allowed to drink all day before long with children accepted in pubs and clubs. Drunkenness will be seen at any time of the day or night on our streets.

Prostitution: Prostitution will be legalized, bringing enormous wealth to the tax man. It will eradicate 'kerb-crawling' as we know it and allow the girls to enjoy limited medical supervision. For years the girls have been 'sitting on gold-mines'- so why not profit from their assets?

THE END.

THE AUTHOR.

Graham L. Storr is now 70 years of age and living with his wife in Nottinghamshire.

He joined the Sheffield City Police in 1957 as a police cadet and became a constable in 1960. From uniform duties he was transferred into the criminal investigation department as a detective constable some 5 years later being promoted to detective sergeant in 1974. He later worked in the regional crime squad and other specialized departments.

Acquiring the nick-name 'Booper' at a very early stage in his service, it was to stay with him throughout his career being used by friends, work colleagues and villains alike.

His reputation as a 'thief- taker' was acknowledged by most officers who worked with him, but his jack-the-lad' persona did not endear him to all senior officers in the force.

Married twice and divorced, seriously injured in a street brawl, he was completely at home among the criminal underworld of South Yorkshire, which eventually led to his downfall.

Storr would not accept the many officers promoted in the force entirely due to their freemason connections, seeking to vilify them publicly whenever he got the chance, thus affecting his career chances.

In 1982 he was suspended from duty at the start of a massive criminal investigation launched by the South Yorkshire police into major fraud and other offences. The book describes how serving police officers criminals and city businessmen were implicated in crimes and other malpractices that led many to prison.

In 1984 Storr was convicted of corruption and other offences and sentenced to 5 years imprisonment. No other police officer ever appeared in court following the enquiry which aggrieved the author compelling him to write his memoirs whilst locked in a cell sometimes for 23 hours a day.

Storr was released in 1987 returning to South Yorkshire where, after marrying his partner, he successfully carved out a career for himself in industry until his retirement.

Having nothing to lose with his image and integrity destroyed, the author has been able to write with humour and heartache, frankness and honesty a comprehensive record of 'real' policing in the sixties. As he points out, no other ex-police officer has served two masters in the way that he did and recorded events. Judge for yourselves.